Losing It All to Sprawl

THE FLORIDA HISTORY AND CULTURE SERIES

Florida A&M University, Tallahassee
Florida Atlantic University, Boca Raton
Florida Gulf Coast University, Ft. Myers
Florida International University, Miami
Florida State University, Tallahassee
University of Central Florida, Orlando
University of Florida, Gainesville
University of North Florida, Jacksonville
University of South Florida, Tampa
University of West Florida, Pensacola

Florida's Space Coast: The Impact of NASA on the Sunshine State, by William Barnaby Faherty, S.J. (2002)

In the Eye of Hurricane Andrew, by Eugene F. Provenzo Jr. and Asterie Baker Provenzo (2002)

Florida's Farmworkers in the Twenty-first Century, text by Nano Riley and photographs by Davida Johns (2003)

Making Waves: Female Activists in Twentieth-Century Florida, edited by Jack E. Davis and Kari Frederickson (2003)

Orange Journalism: Voices from Florida Newspapers, by Julian M. Pleasants (2003)

The Stranahans of Ft. Lauderdale: A Pioneer Family of New River, by Harry A. Kersey Jr. (2003)

Death in the Everglades: The Murder of Guy Bradley, America's First Martyr to Environmentalism, by Stuart B. McIver (2003)

Jacksonville: The Consolidation Story, from Civil Rights to the Jaguars, by James B. Crooks (2004)

The Seminole Wars: The Nation's Longest Indian Conflict, by John and Mary Lou Missall (2004)

The Mosquito Wars: A History of Mosquito Control in Florida, by Gordon Patterson (2004)

The Seasons of Real Florida, by Jeff Klinkenberg (2004, first paperback edition, 2005)

Land of Sunshine, State of Dreams: A Social History of Modern Florida, by Gary Mormino (2005)

Paradise Lost? The Environmental History of Florida, edited by Jack E. Davis and Raymond Arsenault (2005)

Frolicking Bears, Wet Vultures, and Other Oddities: A New York Journalist in Nineteenth-Century Florida, edited by Jerald T. Milanich (2005)

Voices of the Apalachicola, compiled and edited by Faith Eidse, Northwest Florida Water Management District (2005)

Waters Less Traveled: Exploring Florida's Big Bend Coast, by Doug Alderson (2005)

Saving South Beach, by M. Barron Stofik (2005)

Losing It All to Sprawl: How Progress Ate My Cracker Landscape, by Bill Belleville (2006)

Losing It

University Press of Florida

Gainesville · Tallahassee · Tampa · Boca Raton
Pensacola · Orlando · Miami · Jacksonville · Ft. Myers

All to Sprawl

How Progress Ate My Cracker Landscape

Bill Belleville

11 10 09 08 07 06   6 5 4 3 2 1

Unless otherwise noted, all photos are by Bill Belleville
A record of cataloging-in-publication information
is available from the Library of Congress.
ISBN 0-8130-2928-7
The University Press of Florida is the scholarly publishing agency
for the State University System of Florida, comprising Florida A&M
University, Florida Atlantic University, Florida Gulf Coast University,
Florida International University, Florida State University, University
of Central Florida, University of Florida, University of North Florida,
University of South Florida, and University of West Florida.

University Press of Florida
15 Northwest 15th Street
Gainesville, FL 32611-2079
http://www.upf.com

For Zona Mathews Beckwith,
and Mike Durak, and their families

It is as if the residents of the disappearing town are hanging onto pieces of it, because that's what you have left when a community falls apart, pieces, and between all the pieces, you have the ghosts who knew the place when it was less rudimentary and more whole, who are eternally present, inhabiting the town's hollows like wind and weeds.

Wendell Berry

Contents

Foreword

During the past half century, the burgeoning growth and increased national and international visibility of Florida have sparked a great deal of popular interest in the state's past, present, and future. As the favorite destination of hordes of tourists and as the new home for millions of retirees, immigrants, and transplants, modern Florida has become a demographic, political, and cultural bellwether.

A state of vast distances and distant strangers, Florida needs more citizens who care about the welfare of this special place and its people. We hope this series helps newcomers and old timers appreciate and understand Florida. The University Press of Florida established the Florida History and Culture Series in an effort to provide an accessible and attractive format for the publication of works related to the Sunshine State.

As coeditors of the series, we are deeply committed to the creation of an eclectic but carefully crafted set of books that will provide the field of Florida studies with a fresh focus, and encourage Florida researchers and writers to consider the broader implications and context of their work. The series includes monographs, memoirs, anthologies, and travelogues. And, while the series features books of historical and cultural interest, we also emphasize research on Florida's environment and politics. We want each book to retain a distinct personality and voice, but at the same time we hope to foster a sense of community and collaboration among Florida scholars.

In Losing It All to Sprawl, Bill Belleville takes readers literally and figuratively into his back yard, a postage-stamp tract of Florida west of Sanford in Seminole County. Alternating between contemporary clashes with developers who covet his and his neighbors' property on Sewell Road off S.R. 46 and flashbacks to Seminoles, sawyers, and celery kings who once roamed the Wekiva River Valley, Belleville weaves a narrative that is intensely personal. Most of all, it is about his relationship with the land and neighbors and the place he called home for fifteen years.

A powerful sense of place pervades Belleville's writing: Blackwater Creek and unnamed springs, ladderback woodpeckers and marsh wrens, cracker houses made of heartwood cypress and dreams lost to urban sprawl. One can well imagine future literary tourists wandering along Sewell Road searching for familiar landmarks—the coquina rock pond, flower beds, and yes, the one-eyed bunny. Losing It All to Sprawl reinforces Belleville's reputation as one of Florida's outstanding writers.

Gary Mormino and Raymond Arsenault
Series Editors

Acknowledgments

My greatest appreciation to Zona and Art Beckwith, and Mike and Carolyn Durak, who graciously offered information that was indispensable to telling the story of Sewell Road. My heartfelt thanks to Lisa Roberts, a thoughtful editor and a wonderful companion whose encouragement and inspiration helped make this book happen. My gratitude also goes to those who provided helpful information or support, including Jennifer McMurtray of the Defenders of Wildlife, Dr. Steve Phelan, Russ and Katie Moncrief, Nancy Prine, Joe Newman, Clay Henderson, Jeff Klinkenberg, and Susan Brady. Thanks to those along the way who have enriched my life and made the writing go just a little bit better: E. T. Prickett, Dr. Colin and Bonnie Freeman, Dr. Bobby Boswell, Bob Giguere, Teri Sopp, Lee and Mindy Hanna, Leslie and Michael Poole, Virginia Maxwell, Janisse Ray, Michelle Thatcher, my daughter, Beth, her husband, Chuck, and grandboys Ray and Will Crawley.

Preface

When I step into my backyard at 8 a.m., I see the mist rising from the ground, everything all silver now from the reflection of the new sun, small cobwebs left in the shape of tents between the blades of grass from last night's tiny business. The dew is heavy and splashes when my little sheltie runs through it, leaving a wake like a boat keel does in water. I see his warm breath puff out in front of him as he romps, a little dragon breathing smoke, looking for the rabbits that forever taunt him, at least two hops away before he smells them.

The saucer-sized white blooms that burst open on the giant cereus cactus by the coolness of late night have gone black and fallen. A monochrome of green, the cactus reigns over a corner of the yard like a thick, stocky tree. Back inside its limbs, mockingbirds flit about, chasing the anoles, little lizard chins all puffed up with red to impress each other.

The vines of the wild blackberry trail back into the subtropical thicket that consumes the rear of the yard, winding back through the elephant ears and guava bushes. Under the broad banana leaves, the small fruits are fat and green, while the Hamlins and sour root stock have turned just like the little pumpkin-colored kumquats that fill the two trees in the front, near the coral vine that meanders up the side of the porch.

During seasonal changes here in Florida, the leaves of the sweetgum go yellow and red, and the fingers of the golden polypody fern become streaked with burnt umber. Up high, the berries of the sabal palms hang in clusters under the lowest fronds. In the small coquina rock pond, native gambusia move about more slowly just below the water's surface, amidst the hydrilla and the roots of the river iris I once collected from the St. Johns.

I don't spread bug poisons about, so I see lots of caterpillars everywhere, have to pick them off my habanero pepper patch by hand sometimes. They don't die or go away, but sneak off and hide somewhere, spinning a chrysalis of silk and inside, perhaps dreaming of one day waking up with wings with colors and the chance to fly. And then suddenly, here they are, bright aerodynamic leaves, rising and falling in the yard, a newfound surprise every time: the black swallowtail, the Gulf fritillary, and the zebra longwing, as dazzling as they were when William Bartram first saw them over two hundred years ago, blown up fresh from the tropics.

This is the last remains of an old farm spread in northern Seminole County, barely an acre left now, at the end of a dirt road. The two-story house here is mostly of heart cypress, so dense that I have broken circular saw blades and countless nails as I've gone about the never-ending chore of keeping it livable.

It is a fine old Cracker-style home raised up off the ground a few feet, molded-steel roof overhangs, gables everywhere, porches to the front and back, richly aged hardwood floors and brick fireplace. Built solid in the late 1920s, it was designed to be naturally insulated, cool from cross ventilation and the shade of well-planted trees, bushy magnolia and water oak, back in the days when it took resourcefulness and common sense to live in Florida and not air-conditioning and bug spray. It is a place where I can go and sit quietly on the worn stone bench with the hearts in the side, next to the massive stand of bamboo, and listen to the wind coax music from the hollow reeds, hear the first sounds of the chuck-will's-widow at dusk, wait for Orion and the Pleiades to appear. Falling stars arrive as a hat-trick of a surprise, streaking their way across the night sky with no preamble.

Now that the leaves of fall have thinned, I can see abandoned nests in the low boughs of the trees, close up. Cardinals, who seem to be smart, brave birds, make fine ones, weaving thinner threads of plants atop thicker ones, nice and soft for the eggs. Blue jay nests seem tossed together from twigs as an afterthought, mindless squawks manifest. Of them all, it is the intricate, cocoonlike assemblages of the little marsh wrens that always stop me in my tracks. Once a mamma wren built an entire one inside the utility room next to the big old wooden garage, flitting in and out from the open space under the rafters with pieces of her home in her mouth. I found her there one day, back on a dusty shelf at eye level, resting on her eggs, and I felt like an intruder.

Another time, I watched in fascination as a screech owl, a tiny raptor with hornlike tufts on its head, raised a family of four owlets in the hollow trunk of an old queen palm. Sometimes, right at dusk, I would sit outside on the worn concrete bench and see her swoop in low, something wiggly in her mouth to feed the brood. Later, at least two families of ladder-backed woodpeckers used cavities in the palm for the same purpose. I could hear their sharp calls there, morning and just before dark.

Sometimes the confrontations of nature evolve before my eyes, a nature documentary with no on or off switch. Once I saw an orange-and-black corn snake up high in a cedar tree with a massive bullfrog in its mouth, the frog screaming like a little kitten. I shook the tree, the snake opened its mouth, and down came one fat, grateful bullfrog with a resounding thud and a croak. On another day, I watched a half-grown gopher tortoise come barreling through a remote portion of the yard in his distinct wobble-crawl, entirely perplexing a baby possum that had strayed too far from its nest.

Being part of an experience like this requires a dose of commitment, a desire to slow down and leave things as they are. I have a country neighbor who lives in another old Cracker house nearby. He's connected here, and understands. He is a big, heavy man who does big politically incorrect things like hunt and fish and drink Jack Daniels whiskey and eat too much of all the wrong kinds of food. We have brief conversations in the street in passing every few months, and recently, during one of those, he stopped midway in a sentence and said "red-shouldered hawk."

We both looked up then, searching for the shrill whistle the hawk makes, up high in his orbit as he searches the ground for little things that move. And sure enough, there he was, in the midst of a wide elegant swoop, like a finely crafted Chinese kite, except without the string. We both smiled then, at the hawk and each other and the notion that something that wild can still exist here, just over our heads.

Yet this picture I've just painted has begun to change in the last few months. The bulldozers have been scraping the epidermal layer off the earth not far away, preparing for a brand new mall, a shoppers' paradise that will bring jobs and money and people and their cars. The road my dirt lane connects to is being paved and widened to accommodate all this busy commerce.

You can hear the high-pitched buzzers go off and on all day as the heavy machinery moves forward and then into reverse. Up from the ground go the palmettos, the sabal palms, the southern red cedar, and the sweet bay, shredded and piled and burned like rubbish. The few gopher tortoises that weren't buried alive make a run for it, lighting out across the new highway for safe ground, trying not to become roadkill. I've rescued three of them so far, turning them loose at the edge of my backyard, where they march off into the 20 acres of dead citrus grove next to the house.

Someday the old grove will go too; there is a proposal for it to become a multifamily development of some sort, probably to hold the swarms of minimum-wage workers who will staff the retail stores in the mall. The hawk has suspiciously disappeared, although I hope not for good. I wonder how much longer it will be before the flood of new mall lights dims the blackness of the sky, snuffing out the constellations, the falling stars.

The other day, a fast-talking realtor called to see if I wanted to become part of a "package deal" for some big retail business that had its eye on the area. Before he even heard my answer, he told me that he knew for a fact that everything in Florida was for sale. Even if I stayed, I would be up against the back of one shopper paradise or another, dumpsters full of consumer detritus, lots of noise. Just wouldn't be the same.

And I couldn't argue with him on that one, because I knew that it wouldn't be, knew that growth with no natural ethic to accompany it is a maelstrom, knew that's why this state was losing its connectedness, its link between people and the land. Florida is for sale, has been for a while now, and it makes me sad as hell. I'll stay as long as I can, but one day soon it will all go: the marsh wrens and the butterflies, the cactus and blackberry vines, the old Cracker house, the feeling.

And I wondered if the hawk should ever come back, just on a random flyover one day, singing its high, sweet whistle way up in the sky, if anyone here where this dirt street once was will even remember the kind of bird he is, or care enough to stop, just for a moment, and smile.

Introduction

Growth only for the sake of more growth is the strategy of a cancer cell.
Edward O. Wilson, biologist

I have kind of an alacrity in sinking.
William Shakespeare, playwright

I have been sinking into Florida for decades now. True, I wanted a place that would absorb me, envelop me, and draw me into its own lush geography. And that is what I have found. Florida, the land of fountains of youth and founts of luxuriant illusion, has fully captured my imagination and pulled me deeply into her. She used the same native art to seduce naturalists William Bartram and André Michaux, landscape painters William Morris Hunt and Winslow Homer—the same artistry that finally converted a Yankee intellectual named Marjorie Kinnan Rawlings into a bold writer who articulated the fine distinction of place far better than the people who had lived it for generations.

However powerful its grip may be, all that sinking is just allegory, a suggestion of something with deeper meaning. In fact, there is a more literal sinking taking place here. It is of the sort that has no metaphor attached to it for it draws you down to a place below sea level where it is just not safe to be. In this reality, the terrain of this verdant land of flowers—the moist state with more wetlands and springs and lakes than any other—is drying up. As it dehydrates, its soils slough off in entire plats. Some of it dissolves into the atmosphere, leaving a subsiding natural terrain just slightly less than what it had been. Other chunks—far more melodramatic and menacing—collapse as "sinkholes" into a limestone underworld that few know and fewer ever see.

It was natural that I would come to this Florida as a young adult to sink because wonder and dark mystery and holes in the ground have always struck me as the same thing. And too, others in my family have sunk here before me. The most notorious was my maternal grandfather, who, on becoming wealthy by devising a refrigeration method to cheaply ship sweet Wauchula-grown strawberries up north in the winter, promptly divorced my grandmother and married his young secretary. From his seasonal home in the rural interior of the peninsula, they traveled to France, where he promptly died of a heart attack, leaving my grandmother with two adolescent children and little else. Nearly all his fortune went to his new bride, who promptly sunk him 6 feet into the ground, and that was the end of that.

But it wasn't truly the end at all. There was enough of the raw glamour of this mid-twentieth-century Florida left in my mother's own dreams to bring us back to La Florida from the rural Eastern Shore of Maryland. When I was eight, we packed into our old Woody station wagon—Mom, Dad, my brother, and me—and drove here to visit. It was then that I drifted atop Silver Springs in a glass-bottom boat, saw a black hole in the ground that spit out water as clear and preternaturally blue as Windex. Our guide narrated with a theatrical rhythm, like a Slinky stepping its way down the stairs. Both The Creature from the Black Lagoon and Sea Hunt were once filmed here—indeed, part of an old set was still submerged. On the junglelike shores around us, rhesus monkeys left from a decades-old Tarzan movie shoot still romped. The air was thick with fictional celebrity.

I had just read The Pink Motel, about a young boy whose average American family inherits a decrepit Florida beachfront motel full of wonderfully eccentric guests. On our own real-life trip, we were just coming for a vacation, but I was no less dazzled with the possibilities of Florida than my counterpart in The Pink Motel. There was something at once seductive and outlandish about our whole experience that day, as if we—having brushed up against the fame of the Tarzan monkeys and the Sea Hunt set and the ghost of the Creature—were all part of some Saturday movie matinee. And I felt a little famous myself, just being here. This Florida was as far removed from my linear Beaver Cleaver childhood as I could imagine. The whole state, in fact, seemed like one giant Pink Motel, a place where rassling alligators was a real vocation and the landscape was defined by either a junglelike wilderness or a stage set. I dreamed of returning to tramp through this jungle and to sink down into dark aquatic crevasses under the springs to see where they went. There was only the slightest hint of a real-world constraint—that the entry, the descent, would also have to be followed by an ascent. At the time, it just didn't seem that important.

I have lived here for over three decades now, and in that time I have taken the yearning to sink as literally as I could. I have submerged into such springs wearing scuba tanks—once even venturing into the black maw of Silver itself with a diver who was mapping its underground route. There I found cavern walls lined with prehistoric ocean sea biscuits, saw a fossilized clam as wide as a dinner plate. I rolled a basketball-sized limestone rock over on the floor of the cave, and a tiny albino arthropod, a cave-dwelling shrimplike creature bereft of color, flitted out like a wisp of muted light. The little shrimp was as yet undescribed. Like most troglodytic life, it was endemic to this cave, living nowhere else on earth. When I emerged from the dark cavern mouth in my neoprene suit and tanks that day, I looked up to see scores of curious tourist faces pressed nearly against the glass bottoms of the tour boats. The boats were not unlike the ones I had ridden so long ago, except now they were fiberglass instead of wooden. My own senses were still reeling from finning over a forever-dark Jurassic sea bottom on permanent ebb. And the moment became vaguely hallucinogenic, as if I were here but also someplace else at the same time—part of me was an adult emerging from a place I'd always wanted to be, while another was the child in the boat, wishing for the moment to finally happen. I could only guess how the tour guide's melodramatic spin had ignited the guileless expectations of his passengers on the other side of the glass. Looking up, I wondered if they thought of me in the same way that I had thought of the submerged stage set of my own childhood boat ride here—as something so outlandish that it blurred the cusp between fiction and fact.

But descending into a water-filled hole in the rock, even one surrounded by tour boats, is a conscious choice. Other sinkings are less so: the way my backyard now sinks when one square meter after another—bereft of the groundwater that once supported it—gradually gives way as small limestone chambers beneath it slowly cave in. Unlike the great, sudden-collapse sinks, these events are slight and gradual, and unless you are here to watch them day by day, they are nearly indecipherable dips of subsidence in the landscape.

After all, our subterrain, that soft limestone called karst, is nothing but a giant slab of sedimentary rock configured like Swiss cheese, veined with clear, cold water. Some sinkings then are perfectly natural, the product of time, climate, and the seismic jostling of the earth. Indeed, most of our lakes here have been created from sinks. Except that now the rate at which sinks occur has accelerated at an alarming pace, and that acceleration comes from allow-ing—even encouraging—residents to settle in places where they ought not to be. The orange and its blossom are on the state license plate, but the groves that helped sustain the true scent of La Florida for so long are disappearing. A more accurate icon might depict a sunburnt tourist in mouse ears, beckoning from the edge of a sinkhole.

Odd as it sounds, there is still some symmetry to it all. Modern tourism, after all, is the natural derivation of how Florida first introduced itself to the world, with its early prototourists riding steamboats for miles up rivers like the Suwannee and the St. Johns. Serious "improvement" to the terrain, although tried for years, didn't fully arrive until technology caught up with its ambitions. And then it settled in with a vengeance, its promoters intent on luring back those same tourists to settle in as homeowners. Like the demonic brooms in the Sorcerer's Apprentice, this growth-driven economy seems to have taken on a life all its own. As a state, we experience a net gain of seven hundred residents a day, and they are being invited to live just about anywhere a developer wants to put them. That includes the soggy floodplain that holds our wetlands, and the hilly, upland terrain that collects rainfall to "recharge" the underground rivers we call the aquifer. Bereft of life-giving wetlands, the landscape begins to sizzle in the warm Florida sun. Without its historic recharge—and stressed with the oversized thirst that lots of people bring to any warm place—the veins of this aquifer dwindle, desiccate, settle down upon themselves.

All of this is no secret, of course. And today the fundamental notion of Florida's unique, finite ecology is better understood than ever. Yet, despite pleas from those who stress the need to balance use with preservation, the itinerary that guides the growth of Florida is a sink itself, one colossal politicized hole where common sense used to be. And the condition that results is called sprawl. Certainly this is happening all over the country with various degrees of wretched efficiency. The damage to the natural systems here is just more obvious because Florida is not unlike an island. You can think of it, in fact, as a three-sided island, one gigantic sandbar stacked atop other sandbars, which in turn are layered over sand, gravel, bone, shell, coral, clay. We have no distinct geofault line like California that threatens to dump half of the state into the sea when it goes. Instead, we have a series of subtle minifaults, each following paths of fissures in the limestone below—and each blowing itself out when its water level recedes, slowly, over time. The truth is that sprawl is sinking us here in Florida, and it is taking just about everything along with it as it goes, swallowing up the intricate weave of geography and culture, painstakingly shaped over time.

Now the place where I live is in the crosshairs. My traditional Florida Cracker neighborhood has become an abrupt transition zone between the old and the new, and the transformation is whiplash swift—the stasis mutating nearly overnight with little grace. The landscape around me is being scraped clean of sabal palms and live oaks, red cedar and longleaf pine. Each day the big yellow bulldozers and backhoes rumble ever closer across the rich dark earth of what was once a seasonally wet river delta, snapping trunks and limbs like so many pick-up sticks. In their place go malls and plazas full of fancy, pretty things, a shopper's paradise.

Do you know that we have insurance policies customized for termites and sinkholes in the Sunshine State? I keep my home up the best I can. But when the future of the place is uncertain, I let some things slide—such as the termite coverage. We are hot and wet and full of bugs down here—indeed, Florida is an entomologist's dream. But, left untreated, the wood in the homes slowly vanishes. I walk between the kitchen and the parlor now, and as I do, the floor there sinks ever so gradually under my feet as if it were made of balsa. I crawl under the house to see about this, and as my fingernails dig easily into the wood supports overhead, the detritus of termite dust falls on my forehead. I creep out and back up into the bright Florida sunlight, a little stunned by it all. As I do, I feel the ground under me giving way as well. It is settling by mere degrees, nibbling at just the lip of my shoe soles now.

So there you have it: My yard is sinking, my house is sinking—even my entire state is sinking into the perpetually sucking, bottomless drain of uncontrolled growth. I wonder now what to do, and the choices are deceptively simple: I can pack up and head for the hills—or I can sink down with it and chronicle the journey with some measure of alacrity, riding the ever-fragmenting natural Florida landscape like an elevator on slow-motion free fall. I make my decision, reminding myself to be careful to leap out before it finally plummets through the soft earthen bottom of the shaft, taking me down with it.

Chapter One

For never they build their abodes except where there are wood and water.
Alvar Nuñez Cabeza de Vaca, providing the earliest description of how Florida Indians lived,
after a 1528 expedition to the peninsula

It was 1990, a dazzling sunny late spring Saturday afternoon in central Florida, and I was driving down quiet State Road 46 toward the interstate a few miles away. I was renting a home in downtown Sanford then, and in the four or so miles between it and the interstate, the two-lane country highway was mostly given over to farm fields, cow pastures, and splotches of remnant native woods, interspersed with modest homes, a junkyard or two, roadside produce stands selling fresh vegetables and boiled peanuts, a few convenience stores, and the occasional anomaly like a ramshackle cement-block building that advertised "wholesale rattan furniture." In the midst of all of this, a white plywood board with hand-painted red lettering—"House for Sale"—caught my attention. It was propped next to a narrow, wooded dirt road off the highway. The mouth of the street was flanked by two simple wood-frame homes. A small green county sign identified this as "Sewell Road," and a larger geometric yellow sign warned "Dead End." Even though I had driven S.R. 46 many times before, this was a side street I didn't even know existed. I braked and turned onto Sewell to see what this was about. I didn't know it then, but I was about to enter into a relationship that would transform my life.

I drove down the dirt road a few hundred yards, passing only four other homes, all on the westerly, or right, side. The road ended at the edge of an old citrus grove that had been burnt to the ground by the last hard freeze five years earlier. There was no fancy cul-de-sac to turn around, simply a green foliage wall where the dead grove was busy being colonized by native trees. On the easterly left side was a two-story white house with blue shutters behind a chain-link fence that itself was covered with a trailing vine with violet trumpet-shaped blossoms. Several well-tended ligustrums bushed up on the inside edge of the fence, and two large kumquat trees stood on either side of the little sidewalk leading to the front door. This was the house that was for sale.

I pulled through an open gate in the fence into a gravel driveway, nosing up next to the old wooden two-car garage. I saw that its two huge sliding doors were made of narrow, one-inch-wide batten boards that builders today sometimes call "boxcar" or "railroad" siding because it was once used to line the interior of boxcars. Although well kept, the home seemed unoccupied. I got out of my jeep tentatively. Country dogs are usually more pragmatic than their townie counterparts, and sometimes don't even bother with the lavish prelude of barking before they get right down to business. But there were no dogs, and I walked around the acre or so of land surrounding the house by myself, taking it all in.

The yard was full of mature orange trees and a massive stand of bamboo and a cactus the size of a panel truck. There was a substantial barbecue grill made of red bricks under a tin-roofed pavilion in the back and an empty coquina-walled fish pond that rose up out of the side yard like a miniature Spanish fortress. Flowering pink coral vine and blue plumbago were vying for space below the metal jalousies of the enclosed front porch, overwhelming a ginger-colored lantana there. Oddly, there was also a small, shallow swimming pool near the cactus on the north edge of the lot, and it was choked with duckweed and lotus lily and papyrus palm. There were two brick chimneys on the house, one on the north wall and a smaller one to the east that looked as if it may once have serviced a wood stove in the kitchen. The roof was molded steel, all silvery and bright in the spring sun.

The lot was bordered by the dead grove to the south, by another older wooden home several hundred yards behind it to the east, and to the north—on the 5 acres or so of land between the home and S.R. 46—by a small forest of young longleaf pine, all likely spawned by the few remnant longleafs still left in the neighborhood. Inside the little pine forest was a livestock shed and another smaller enclosed workshoplike building, walled in with pecky cypress siding painted aluminum and capped with a tin roof. Based on the size of the few magnificent conifers that still towered high above, I guessed this was likely a pine flatwoods once, a seasonally flooding transitional zone between the lower wetlands of the St. Johns River a mile or so to the north and the gently rolling hills of the uplands to the south. Although it has been greatly modified over the centuries, a pine flatwoods is the most common ecological community in natural Florida. The terrain itself is nearly level and usually underlain by a "hardpan" that keeps waters from easily draining through the upper soils.

To the degree that one can have deep and instinctual feelings for a place, it was every bit of that—love at first sight. There was something vaguely romantic about the house, about its yard, about how it was tucked away here on what seemed to be a secluded country road. Best of all, it existed well outside the bounds of the extruded walled developments that were increasingly suffocating the true nature of this part of the state. The homestead seemed to be from the era of Cross Creek, the rural hamlet outside of Gainesville that Marjorie Kinnan Rawlings had immortalized in her own books and short stories. The Creek, as Rawlings referred to it, gave her both solace and inspiration. She once wrote: "We need the song of birds, and there is none finer than the red-bird. We need the sound of rain coming across the hamaca, and the sound of wind in trees. . . . We need above all, I think, a certain remoteness from urban confusion." There were redbirds—cardinals—here because I saw them in the yard. There was the sound of the wind in the tall pines because I heard it. And certainly the house and its yard promised a fine antidote to urban confusion. Civilization was taking its toll on me, and whatever else this end-of-the-road house would be, I figured its authenticity would at least help satisfy my very real need for a sense of place in Florida. I jotted down the telephone number on the sign, called the owners, and after meeting with them, struck a deal to buy it.

I had lived in Altamonte Springs in southern Seminole County for nearly fifteen years. While I enjoyed a home there on a quiet winding street canopied with the foliage crown of old oaks, the city of Altamonte itself was not a real place. My street seemed momentarily safe because it had been "built out"—not as a tract neighborhood but as an eclectic composite of uniquely styled homes, each constructed over several decades by different owners. In typical Florida fashion, my home there was on the rim of an ancient sinkhole, its slopes forested with mature hardwoods. The presence of the old earthen depression gave me an odd sense of security since it is unusual for sinks to collapse more than once in the same place—just as lightning, so the folk wisdom goes, rarely strikes the same spot twice.

The man I bought it from was a builder who chose the best materials to construct a split-level cedar home that sort of walked its way down the upper-sink slope. The backyard descended first into a thick hammock of saw palmettos and skinny, twisted old oaks that, after it left the property line, became even steeper in grade until it bottomed out at the base of the prehistoric sink. A family of gray foxes lived there somewhere, along with raccoons and possums, all likely chased out from other places. Good split-level homes were hard to build, and the sloping terrain that formed the bowl of the sink was simply unsuitable for the cookie-cutter models that blighted most of the rest of Altamonte. While the house and its surroundings offered some comfort, it was of the most transitory sort: To travel anywhere beyond its yard meant I had to venture out into the heavily congested road that bisected the town, a demon of a highway alternatively named S.R. 436 and Semoran Boulevard.

I had moved into that first home with my young wife thinking that we would soon know most of our immediate neighbors simply because they lived nearby. In fact, in all our time, we really only got to know one. He was Benny Bennett, a spry, independent retiree who made as few compromises as possible with age. I remember Benny putting new shingles on the roof of his home by himself once, up in the warm Florida sun with a hammer in one hand and an Old Milwaukee in the other. Benny's wife had passed away, and he was living out his last years here, puttering about with projects like roofing and inventing motion-sensitive buzzer gadgets to spook away birds when they pecked at the fruits on his persimmon tree. He seemed perpetually to be eighty years old—eighty when we arrived, and eighty when we left.

The other neighbors were much younger and seemed afflicted with the rootless sort of disenfranchisement that comes from living in a place where everyone is new and the only constant is change. They scuttled about like rabbits in the shadows, coming and going. When we moved in, only Benny came to welcome us to the neighborhood; afterwards, few even acknowledged we were there. Unlike traditional towns in the Old South, we didn't know each other's kin. Professional movers did a brisk business, transporting buyers and sellers in and out of their homes every couple of years or so. Lawton Chiles, a former governor, once warned that Florida ought to stop acting like a large "crowd" of disassociated people and start acting more like a state, with all the necessary interpersonal connections and responsibilities that entails. As a microcosm, our neighborhood was a small crowd of people living in one place, not just dissociated from each other but also disconnected from historic geography. As local newspaper columnist and author Jim Robison noted in his book Flashbacks: "Many non-natives . . . assume the area has no history, that the human occupation of eastern Central Florida begin somewhere in the 1960's when Walt Disney made the decision to launch his world."

Certainly, Altamonte Springs had a very real history, and it was not dissimilar from that of other settlements in the Florida interior. The little village had been founded in the 1870s as Snow Station, a whistle-stop on a railroad line. It grew up around a spacious winter hotel with open verandahs and a little spring that bubbled from the base of a nearby gazebo into a clear, sandy-bottomed lake. Victorian "cottages" housed more affluent visitors, nearly all of whom arrived in November at a local rail depot and left by springtime. The natives who stayed year-round farmed orange groves and drained sap from the tall longleafs to make turpentine. Although the business of logging mature pines and cypress was underway, the region still had most of its first-growth forest intact at the end of the nineteenth century.

Yet, by modern times the place had changed so fully that it had become unrecognizable. As one local historian noted with no trace of irony: "It was the first community to take advantage of the retail and residential growth opportunities made possible by I-4 and the widening metro Orlando economy." In other words, it was the regional archetype for sprawl. Not long before I arrived, city leaders—eager to ride the coattails of Orlando's nascent boom—even allowed the spring for which the town was named to be paved over, bucolic enchantment capped with an asphalt parking lot that eventually would hold expensive autos driven by software technicians. A large mall opened in 1974, and it in turn attracted strip plazas, all feeding off the mall's inducement to consume. The few historic cottages that still remained were razed—or, in a few cases, actually put up on wheels and moved a few miles north to Longwood, where sprawl then was less menacing. Except for the random sabal palm at roadside, this Altamonte Springs could have been plopped down almost anywhere on the map. Sprawl had consumed and homogenized it and robbed it of what made it distinctive. It seemed to actualize the comment that Gertrude Stein once made: "There is no there, there." Altamonte Springs had become, as a local newspaper reporter once confided to me, "the only shopping mall in America with its own mayor."

Within this transience, there were some hilariously disparate Florida moments, although they surely were not planned as such. At the edge of the mall's gigantic asphalt parking lot, a Caribbean-themed chain restaurant and fern bar was built with a wraparound porch that overlooked a congested highway on one side and masses of parked cars steaming in the hot Florida sun on the other. It became a very popular and trendy bar, and I would drive by and see patrons packed onto the porches—buzzed after a couple over-priced margaritas, awash in canned Jimmy Buffett music, and apparently not the least troubled that they were surrounded by an acrid, unrippling, petro-based sea of commerce and not the Caribbean Sea itself.

Once bright with the promise of staking out new territory, my life eventually began to devolve in Altamonte. Finally, my wife and I divorced, and we sold the sink-sloping tri-level and went our separate ways. I moved to Folly, a little sea island off the coast of South Carolina, where I rented an ocean-front home for a year. The irony of the island's name was not lost on me for I moved there with no "job" other than my itinerant article writing and with no long-term expectations except to fulfill the terms of my year-long lease. And, after all, it was a coastal island, prone to fits of losing tons of sand from its beaches and shoals as it slowly washed itself away into the sea—how long, really, could any of us live in such a place?

Still, I found Folly to be a refuge where I could hunker down, lick my wounds, and in moments of clarity, try to decide if I even wanted to return to Florida at all. Certainly there was an unintended consequence of the experience: Living on an island for a year reminded me of valuable lessons in learning to pay attention to how the natural world works. Emerson once wrote that books and nature belong to those who can see them, and I wanted badly to see. A busy beach town for locals in the summer, Folly was quiet during the winter season. I lived on the northern end, where the island narrowed into a peninsula that was surrounded on one side by marsh and on the other by the ocean. It had it nearly to myself. I surf fished and walked the beach alone at night and gathered sand dollars at dawn. A teacher and poet who lived farther inland came to visit on the weekends, and she and I would plan our nights by the meteor showers in the pitch-dark sky. When one was scheduled to arrive, we would sit out on the boardwalk that trailed out from my porch over the dune and look on with astonishment.

On Folly, I watched the seasons carefully begin and end, and saw the way tides and wind defined reality more precisely than any human presumptions ever could. I thought of my best memories of what Florida had always been—of why nature had fascinated me on my early visits here as a boy, and why I so loved the mystifying boggy places that gifted it with such a rare character. After trying with great difficulty to make a responsible, intellectual decision about where my life should go, I finally gave in to my heart and came back to Florida simply because it seemed like the right thing to do. Folly would continue to wash away, but it would have to do so without me. I knew if I were to return, though, I would have to find a place that made sense to me, a place not closed in by apartment complexes and franchise restaurants and malls. Since I made my living as a magazine writer, I would also have to be vigilant and not work just for money but to solicit assignments that helped me better understand how the natural soul of the landscape itself had been layered and informed by its history.

While Sanford was the county seat of Seminole, it was a pleasantly retro little town not yet consumed by the ever-spreading sprawl of the Orlando metro area to the south. It reminded me more of the quiet country place on the lower Eastern Shore of Maryland where I had grown up. Its allure as a slow-lane refuge was not lost on others. In the 1970s, I had interviewed Carl Langford, then mayor of Orlando, for a feature article in a newspaper. Langford was a shrewd country boy with his own down-home style. Once to make some now-obscure point, he put on a red Superman costume and descended the steps of City Hall, cape furling behind him. Since he was also bald, a bit pudgy, and mustachioed, the effect was particularly striking. I don't remember the occasion, just the fact that he was confident enough in himself to poke a little fun. When I spoke with him, Langford knew that his city had outgrown him, and he was right. He longed for a quieter way of life, one he still saw when he visited the town tucked away on the south shore of Lake Monroe in northern Seminole County. "There's a small-town atmosphere in Sanford that we [Orlando] don't have anymore," Langford lamented. "They're living a slower life up there. . . . They don't seem to be frustrated as much as we are down here. It reminds me of how it used to feel in Orlando." When Langford left office, he also left town, fleeing to the relative solitude of the hills of North Carolina. He wasn't alone; natives were leaving in droves for the more remote hills of the Southeast to recapture what they once knew here. Langford's office was subsequently held by a succession of buttoned-down corporate players, lawyers, and developers, none of whom ever dressed up in a Superman suit.

The for-sale house I had stumbled over on Sewell Road was clearly of Cracker origins—what some architects today call "vernacular wooden Florida design." There are many ways to explain such a structure, but the most vital is that it and many others like it were built before air-conditioning muted the realities of living in a place like Florida. The house was constructed from dense, heavy, heart cypress, which provided its own measure of natural insulation, and it was up on concrete blocks to allow air to circulate under it.

Its elevation also kept it above the low ground, preparing it for that special Florida moment when monsoonal summer rains overwhelm the earth's ability to absorb them. Its roof was metal so that it would reflect the sun, and its generously wide gables and overhangs would shelter most of the windows from the overhead glow. Two giant deciduous hardwoods also stood guard, providing more shade—a southern magnolia to the front and a water oak to the side between the house and the garage. The structure was more rectangular than not, and most of its girth was arranged on a north-south axis for good reason: Its exterior walls could absorb solar heat from a low winter sun while also avoiding the scorch when the summer sun was high overhead. The main heat-giving fireplace was on the north side, the side with the least amount of sunlight. By design and configuration, lumber would remain dry and less prone to the premature rot of humidity. Architecturally, the style would likely be described as a "double-pen" Cracker house, with chimneys against outside walls and simple rooms opening into shady porches.

When the old windows were raised to catch the cross-ventilated breezes, the structure was designed to stay cool and pleasant throughout the entire year, except for a few weeks in late August when nothing short of a bomb would move the heavy air. Designers today call this style "passive solar" because it is energy efficient without the use of high-tech hardware to help make it so. In fact, its design was far less a function of aesthetics than of utility. As such, it was equipped to withstand the hot, humid Florida weather far better than the more modern hermetically sealed block and stucco ranch homes that require thick insulation and a constant running of the central air or heat to make them inhabitable. The place made wonderful sense—in fact, it had a very real vernacular wisdom literally built into it. While I wasn't required to live an air-conditioning-free existence like those who were here before me, I chose to do so simply because I could. Certainly I was eager to simplify my life. I couldn't turn back the clock, but I could occupy a place built to articulate the historic realities of its geography.

I learned all I could about the logic of this structure, and as I did, I found a champion of the theory of Cracker design. He was an architect-professor from the University of Florida named Ronald W. Haase. Professor Haase defined vernacular as "the native language or dialect of a particular region or place." In a book he wrote on the style, Haase said: "In Florida, it is the Cracker house that has most mediated between the man-made and the natural." I liked that a lot. Haase also lamented that the Florida Cracker style had not been recognized and honored as fully as the New England saltbox or the southwestern adobe ranch, the Spanish Mediterranean of St. Augustine or the Moorish boom-time hotels of Tampa and Palm Beach. Despite its lack of celebrity, the humble, modest Cracker design still had a simple grace and beauty all its own. Haase even championed its revival, noting that its pragmatism offers a badly needed remedy to the stark meaninglessness of modern and postmodern design. As for the original Cracker homes that still remain in central and north Florida, Haase noted poignantly: "They will all soon be gone."

State Road 46 was the pavement that connected Sanford with Mt. Dora, a little chocolate box of a town stacked on gently rolling hills another 32 miles to the west. In the early 1960s, when S.R. 46 was no more than a single-lane country road, it had been bisected by an interstate stretched between Daytona and Tampa. It was an expressway that originally was to link Jacksonville with Tampa because they were two well-established port cities on the coasts. But the ambitions of Orlando city leaders—coalesced by Martin Andersen, the powerful owner-publisher of the daily newspaper—prevailed. And the quiet, former cow town of Orlando in the interior of the state was dutifully intersected by Interstate 4. The Florida Turnpike arrived not long afterwards for the same reason. Walt Disney, after flying over Florida to scout for good road connections to site his planned new mega-attraction in the 1960s, looked down upon the cattle pastures just southwest of Orlando, saw I-4 and the Florida Turnpike crisscrossing each other, and thought: Great roads; cheap land. I could do this here.

Despite the purposeful pro-growth determination found nearly everywhere else in central Florida, Interstate 4 had scant effect on Sanford. In fact, there was so little hope for development here that the access and exit lanes were designed as "farm ramps" of the sort that directly deposited vehicles from the interstate to the local road, without needing the fancy traffic enhancement of a cloverleaf. Sanford, as the southernmost port for luxury steamboats on the St. Johns River, was once the bustling heart of central Florida. But it had weathered a couple of nasty economic crashes that had almost taken it down for good, and it had circled the wagons. For Sanford leaders, growth meant modestly spreading beyond the historic downtown and allowing new shopping plazas, sub shops, and auto repair garages to be built on nearby U.S. 17-92, a humble goal by modern Florida standards. By the late 1980s, its people were unpretentious farmers and merchants and small-town professionals, and they seemed to have no designs on being anything else. They enjoyed, as the former mayor of Orlando once wisely observed, a slower, less frustrating way of life.

Sanford was located on the shores of the north-flowing St. Johns River, where that waterway dilutes into a 15-square-mile lake that the Creeks called Wepolokse; the Spanish, Valdez; and the Americans, Monroe, for the fifth U.S. president. The name given it by the Timucua and Mayaca and those who preceded them has been lost to time. Although the river begins much farther south, just inland of Vero Beach, it was wilder down there, winding through a treeless marsh rather than a hardwood swamp. More to the point, the upper river was undredged and given to constantly redefining itself through a series of braided shallow streams and sloughs, most of which would open and close depending on rainfall and the surreptitious dynamics of stream flow. When the naturalist William "Billy" Bartram first oared and sailed up the St. Johns in 1764 with his father, John, they ultimately ran into the convoluted maze of Puzzle Lake not too far south of here and thought they had reached the river's headwaters. But the river meandered far beyond Puzzle Lake, another 100 miles south to Lake Hell n' Blazes. For the lonely cartographer who didn't find his way to that navigational headwater until the early twentieth century, Hell n' Blazes must have been an untamed place that begged the harsh reality of its name.

As for Lake Monroe, its very first European settlements were marked by a flamboyant flavor that overreached so grandly that its founders eventually ended up inflicting sucker punches on themselves. By the middle of the twentieth century, Sanford, which proclaimed itself the "Gateway to South Florida" during its steamboat era, had developed a sort of attitude, a kind of reverse snobbery that acknowledged that it had been the heir apparent to the prosperity that now defined Orlando—its former down-on-its-heels, land-locked country neighbor. But now it had been removed from competition, whether by design or not, and there was no need for argument. Sanford had been here first and was once bigger and grander. End of debate.

And so, by the time I moved to Sewell Road, tourists whooshed right on by on I-4 without a second thought as to what the Sanford exit might offer. The normally frenzied "business corridor" at the conflux of S.R. 46 and the interstate was instead a backwater slough off the main stem that seemed not to go anywhere. It puddled up into a Stuckey's, a Waffle House, a broken-down pre-fab motel, a gas station, and an ex–gas station turned craft shop—Cathy's, it was called. Cathy's specialized in the handmade wooden birds with legs that tapered to a pole that you stuck in the ground. Their wings were attached separately, and in a light breeze, they would spin around in a manic blur. There were brightly colored cardinals and flamingos and blue jays, and every time I drove past, their wings were spinning so fast they seemed as if they might take flight. A friend once came to visit with one of the flamingos as a gift, and, finding me not at home, she left it stuck in my yard, its wings endlessly whirling madly in the slightest breeze. Less than a half mile from the I-4 exit, cows grazed in pastures, and farmers still grew cabbage and melons and beans in big, flat, open fields. Just across the street on the corner of Monroe Road and S.R. 46, a tumbledown roadside stand sold oranges, tangerines, okra, boiled peanuts, and jars of homemade sugar-cane syrup. Nearby, on a small street named Reinhart Road, a worn block and wood-frame kennel advertised itself as the "Pet Rest Inn." Sewell Road fit here, wedged in between the cow pastures, the row crops, and the citrus groves, a little world within a world, less than a mile from the interstate.

Although I had moved to the edge of the unincorporated little farming community that was called Lake Monroe, my address was Sanford, even though that city was 4 miles away. Sanford, like much of Florida, had two distinct histories: One was the warm fuzzy chamber-of-commerce version that reveled in its old brick streets and Victorian-era storefronts, and the homespun civic attributes of all who had ever lived here. The other was more raw, and accurate.

Sanford itself had been named for the brilliant and asthmatic "Major General" Henry Sanford, an honorary officer but a real-life foreign service diplomat who founded it by the sheer act of buying 20 square miles of land for development in 1870 via his Florida Land and Colonization Company. Sanford was a Connecticut lawyer who had been the U.S. ambassador to Belgium. On his foreign service tour, he became aware of that country's colonization of the dense tropical fretwork of the Congo. Back home, he decided he could do the same with this strange new subtropical jungle called Florida. By 1880, his colony in Florida featured a 200-room hotel, a telegraph service, two banks, eight churches, four newspapers, and three steamboat piers. It eventually consumed the original village of Mellonville, situated on the site of an old Seminole War fort just to the east on Lake Monroe. Fort Mellon, named for a commander killed during an attack there, had been aimed at controlling, harassing, or eliminating the Seminoles, whose main offense was living on the land the new settlers wanted. Sanford's namesake city grew and grew until its population outnumbered that of landlocked Orlando. Henry Sanford considered Orlando a backwoods cow town that stood in the way of the ambitions he had to make his new colony into the transportation hub for all of south Florida. It was Sanford who urged his friend, the Philadelphia saw-blade heir Hamilton Disston, to buy otherwise "useless" wetlands in this waterlogged state, drain it, and then sell the "reclaimed" land to homesteaders. (Disston, who launched his draining operation from Kissimmee to the south in 1881, planned to drain the entire Everglades, starting at its headwaters just below Orlando.)

Henry Sanford was fluent in German, French, Spanish, and Italian, but he was less conversant with the vernacular of the place. Although Sanford only lived here seasonally and had little local knowledge of the geography or culture, he never fully entrusted his local agent to be in decision-making sovereignty of the settlement. Ultimately, his land business—which sold 10-acre tracts for $25 an acre—failed, as did his newly planted citrus groves. In the end, Sanford died leaving his young wife in great debt—not to mention a backwoods fiefdom bereft of its monarch. His wife, who much preferred Europe to her late husband's town, spent the last decade of her life trying to pay back his debts. She described it as "a vampire that sucked the repose and the beauty and the dignity and cheerfulness out of our lives."

In a way, poor old "Major General" Sanford functioned not unlike the nineteenth-century British who imperialistically carved out little crown colonies throughout the world. When they left—deposed, bankrupt, defeated—they departed with such haste that the transfer of managerial autonomy to their colonial subjects was a distant concern. To those practical-minded Crackers who lived unassuming, hard-working lives, Sanford's grand ambition must have seemed as alien as the Belgian king's aspirations to "civilize" the Congo had to the natives there.

At least Henry Sanford had selected his colony's site for all the right reasons. He wanted to settle the southern shore of Lake Monroe because that dilation of the St. Johns was the most prominent geographic and navigational feature in the interior here. Indeed, that was how Florida had been organically settled—by early migrants like the Timucua and Mayaca, the Calusa and the Tequesta, and all the unnamed Indians who preceded them for twelve thousand years or more. These earliest Floridians decided where to live by choosing a high bank to stay dry, a waterway to transport them, and a wildlife habitat with fish and game to feed them. They could trek into the swamp or scrub to hunt, but living too deep in the wetlands or too far away from the rivers atop sandhills made little sense.

At first, these earliest Paleo-Floridians migrated between the coastal lagoons and the newly birthed inland springs and rivers. Finally, after glaciers from the last Ice Age fully retreated, and the arid peninsula of Florida became moist with a newly invigorated hydrological cycle, they began to live more permanently on the banks of sure-flowing rivers like the St. Johns. They stayed close to the navigable water because it offered great efficacy to be there. The river brought them snails and fish, alligators and gar, even manatees. They could paddle it to travel from place to place, to trade, hunt, explore. It gave them time to consider their lives, to invent mythology, to pay homage to their gods, all of which were manifest around them in the woods and sky. Here, they discarded their refuse, building up garbage and burial middens of shell and bone and sand along the shore until, finally, the St. Johns—of all the rivers—became home to the most generous collection of such middens in North America. And the lake now mapped as Monroe was the lush cornucopia that splayed out across its midsection. Even until the late nineteenth century, Carolina parakeets flew overhead in great shoals of green, immense ivory-billed woodpeckers hammered loudly from the cypress, panthers and bears moved warily in the understory of needle palm and wild grape vines. Monroe was shallow and so clear you could see the eel grass growing on the sandy bottom below. It was sweet, fed with fresh upland water and springs. If you were thirsty, you could cup your hands and drink from it. For Indians and the white pioneers who followed, it was a splendid place to live. When early settlers moved away from the lake, they did so because they found land that was productive and useful for them.

Sometime between the time Henry Sanford died and when I arrived in Florida in 1973, the idea of settling in places based on the wisdom of appropriate geographic features went all to hell.

Highways and roads now decided how the landscape would be developed. If there were no roads, they could simply be built to open up the countryside to where developers had bought cheap land. Marketing and advertising could reshape the image, and landscapers could shrub it up with non-native palms and flowers, all of which require intense amounts of water and chemicals to keep them alive. A new arrival, paying attention only to brochures and billboards, would think they had descended into a fantasyland of a place—a climate-controlled community of neatly manicured yards and guarded entrances and some trees—but not too many, because snakes and grove rats could hide in them. Irrigators, exterminators, and the people who make a living spraying poisons on lawns flourished. The common-sense method of selecting a place to live based on its ability to sustain people was forgotten. Florida, which boomed first with newcomers in the 1880s and again in the 1920s, was booming again in the 1960s. In retrospect, the Orlando Sentinel observed at the beginning of 2000:

"Florida had no single event—no Gold Rush—that drove masses south. It was a steady stream of people lured by a string of promoters, warm climate, miles of coastline, vacant land and natural resources—all spelling potential opportunities. . . .

"They have made Florida the U.S. southern frontier much the same way that California was America's new beginning in the West a century earlier. . . . Wave after wave of newcomers has accounted for 80 percent of the state's population growth, and in some decades it has been as high as 90 percent."

Then, in full consideration of how this state had been so fully rearranged by people who were lured or decoyed by tourism and real estate brochures and promotional hype, the paper went on to name a single individual who most defined modern Florida, and they lionized him as the "Man of the Century." The Man of the Century was "The Newcomer."

Who could argue? After all, I had come here myself seeking my own fortune. No matter that I was lured by the half-remembered nascent romance of childhood. The point was that I was here, and I needed a place to live.

Chapter Two

Enchantment here is different things for each of us.
Marjorie Kinnan Rawlings, Cross Creek

I moved into my home on Sewell Road with a U-Haul truck and the help of a fishing buddy and a hired transient I found loitering at a local labor pool. We loaded all the furniture and boxes from my rented house in Sanford and then trucked it to Sewell, the three of us working up a good sweat over the course of five hours or so. Then they left, and I began to settle in.

My first dilemma was deciding where to put the bedroom. Except for the natural, heat-mitigating value of the wood, houses of this era did not have insulating padding behind the walls. The ceiling, originally made of batten board cypress, had in more modern times been covered with a series of soft, 1-by-3-foot fabric-board tiles that seemed pressed from wood and paper, a sort of hamburger of fiber shards. These "tiles," now painted white, gave the ceiling a decidedly fifties look, like a drop ceiling that didn't fully drop. I realized that the tiles were glued atop the original batten board to provide a sort of external insulation. It was an organic extension of ad hoc design—it was there because, aesthetic or not, it worked in some way. In the long, rectangular living room, heat from the fireplace had likely loosened the glue binding the tilework, and the ceiling had begun to sag. To fix this, thin circles of roofing aluminum slightly larger than silver dollars had been nailed into the ceiling at the edges where two or more tiles abutted each other. The result was singular in its effect, and once a visiting friend commented on the unique nature of "all those little flying saucers in your ceiling."

The kitchen had its own distinctive appeal. The original pipe that once connected a wood-burning stove to the chimney was flush in the wall and capped with what looked like an old pie tin. Opposite it was what must have been the state of art in cooking in the 1950s, a white enameled gas stove, its brand name proudly inscribed on a corner in lime-green letters—the Ultra-matic Caloric. In addition to its gas and oven burners, it was equipped with other modern functions, such as a round-faced clock with a plastic timer dial and a small built-in fluorescent light. The burners and oven worked great, but

I could never seem to get the clock or light to return to life. Nearby was a set of double porcelain sinks with sideboards. You could swing out the two side-hinged cypress-framed windows over them and let in a light breeze, sometimes filling the kitchen with the scent of the orange blossoms when the trees were in bloom.

The dining room was between the kitchen and living areas, and its walls were covered with the wide board paneling of real knotty pine, lustered a warm ginger tone by age. Hidden under its burgundy-colored carpet was a hardwood floor. Sometime in the last thirty years, a set of industrial-quality sliding glass doors had been installed between the dining and the living rooms. The doors, which seemed entirely incongruous with the integrity of the 1920s-era home, were adorned with two large decals of sailboats cutting through the froth of water. I soon realized that the decals were there not for décor but to alert occupants to when the thick, clear glass doors were shut. Sailboat floating in the ether chest-level from the ground? Don't walk into it. The doors, I figured, provided a heat barrier that allowed the bottom floor of the house to be divided into two manageable zones: During cooler winter months, the fireplace and small gas heater in the living room would keep that immense rectangle cozy; on the other side, the heat from the gas stove could do the same. When only one zone or the other needed to be heated, the doors could be shut, thus saving valuable energy.

A few days after the move, Mike and Carolyn Durak stopped by for a visit. Mike, who had grown up in the house, had sold it to me on behalf of his father. In a way, I now realize they were also saying good-bye to a place they had once loved. Carolyn, a retired elementary school teacher, had a delightful, infectious exuberance. Mike, with an education in geography, had worked for the Central and Southern Florida Flood Control District, among other agencies, and taken an early retirement from the Seminole County government. Lanky, bright, intense, Mike had used his knowledge of road building and its impact on the land to help steer roads away from sensitive places like seasonally flooding wetlands in the county. He and Carolyn now lived in a newer ranch-style home on nearby Monroe Road on the north side of S.R. 46 and owned some 16 acres of woodland and creek nearby. But they had bought several hundred acres of land in rural Tennessee and would be relocating there soon. Their dad, Michael Sr., had moved out of the Sewell Road home; he was living with them now and would be going to Tennessee when they did. Both Mike and Carolyn had a sort of self-reliant can-do spirit, and they seemed excited about the prospect of starting a new country life in another southern state that was not plagued by sprawl. Yet Mike couldn't hide a sort of resentment he had for the change that was sweeping over Florida. He hinted that it was virtually unstoppable, and that rather than spend the last years of his life fighting it, he would—like many other Florida natives, including the former Orlando mayor—resettle in a place that somehow reminded him of the rural and quiet life he once knew.

We walked around the house, and Mike helped me crack the code of its lifeways. There had, indeed, been no single bedroom. In fact, he and his mother and father had seasonally migrated around the house, sleeping in different rooms depending on how comfortable each was at the time. Sometimes they nested upstairs; sometimes in the room between the kitchen and the pantry, sometimes out on the enclosed porch to the rear. The wooden wall on that porch reached only to the waist; panels of jalousie windows filled the space between there and the ceiling. I noticed the lower two slats of each window were made of a cloudy glass that—with the low wall—helped block the more sensitive private anatomies of bodies from an outside view.

The Duraks had left some furniture and knick-knacks behind, including an inexpensive dining room table and chairs, a wrought iron floor lamp, a dandy beige-colored living area rug bursting with roses, a huge gilded frame mirror over the fireplace, a chest of drawers with strips of wormy maple veneer, a tiny dish with a flamingo hand-painted on it, and an art deco vase that I thought was worthless kitsch but that later turned out to be an expensive collectible. In the kitchen, there were metal drawers full of clean rags, which were routinely washed and re-used in place of paper towels. The walls and woodwork around the doors and windows were uniformly painted lime green, a color that had been the rage in Florida a few decades ago. Indeed, the green seemed to be the exact same color of the logo on my Ultramatic Caloric stove. The window glass was delightfully uneven and refracted images on the other side with a slightly wavy effect. The living room fireplace was outfitted with a "Heat-A-Lator" that helped passively recapture some of the heat that would otherwise go up the chimney and blow it back out through graded metal vents. Mike told me that his parents would hide money around the house at Easter—more fun than searching for Easter eggs—and the grandchildren would run and hunt for it, looking in drawers and under beds and in closets. The Duraks said they had scoured the old house just last week and found thirty or forty dollars still squirreled away from a forgotten Easter, and figured they had it all. Months later, I was digging around in the back of one of the rag drawers for a wipe cloth to use and found three ten-dollar bills. I had put most of my savings into purchasing this house, and so I accepted the gift gratefully and certainly with as much enthusiasm as any little kid may have had at Easter time. I regarded this newly discovered money much like I regarded my homestead, as a gift, passed down generously through time.

We toured the backyard and stopped inside the open tin-roofed shed that covered the handsome brick barbecue. In the corner was an old wringer washer; I saw the shed had been wired with electricity and even plumbed for water. The drain for the washer went into a ditch at the base of the shed, and from there it flowed into another ditch that ran along the perimeter of the property. The shed had corrugated green fiberglass sheets around it to block the winter wind. There was a handmade cypress bench and a cart with wheels from Mike's old baby carriage, both painted lime green. The cart had ferried hamburger and ketchup and buns from the kitchen for family cookouts. Nearby was a small coontie, an ancient palm-like cycad that seeds without flowering. Its tuberlike roots, ground finely, were used as flour, first by the Timucua and Mayaca, and later by the white settlers. It is a striking little shrub with glossy green pinnate leaves, most notable now for its use for landscaping—in fact, it was even listed by the state as commercially exploited because of this particular utility. In all my wanderings through the woods in Florida, I had never seen a coontie in the wild, and it pleased me that one was growing in my yard.

The Duraks named the plants and flowers for me—the "Easter bonnet" flower that grew in a vine until it covered the chain-link fence next to the road; the two meiwa kumquat trees that flanked the front door, their little fruits as round as miniature oranges; the figs and yellow Cattley and red Cattley guavas out back; the elderberries; the poinsettias from Christmases long ago now growing wild, 6 and 7 feet tall. And the centerpiece of the yard, the giant tropical cactus that was as big as I've ever seen it anywhere in Florida. Cereus, they called it, Queen of the Night, and in the warm months it would sprout magnificent lilylike blooms that didn't open until nearly midnight and then closed by early morning. Next to it was a prickly pear, a much smaller cactus with flat pads and yellow blossoms that were open by day. Antillean in origin, the prickly pear had been recorded long ago by naturalist William Bartram when he explored Florida. A compact bush they called a Georgia rose was growing next to a white stone bench. It was an antique that bore tight little flowers, each with a delicate rose scent. Behind the rose was a large clump of green studded with tight, red, crepelike buds. It looked like a hibiscus with blossoms that never opened. Carolyn called it a Turks-cap and showed me how to pull the blooms off and, if the hummingbirds or bees had not yet been there, to suck out faint traces of honey-flavored nectar. A real hibiscus bush grew up against the back of the house, nearly hiding a propane gas tank there. To the sides and back, the land was encircled with a hog-wire fence. Rawlings, when she lived at Cross Creek, kept both a Turks-cap and a hibiscus near her Cracker house, just inside her own hog fence. It didn't take a stretch of imagination to picture her living here, for this house and hers were of the same era.

Next to the cereus, there was a 2-inch-wide pipe that capped off an artesian well. The well had been drilled down into the surficial aquifer only 15 or 20 feet deep, a water source that was under so much pressure from the uplands that poking a hole into its limestone and clay casement was enough to bring it spouting up out of the ground. A faucet had been put on the capped pipe so it could be open and shut. When Mike twisted the faucet, I could smell the strong scent of sulfur from the pipe, but the groundwater no longer had the energy to surge upwards. A huge, 3-foot-high concrete pipe was stuck perpendicularly in the ground next to the well, but Mike was unsure of how the culvert had been used. At the back of the yard was an immense stand of bamboo, and hidden behind it was an old tin-roofed shed that had once been a chicken house. I lifted the hinged metal lid that covered a narrow tier of the shed and inside saw six wooden citrus boxes, each of which once held a nesting hen. Birds routinely lived around and migrated through the land here, Mike said. Woodpeckers, owls, mockingbirds, cardinals, wrens, and, by winter, flocks of warblers and robins. A chuck-will's-widow, seldom seen, was always heard calling at night.

The derelict swimming pool sat just to the north, and I wondered about its history. Mike said his father had built it for his mother. But she couldn't swim, so he built it shallow, 3 or 4 feet or so, about the size of a kiddie pool, except it was made of porcelain tile and looked like a miniature in-ground swimming pool. When his father needed to filter the water, he brought out an old hand pump made especially for cleaning little ponds or pools. I guess they made things like that then. By now, Mrs. Durak had been dead for a few years, and her husband couldn't much bear to deal with the pool, so he had let it go. It was full of giant bullfrogs, and a native version of the lotus lily, along with lots of pond scum. Gambusia, the little native minnow called mosquitofish because of its taste for mosquito larvae, were thriving there now. The gambusia were an early form of mosquito control; county agents would drive around with great vats of water with mosquitofish that they dumped in the cisterns of the country homes. Later, I learned that Mrs. Durak's ashes had been spread under the cereus. I could imagine her as a younger woman, soaking in her pool, perhaps by twilight, the heady scent of orange blossoms wafting across the landscape, cereus ready to decorate itself with its gigantic lotuslike white blooms. Perhaps the chuck-will's-widow called out its ineffably sweet four-note refrain from the woods nearby, punctuating an otherwise still and lonely country night.

The swimming pool was on the remaining undeveloped land between here and S.R. 46 that the Duraks were keeping to sell speculatively. It had once been an open pasture where cows and horses could graze, but by now the land beyond the pool was mostly full of newly sprouted longleaf pine. When I first saw the pool, I had hoped they might lease the immediate land around it to me, and I could clean it out and use it, perhaps to grow catfish— a half-baked dream I once had as a backyard fish farmer, finally come true. But the Duraks' lawyer warned them that the old pool was a hazard to any neighborhood child who might fall in and drown—and "hazard" to lawyers translates into liability. The pond would have to be destroyed before the Duraks left town, and one day it was, a backhoe driver entering through a wide gate in the front fence on Sewell, scooping up a mature citrus tree that was in its way, and then crushing the walls of the pool into itself. Mike had come out to watch, and as the pool was being crushed, he looked away absently and said, "Mama's rolling over in her grave." Then he and I chased after the giant bullfrogs that were leaping away from the path of devastation.

Back on the other side of the house near the driveway, a wooden arbor supported a purple wisteria vine, a vine so old it was now thicker than my forearm. Next to it was the most striking landscaping touch of all—the handmade pond that looked like a miniature Spanish fortress. It rose up out of the ground for several feet, its mineralized walls cobbled from mortar and coquina and limestone. I looked closely at the edges of the rim and saw that marbles—the kind kids play with—had once been pressed into the mortar there. "They were mine when I was a boy," Mike told me. The pond was tiered into two reservoirs—a lower one that also scooped down a couple feet into the ground, and a higher one just behind it that reached to my waist. The upper pond had a lip in its middle, and it appeared that the cold artesian water from a well first filled it and then overflowed as a waterfall into the one below. Goldfish had lived here, swimming among native lotus lily pads that bloomed white. Mike's mom could clean greens and peas and corn at the big double sink in the kitchen and, looking out through the open window, watch the pond, its waterfall, and the flashes of gold below. The artesian well that fed the pond came from a different source than the well by the cactus, and the pipe feeding this one had dried long ago.

By now the pond was parched, its walls cracked, and a 5-foot-tall laurel oak was growing out of its bottom. Mike suggested I simply tear it all down and remove the stone. But I had bigger plans: I would chop out the tree, patch the pond with concrete, and even though I could no longer tap the artesian well, I could fill the newly sealed pond basin with water from the garden hose. In fact, I had kept the frogs that escaped the Apocalypse of the pool alive in PVC buckets until I finished reconstructing the old pond. When it was ready to occupy, I filled it with water and native lotus lilies and dumped the buckets of frogs into it. They croaked and splashed with great frog abandon. Later, I added some gambusia that I scooped out of the flowing ditch at the back of the property, along with a few crayfish. One morning I saw a little green heron standing on the edge of the pond rim, picking out his dinner, one gambusia at a time. He was a study in patience, his movements stop-framed and nearly imperceptible except for the final lunge he made with his pointed beak into the water. I wondered if other green herons before him had known of this fishing hole.

When I had time, I poked around in the two-car garage and found a wooden milking stool, left from when the Duraks had a small farm here on their land. Scattered about in the garage were also piles of wire and scraps of wood and some of the original milled siding, materials that could have been used to jerry-rig a number of useful things out here on a farm. In one corner was an old water pump and a kerosene grove heater used to keep the citrus trees from freezing. In another, there were three old dust-covered bamboo fishing poles, likely cut from the stand that hid the chicken coop. Equipped with a short string line, a hook and bobber, they made dandy cane poles. And now they were left here in the garage, put away one final summer afternoon and never picked back up again, representing all that is so familiar, all that once was so routine that it seemed as if it might go on forever. And then one day, the tiny gear wheels of our lifeways move, ever so gradually, and the future shifts, as subtle and imperceptible as that of the motion of a green heron, and nothing is ever the same again. I didn't have the heart to throw the cane poles away, and simply left them hanging there in the corner of the garage.

The Duraks seem to take a very real pleasure in being able to hand the place over to someone who would care for it. It really was a fine homestead, out here at the end of a quiet dirt road, and while the area had changed enough to chase off the Duraks, it was still serene and charming enough to offer comfort to me. Mike and Carolyn came by a few more times before they left, and once Mike's dad came with them. The senior Durak told me about an underground conduit system he once built that drained the water off the patio between the garage and the house, and how once when he was cleaning it, he found a snake inside. He showed me the drain and cautioned me about doing the same. His eyes were still clear and strong then. He looked up at me and spread his arms out. "You can do anything you want with it," he said, and I took that to mean that this house and its great natural amusement park of a yard had great potential, and that I could realize it as I wanted, and have fun doing so, just as he had done. But then I understood that he was turning his home, a place where all his dreams had been grounded for so long, over to me as fully as he could, and in doing so, giving me permission to be here. "I mean it," he said, and I shook his hand and thanked him.

I made some changes, but they weren't drastic. One of the first things I did was to tear off the old green fiberglass panels around the brick barbecue pit, and put up wooden lattice in its place. I used the wiring already there inside to power a ceiling fan that I put in the middle of the underside of the gabled roof. Then I hung a fiber hammock between two of the opposite posts. I had made my own outdoor chickee—in imitation of what the Seminoles once called their homes. It was ventilated on all sides by the seasons, and in the winter, the barbecue grill became an outdoor fireplace that I fueled with dead citrus branches and twigs. Just beyond the northern boundary of my land, I poked around in the shed left behind on the Durak property, the one that was tin-roofed with boards of pecky cypress serving as walls. It was full of small limbs once cut for the fireplace, and when it grew colder, I would push the old wheelbarrow over there and fill it full of mini-logs to make an outdoor fire in the brick grill. The logs Mr. Durak had once cut burned full and bright, and I would sit in front of the diminutive bonfire on the cypress bench, sip a hot chocolate, and be glad that I was alive in my little world at the back of a yard, at the end of a road. At night, a yellow glow shimmered from inside the uneven windows of the old house, and with the canopy of foliage overhead—the sugar hackberry and the magnolia, the sabal and queen palms—I felt as if I were miles away from civilization, living in a time that was no longer the present, the amber glow not electric lights but kerosene lamps. The moonlight lay on the palm fronds like a varnished silver, and the chuck-will's-widow still called from the darkness, unutterably sweet as it always must have been. The traffic out on S.R. 46 was still light, and the trees muted most of it, so there was no sound except that of nature. Cicadas hummed, the night hawk sang, and the evening breeze, when it lifted up off the land, gently rustled the tops of the palms and the pines and the sugar hackberry. I felt as if I were somehow protected, safe inside the lineage of tradition here and blessed with the energy of all that had come before me. My heart was as warm as the embers of the burning wood, fully ignited in mimicry and bliss of another time.

When my dad could still drive, he'd come to visit in his white Ford Ranger pickup from his home in Frostproof. Like me, he'd been lured back to Florida by the promise my mom had felt and later wordlessly communicated to us. It was a promise that stayed alive, even after her death in 1986. Dad had been an athlete as a young man, and even in his late seventies and early eighties, his reflexes and essential athleticism were still there, under the frayed weathered shell that age inflicts on us. His Florida was more straightforward: He wasn't as intrigued by the rivers or swamps or beaches as I had been. It was simply a place where the weather allowed him to be outside most of the year, and that recreation helped keep him healthy into old age.

My dad had a strong, old-fashioned work ethic and liked to help out whenever he could. And there was surely enough to do here to keep him busy. There was an odd room half-separated from the kitchen by a waist-high partition. I would have done away with the partition altogether and expanded the kitchen except one end of it was attached to a load-bearing four-by-four. The floor in this room was covered with a ratty carpet, under which were two layers of linoleum—one of them lime green. I had pulled back the edges of these layers and found an unfinished wooden pine floor underneath, its lumber every bit as bright as the day it had first been installed.

This room had once been a way stop during the seasonal rotational pattern for the Duraks. The extra layers of flooring served the very real value of helping to keep the north wind from whipping up through the floorboards of their elevated house, especially under a sleeping room such as this. I ripped back the layers of floor covering, swept and cleaned the wood the best I could, and then my dad helped me finish it out. To match it up with the other aged hardwood of the house, we chose a cherry varnish, and by the time we were done brushing on three coats, the floor gleamed with the color of a new copper penny. Closets were clearly an afterthought in Cracker houses—the only real one was under the stairs leading to the second floor. So I bought a cedar wardrobe at a used furniture store in downtown Sanford, lightly sanded it, replaced a door that had been split with new wood, and refinished it. It went in the corner of the newly invigorated room.

Although my house was a work in progress, I had settled in enough to give it a sense of home. I set up my office in the knotty-pine dining room and worked here, accepting magazine assignments as I had always done. I began to welcome visitors. My dad had always been accepting and looked forward to coming and working on assorted house projects with me, and it was always great to have him here. Once, at Thanksgiving, I cooked a turkey in a smoker grill out in the barbecue pit, experimenting with chips from citrus, oak, and hickory. When I finally raised the large cuplike lid from the smoker after seven hours, the turkey was completely black on the outside from the soot of all those chips. My Dad, whose own farm-rearing gifted him with a certain stoicism, didn't say a word. But when he saw the charred black bird, he couldn't help himself from uttering a single long, low exclamation, geeeeez-zzzz. When I sliced the meat, though, it was tender and moist inside. We peeled off the skin and had ourselves a fine dinner, sitting around a butcher-block oak table in the kitchen.

For friends and acquaintances, my property was a sort of architectural Rorschach, and each projected onto it accordingly. I soon realized that my home was so entirely out of the mainstream that it simply didn't fit the comfort level of most. Oddly, everyone could understand restoring a Victorian home—indeed, one friend even lived in a Victorian replica. But the Cracker style was more problematic for them. Although grand in comparison to the one-story Cracker homes on smaller lots on my road, its design had no cachet whatsoever in modern Florida. One editor friend, who lived in a walled subdivision with rules about the neatness of grass lawns, had no comment on the house but strongly suggested I should more neatly manage my yard, and especially ought to do away with a dead queen palm trunk that loomed next to my barbecue shed. I had left it up because a screech owl and two downy woodpeckers had, alternately, used it to raise broods of young birds, and it gave me great pleasure to see them come and go in the twilight and at dawn. But these are tiny, sublime pleasures that are sometimes difficult to express. One graphic designer I was dating, more forthright, suggested I tear it all down and start over, and soon after that I stopped dating her. A woman friend, an architect at a hospital, recommended I paint it all white, inside and out, in order to make it look neat and clean. One visitor, a television anchor who read the news, withheld judgment. But later, when she became angry at me over some imagined slight, she said "that explains why you live where you do." Two very bright women saw all its nuances and its context and smiled when they walked around the big, friendly, time-stuck yard; one was a visiting poet who taught at a university out west; the other, the woman I would eventually fall in love with.

I went back to Rawlings to see how she reported her own affinity for place in Cross Creek. It was, as I had found in my own patch of land, an appreciation for enchantment—the vernacular of the house, the coquina pond, the wisteria arbor, the tin-roofed brick barbecue pit, the orange trees, the palms, the bamboo. "To me, it is this," Rawlings wrote: "To feel the mystery of a seclusion that yet has shafts of light striking through it. This is the essence of an ancient and secret magic. It goes back, perhaps to the fairy tales of childhood . . . to all the half-luminous places that pleased the imagination as a child . . . here is that mystic loveliness of childhood again. Here is home."

True, there was an easygoing, rickety, out-of-plumb quality that would scare most left-brained humans back to the geometric safety of the walled subdivisions that were coming to dominate central Florida. Rawlings understood this, too, long before the arrival of such development. She appreciated the uneven quality of the Creek, and how it stood out in comparison to more prosperous—and stylishly linear—neighborhoods, even then. "I think that the shabbiness of the Creek is a part of its endearing quality. I for one might admire, but never truly love, an affluent perfection."

Rawlings was either ahead of her time or wonderfully stuck deep inside of it. Her admiration of shabbiness is reflected in the ageless Japanese concept of wabi-sabi, the celebration of the beauty of things imperfect, impermanent, and incomplete. Its concepts mesh with the core of Zen, and its early devotees were tea masters, priests, and monks who practiced Zen Buddhism in the twelfth century. Material suggestions of wabi-sabi are said to suggest the natural process, to be irregular, intimate, unpretentious, earthy, and simple.

Although the practical-minded people who lived here before me would have gotten a kick out of the concept, I accepted the premise that my land and its house were the result of a certain redneck Cracker Zen. The fact that it was not rendered with the conscious realization of this seemed to make it more so.

I began to meet my neighbors, gradually. There was still none of the welcome-wagon embrace I once romanticized when I first moved to Florida. But this time around, I was a single man living by himself rather than half of a young couple. How I was perceived by the rest of the world had changed. But I could tell there was a certain self-reliant live-and-let-live spirit at work here, and I could certainly appreciate that.

Indeed, a few days after I moved in, that ambience leaked abruptly across my property line. I was in my office at my computer when I heard a loud banging on the door next to the patio. It was a teenage boy with close-cropped hair in denim overalls and snake boots. He was breathless, his chest heaving and his face nearly white. "Mister, I lost my cow." He was clearly disturbed. "Have you seen it?" I told him that I had not yet seen his cow. In that most of my property is enclosed by a fence, I was wondering how such an large animal might find its way in. "You don't know this cow," the boy said, with half of a smile.

The boy left, and I went back to my desk, which overlooks the side yard, the driveway, the wisteria arbor, and the old coquina pond. I started tapping away on the computer keys again when I heard a commotion. It was a cow, and it was running down Sewell Road. When it reached the opening to my driveway, it ducked its head down, banked comically like a large Disney cartoon animal—Dumbo on the loose!—and stampeded inside, brushing up against my truck as it went. I watched speechless as it clopped through the concrete patio between the garage and the house. By the time I got to the door, I saw it running at full speed through the backyard, not slowing a bit for the low hog-wire fence. It took the fence with half a leap, bulling through most of it and rearranging the wire into the sag of a giant U. The cow must have escaped from one of the nearby pastures, where it normally grazed somnambulantly, head down and docile—right up until that special moment when it perked up and made its heroic run for freedom. Afterwards, when I would drive out on Reinhart Road past the pastures where cows still ranged, I would try to pick him out of the bunch, but after that one brief moment of energetic rebellion, he had gone back to simply being a cow, inscrutable, like the others, in his complete bovinity.

I fertilized the few Hamlin orange trees on the property to help keep them bearing, and from the seeds of a guava, grew four new plants. The guavas burst with little, delicate, white flowers in the spring, to be followed a few months later by hundreds of plum-sized fruits. I tried every recipe I could find, but the most satisfactory way of dealing with the little fruits, ultimately, was to pick them off the tree, cool them in the refrigerator, and eat them whole. Wild blackberry vines trailed through the southeast corner of the yard, near the old grove, and I let them chart their own course, picking them when they, too, ripened. I traveled a lot then, flying off to overseas locales to report various environmental stories for weeks at a time. I didn't have the luxury of growing a real garden because it would simply get away from me. I did try my hand at habanero peppers, though, as they were hardy brutes with woody stems. I had seen them growing in Central America, had sampled a hot sauce in Belize made from them, and was determined to handcraft my own. My habanero crops, grown from seed, were a great success, and the plants—still enjoying the rich soil the Duraks had augmented with chicken manure—each bore a hundred or more fruits at a time. At the end of each pepper season, I picked, culled, and washed them, and mixed them in a blender with vinegar, carrots, fresh garlic cloves, onions, and salt. Together it made a fine salsa that was close enough to the Belizean sauce I had once sampled to be nearly indistinguishable from it.

Directly across from me in a small Cracker house is the only truly intact nuclear family still on the street, the Metts. Their modest home is surrounded by a chain-link fence, and in the backyard there is a kennel of beagles, used as hunting dogs. Each dog has a number shaved into its fur so that it will be recognizable in the field. A small wooden sign on the fence has been routed out to read: Blue Diamond Kennels. The man's name is Mark, and he works in law enforcement, although he seldom wears his uniform to or from work. We wave, tentative at first, and every few months we talk, usually in the street. I learned that his daddy grew up nearby, that he has bought some land in South Carolina to retire to one day, and that he goes there often to deer hunt. It is clear that he is proud of his kids, a boy of eight and a girl of ten. His wife, Sylvia, always quick to wave and smile, works as a teacher's aide at one of her kids' schools. During holidays, Sylvia always decorates the modest yard—large peppermint sticks around the sidewalk at Christmas, a carved pumpkin at Halloween, different kinds of bunnies at Easter.

Mark and Sylvia's children sometimes play in the street and occasionally stray over into my yard to see what I was doing. The boy is big-boned and heavy like his father, and because of this, seems much older than he is. The girl, a slender little blonde, one time told me that her brother had once been elected Baby King in a beauty contest for infants. Another time, she yelled to me as I backed out of my driveway, telling me that Bigfoot had been caught. Both children seemed entranced by the revitalized coquina pond. They were polite, sweet kids, and they spoke with just the trace of an Old Florida southern accent.

Just north of the Metts family are O. P. Jones and his wife, an elderly couple who have lived on the road since 1970. I would see the man out every day in his suspenders and work shirt and long denim jeans puttering in his yard, tending to his gardenias and orange trees. He seems to have created a sort of den for himself in a shed in his backyard, and when his chores are done, he spends most of the time sitting in front of a small TV there while his wife stays inside the main house, likely watching her own programs. To the north of them is a Cracker home that looks as if it outlived its usefulness a few decades ago. It is falling apart, and the effect of dissolution is enhanced by the fact that the entire yard is nearly covered end to end with debris—old concrete blocks and lumber, piles of boxes, jumbles of metal that long ago lost their form, wabi sabi turned in upon itself. When I first moved here, I thought the house might be abandoned. Later I would see a pickup with a trailer loaded with lawn-maintenance gear in the driveway. A retired navy vet lived there with a wife who was disabled from a stroke; in the few times she came outside, she used a walker. While he struck me as unsociable, I figured life had dealt him some tough hands. He seemed to care, lovingly, for his wife. In his retirement, he took care of the yards of rich people who lived somewhere else.

At the mouth of Sewell, facing S.R. 46, are two smaller Cracker homes, one with a set of coonties in the yard. The owner of one home died before I moved in, and it was up for sale. A developer had bought the other from the original family and was renting it for a few hundred dollars a month to keep it occupied. Although barely more than 500 feet from my property, these homes were on land closer to the river, and the topography was lower. Ditches surrounded the houses on all sides, leading to the large trench that paralleled S.R. 46. The previous owners clearly understood the wisdom of keeping their own tiny canals open to drain to the north. But the new family of renters came here from somewhere else. Soon they let weeds and trees clog their man-made gullies. When it rained hard, water would flow downstream, as it has always done, and the yards there would flood. One day I drove by and noticed that the two coonties growing in one of the yards had been mowed down to the ground. For the newcomers, it was all wet and green, no distinguishing for nuance.

There was one last room downstairs that needed major tending, and it was separated from the copper-penny room by a doorway with no door. I figured old Mr. Durak was unlikely to throw out anything as valuable as a heart cypress wood door, and so I searched the garage to see if I could find it. I found three there, each a slightly different size, and two painted lime green. Unlike modern hollow-core doors, these were solid heart cypress, and each weighed close to 75 pounds. I finally figured out which of the three matched the framed doorway and then cleaned, scraped, and sanded it, painted it white, and hung it on the original hinges. The room it opened to had been built as a large walk-in pantry, and it was full of heavy wooden shelves and illuminated with a single light bulb in the ceiling. This is where the fruits I had seen growing had been preserved and stacked—the elderberries, the figs, the guavas, the kumquats, and the corn and peas from the garden that was seasonally planted behind the garage.

I had no interest in learning how to preserve fruit or vegetables—besides, I had a refrigerator—so the pantry shelves would go. As I tore out the shelves with a crowbar and hammer, panels of the wall coverings shredded as well. The panels were a version of the soft-tile ceiling, except the material was a sort of primitive Masonite. Under it was the original batten board. I replaced the proto-Masonite on the two walls I had damaged by hanging sheetrock. I then rippled the soft tiles from the ceiling to expose the batten and, after cleaning it, painted it white. I hung a ceiling fan where the light had been, and rewired an outlet from the other side of the wall, where it had done service in a closet under the stairs for the upper story. The pantry was the only room with a truly hideous floor—since, indeed, it didn't have to be anything else but useful. It was roughly hewn soft pine, unevenly cut and painted with several coats of dark brown paint. This I covered with wall-to-wall carpet and pad I had bought to match the room size. This would be my bedroom, especially appropriate since the "new" bathroom was adjacent to it. Boxlike, the bathroom poked out from the original structure on the north side—a more modern addition that was tacked on to replace the original outhouse sometime in the 1940s. I planned to eventually finish out the second floor and relocate my bedroom there, and then to use this as a guest room.

Upstairs, I got as far as installing a toilet and sink, and then three years after I arrived, the first wave of bulldozers came. They were moving earth to build a new mall a quarter mile away, atop high land that had been used to graze cows. The sound of their presence was distinguished not by any rumbling of machinery, but by the loud, piercing safety buzzers that would automatically go off when one of the large bulldozers was moving in reverse. Sharp, high noises like this carry for miles, while the soft furrows of the terrain seem to absorb the low rumbles and groans and clatters. Signs began to appear next to the woods and other Cracker homes out on S.R. 46, direct and stark harbingers of what was to come. They read, "Available."

I continued to maintain my house, to paint it, and to replace things that broke, like the old J pipe under the kitchen sink. But I had been in Florida long enough to understand that the mall would not be self-contained. Instead, it would create a feeding frenzy for land that would spread far beyond its own immediate boundaries. My memory of what had happened to Altamonte Springs when its own mall was built was still fresh.

The Orlando Sentinel heralded the arrival of the Sanford mall. In an article on December 19, 1993, it made several predictions, all of which were reported in a cheery pro-growth fashion. There was no mention of the need for new infrastructure, the expected increase in traffic and crime, and the impacts on the environment, particularly the loss of natural land and the groundwater under it. It was a testimony to how newspapers balkanize information in separate sections and departments, with scant interpretation and wisdom leaking between each.

"Like a key piece in a puzzle, the September groundbreaking at Seminole Towne Center near Sanford has allowed other pieces in the development picture to begin falling into place. The 1.2 million-square-foot mall, developed by Melvin Simon and Associates, isn't scheduled to open until after Labor Day 1995, but builders, developers and planners say north Seminole County already is beginning to see the effect.

"'State Road 46 is largely empty today, but five years from now, you're going to see a big difference,' [Jay Marder, director of planning for the city of

Sanford,] said. 'I have developers coming into my office every week finding out what it takes to get zoning changes approved.'

"The coming development in north Seminole also is expected to have an impact on the city of Sanford, which has long had a reputation as more of an agricultural center than one of Central Florida's hot spots. [Marder said,] 'With the mall and the new road improvements, Sanford and north Seminole County are really beginning to change.'"

For me, the news was far less cheery. I had already seen the "hot spots" of central Florida, had seen how, more often than not, they trammeled the life out of a place. One day, my little acre would become surrounded by stores and gas stations, and eventually the young longleaf pines between my land and S.R. 46 would go.

But, for now, I was still surrounded on all sides by the same landscape that first drew me here. Mall building moved along slowly, and, at first, most of the neighboring land—including my own—remained zoned as agriculture. Although traffic on S.R. 46 gradually increased and new stoplights were installed, cows still grazed at the edge of the mall-to-be. The day when all this would be gone was still uncertain enough to allow me to sometimes delude myself into thinking that it might never come.

Chapter Three

Shepherd Springs stands in a jungle, a dark pool of peculiarly clear water,
that looks golden in the light.

Into Tropical Florida (1887)

To care for nature and to live in modern Florida requires the near-daily practice of what Scott Fitzgerald once described as "negative capability"—the
ability to embrace two diametrically opposite ideas at once, and to still function. In a public document advertising my county's growth potential to bond-
ing brokers, the promotional copy proclaims Seminole does not expect "to
reach full residential build out until mid century." The same document brags
about the significant increase in the average square-foot size of new homes
here. In other words, a demand for resource-guzzling trophy homes and an
availability of native land to be paved over are highly desirable. None of this
would be odd by itself, of course. It is only when my county's official motto
is considered that negative capability becomes realized: "Seminole County,"
it brags, "Florida's Natural Choice." Within the promotional-brochure spin
of this reality: "Seminole County is known for its natural beauty. The lakes,
lush tropical growth, pine and oak trees, clean, fresh air; these are the things
that make living here special, and one of the most desirable areas to live in
Central Florida."

Taken together, these conflicting messages say: We're a beautiful natural
place to live. Come on down and help us build it out. The message is delusional and vaguely hallucinogenic, like a scene from a Carl Hiaasen novel.
Perhaps this sort of surreality is simply ingrained into Florida, as it is surely
found beyond the world of politics and growth: Not long ago, a down-and-
out bandit tried to hold up a convenience store down in Orlando using a
Vidal Sassoon hair curler wrapped in a towel. Although the instrument was
fitted with a tubelike device that could have been dimly mistaken for a gun
barrel, it was difficult not to notice the electrical cord and plug hanging from
the towel. And a man who performed as the Tigger character at Disney was
arrested for groping a teenage girl during a photo-taking session. That was
not particularly weird by itself. But then a lawyer—who also had dressed

up as Tigger for Disney—contacted the defendant, offering his services for defense. He was, he told his client, eminently qualified to represent him because of his own experience as a make-believe character. After giving his closing argument from inside a Tigger suit, the lawyer rested his case. The jury returned within an hour with a not guilty verdict.

Historically, truth has always been malleable here, more akin to Silly Putty than to the tangible karst rock that underpins the landscape. Seminole, once part of a sprawling county named "Mosquito" because there were so many of them, was first renamed "Orange" for the orange groves, which have since been largely uprooted to make way for growth. Regional feuds between Orlando and Sanford over who was better equipped to lead resulted in the northwest chunk of Orange breaking away into Seminole County in 1913. Today you will find lots of mosquitoes in Seminole but hardly any Seminoles. One of the most famous of the tribe to go was the heroic chief Osceola, who, after coming in to negotiate under a flag of truce in 1837, was summarily placed in chains and taken to a fortress in Ft. Moultrie, South Carolina, where, his wildness stolen from him, he eventually died.

Environmental activists who obsess over these paradoxes usually burn out in a couple of years. Some, fearing they will get hit with a reactive "SLAPP" suit from quarrelsome developers when they protest destruction of natural lands, hunker down because they can't afford to hire an attorney to defend themselves in court. SLAPP is a dandy metaphor; it's a chilling slap in the face to citizens who champion the environment. But it's also literal—the acronym stands for "Strategic Lawsuits Against Public Participation." Three-fourths of those sued actually prevail, but these are mostly larger well-funded environmental organizations with money to defend themselves. It is the grassroots granolas with no budget who usually lose by default. Only the truly driven hang on.

Despite my caring for natural places and my lament for their loss, I still have a certain bedraggled optimism. Admittedly, this hope is a speciated version, peculiar to those who live in the crosshairs of growth. It is not particularly rooted in logic. Instead, it is a Florida version of hope, a sort that can only be realized and sustained by seeking a deep, gut-level bond with a wild place—and then to believe in your heart that these places will save us all. A few years ago, author-naturalist Peter Matthiessen came to the nearby University of Central Florida as a visiting author. Matthiessen was lanky, taciturn, a bit cranky. I sat in on a seminar he gave in which he reminded everyone that Florida has more unroaded wilderness than any of the lower forty-eight. There is a reason: Florida kept its wildness longer than most states because its settlers preferred the sunny windswept coast, where 80 percent of Floridians now live. The untamed interior was the last to go, wet, nearly impenetrable, full of gothic dread and inhospitable Indians and rednecks. Today that moist, vine-tugging inland core represents the best of what we still have. Twenty and thirty years ago, a few elected officials with enough wisdom to understand how the growth momentum would one day masticate Florida, asked for voter referendums to support purchase of public lands. The response was overwhelmingly in favor of the concept. State land-buying agents went to the interior, where wetlands and scrub were still affordable. Using funds from real estate documentary stamps for CARL (Conservation and Recreational Lands) programs and from the sale of public bonds via Preservation 2000 (now Forever Florida), they bought as much property as they could. Today, some 26 percent of Florida is held in public trust, almost a third more than in most states.

The nearby Wekiva River has been a major benefactor of this land buying. There is a great backcountry remaining there, and despite the threats—the never-ending attempts to turn nonpublic chunks of it into sterile, gated, upscale developments—its presence still allows me to get wonderfully lost in my own delusion of hope. At this time, about half of the Wekiva basin is protected as public land—over 110 square miles—and most is divvied up between a state park, preserves, reserves, and forests. Indeed, the State of Florida alone has sunk almost $138 million into purchasing this land. It has paid off: Considering the development that rages around it, the Wekiva is like an enchanted, haunted medieval castle in the middle of rows of sterile office cubicles. Not surprisingly, many of the supporters of preserving the Wekiva basin are relative newcomers who, having moved into its woods and finding solace there, now want to defend it from the rest of the world. These NIMBY—Not In My Backyard—activists form a core of resistance against sprawl in the Wekiva basin because they are well educated and affluent. I do not live in its watershed, but I am close and can be on the waters of its main stem within fifteen minutes. In fact, the nearness of Wekiva and its basin figured strongly in my decision to originally move to Sewell.

Ecologists sometimes argue for the economic advantages of preserving a landscape, even if we don't give a whit about a swallow-tailed kite or a gopher tortoise or a wild turkey. Wetlands store water and keep downstream land from flooding, they filter and clean incoming storm water to keep rivers and lakes clear and economically desirable, and they serve as habitat for animals, which, at some point in their lives, can be variously watched, photographed, toured for, shot, or hooked. As for the high and dry hills we call uplands, they capture rainwater, sending it down into the soft limestone karst below, where after miraculous journeys through the rock, it emerges from springs. For nine out of ten Floridians, this upland-gathered water is also pumped into their homes for drinking and bathing. But these are all rational, quantifiable arguments for preserving natural land. When it comes down to it, you either care in your heart or you don't. Perhaps we learn this caring from our parents and our friends. Maybe we stumble upon it ourselves. No matter. At the core of it is an ethic that, once acquired, makes you forever responsible for it. It is not unlike a religious faith: It can bless you, but it requires blessing in turn.

Today I need to renew my own quest for natural redemption and to satisfy my own yearnings for ecological wholeness. To do so, I get into my jeep and drive out on S.R. 46, headed west for 8 miles until I approach the border of the Wekiva. S.R. 46, lightly traveled until recently, is the only major east-west road that bisects the watershed of the river. From 1977 to 1987, two black bears were killed on the road. They were simply ranging over their historic land, as bears had done for centuries, paying little attention to the barren strip of pavement and the foreign, hard-shelled objects that zoomed across it. Over the next ten years, daily traffic as a result of increased development around the basin nearly quadrupled, from 4,034 vehicle trips a day to 14,900. It created a veritable stampede of hard-shelled objects. In that period, thirty-five bears were hit, all fatally.

The landscape that cradles this river system is more correctly called a "basin" or a surface "watershed." When the larger upland area that helps feed its springs is included, it expands by half again into a "springshed." But these are modern terms and have little appeal for me. I prefer the description I have found on maps from a half century and more ago in which the chart shows the river itself as a series of thin, uncertain lines. It squiggles its way through a terrain usually rendered as tiny, fluffy clouds, all crammed together. The old-fashioned serif titles on these maps describes this ominous landscape as the "Wekiva Swamp," and clearly the clouds are intended not as clouds at all but as treacherous unknown territory that is wet and forbidding. I like that a lot.

I am anticipating the most simple and primal joy of all on my journey to the Wekiva Swamp today: As a boy, when I roamed widely through the forests near my country home, I returned time and again exhilarated with the experience. My dad had grown up in the boonies himself and understood this. Before I set off on my adventures, he always cautioned me to be careful—but never to be afraid. It was the best advice a parent could give a headstrong child who wanted to roam as far as he could in the course of one day. The woods enthralled me, gave me adventure. Sometimes, with the deep, ever-changing shadows and the sudden rustling of branches, they also scared me. And I realize now this intimation of fear was not a bad thing, for it too was rooted in the veneration ancient humans have always engendered for the environment in which they live. Or as Rawlings once wrote: "There is of course an affinity between people and place. . . . We cannot live without the earth or apart from it . . . and something is shriveled in a man's heart when he turns away from it and concerns himself only with the affairs of men." The Wekiva, woods and springs, river and swamp, is a great salve against the shriveling of the heart. It also allows me to be a kid again, and there is comfort in that greater than I can say.

I can trek these woods alone, and often do. But like my adolescent exploring, I have the most fun when I go with a friend who is every bit as excited as I to anticipate what is around the next bend. The adult version of my trekking buddy is Steve, and we have made plans to meet here. By the time I arrive at the Lower Wekiva River State Preserve at the edge of S.R. 46 today, Steve is already at a small trailhead kiosk, looking over a poster identifying animal tracks. I had seen this poster before, and knew there was lots on it—snow hare, wolves, grizzlies—that just isn't found where we live.

This is peninsular north central Florida, after all, and we are off the grid. Our black bears are a subspecies, and our Virginia white-tailed deer, also smaller than their mainland kin, may as well be. We have scads of endemic plants, and droves of ancient-looking wading birds with erector-set feet. Over time, lots of animals and plants have migrated onto this geographic cul-de-sac, and then, instead of turning back, have changed themselves into something other than what they had been. Florida often gets left out of mainland textbooks, omitted from wildlife posters, celebrated for all the wrong reasons. We're an appendage to the continent, a sort of ecological novelty. For most of our tourists, natural Florida is animatronic megafauna, leaping and roaring out at you from a safe Jungle Safari ride. The trick is to find the authentic in all of this, and then to celebrate it.

Steve greets me warmly, a good honest smile, really glad to see me. Lean, beard as wild as Muir's or Abbey's, straw hat tattered, worn t-shirt with an imprint of a Florida black bear on it, faded jeans, and hiking boots. He graduated from the seminary years ago but, before he could be ordained, figured out the church was as political and fractional as the rest of the world. He retreated into the academy and Chaucer, married a poet, and has spent most of his life since teaching. But the gentleness of spirit that first drew him toward priesthood remains, immutable. "We've picked a fine day," says Steve. "A good day for bears to be in the woods." Then he laughs with complete joy. His voice is deep and resonant, his laugh rolling and exultant. There are, of course, more than bears to be found here in this early Florida winter—wildflowers, deer, gators, maybe a pygmy rattler if we're lucky. Life goes on outdoors in Florida, even in the wintertime; it's just not as lush or obvious as the warmer months. Then again, all of the real Florida itself always requires a closer look, a slowing down to read the nuances between the big, fat tropical blossoms and the storybook vines and mosses and ferns.

Steve and I usually kayak, getting out once a month or so on the nearby blackwater rivers and creeks that vein through our landscape. Our times together are distinctive in that they allow us to connect with all that is real in this otherworldly place. It is not unlike how I used to feel in the best moments when I was in church as a child, verging on the edge of rapture and bliss. In my church, the light glowed in the century-old stained glass windows, illuminating Jesus and Mary and the Apostles until it assumed the luminous energy of God himself. I would sit in the dark mahogany pews with my parents and younger brother, tiny clatters and coughs amplified into great echoes by the acoustics of the cavernous room. The voices of the choir, augmented by the music of Brahms and Bach, seemed like messages from the angels themselves, and my skin felt as if it were vibrating with the divine force of it all.

As I grew up, I wondered where the real Christ was behind all the iconic devices and flowery liturgy. I had first read about Him in Sunday school, learning of a crucifixion both agonizingly painful and glorious, and I believed it and it made me sad. I was not to be sad, the teacher told me; it's all over now, because it happened a long time ago, and anyway, we are better people for it. I couldn't much understand that, and kept looking for signs of a real Christ somewhere beyond the one that glowed ever dimmer in the stained glass windows. When I got older, God became a metaphor for all I could never understand, the depth of the feelings finally dissolved, replaced by the rhetorical mask of theology. I yearned for the real, still do. Nature writing, the celebration of the sacred in the natural world, has become a genre now. In dire need of divine leadership, we have allowed its practitioners to assume the secular form of shamans and priests. But, like their counterparts in the traditional world of religion, there is as much concern for celebrity as there is for the kindness of spirit. Self-absorption is no stranger to any art, but it seems most ironic when found in context with a search for the transcendence of a natural landscape, revealed in the mosaic of its tiny miracles. There are some contemporary writers who have side-stepped this affliction, but honestly, Whitman and Thoreau and Emerson, in their pure selfless delight for nature, have expressed a truth without the hubris of modern chest-pounding. Their words and deeds are urgent and real today, almost as if they were still alive and walking on the trail next to me.

I have learned a little of how to behave and how sometimes to express values that matter to me. But really, I am probably more feral than I want to admit. I seem to be most actualized when wandering through the woods or scuba diving somewhere under the water. In the past, when women suggested domestication, I shuddered. Somehow I feared being tamed, feared having my own swamp drained and turned into a slab of geometrically ordered asphalt. But I do have the capacity to learn, however painful and slow it has been. There is a fine woman in my life now, one who truly cares for me, and I have finally found the courage to respond in kind. In the midst of the greatest transience I have ever known, of living in a place that mutates almost daily, I am learning to finally let go, and to allow the peace and intimacy of the moment to settle in.

Still, I am human and have great human appetites, some of which I am still learning to temper. I stayed up late last night and didn't much feel like getting up early this morning to load the kayaks, fiddling with knots and tie-downs. A simple thing, this sleepy languor; yet it informs a choice that allows an entire day of our lives to unfold in a different way. Instead of paddling 12 miles or so through the flowing swamp, we will walk nearly the same distance. But our trails will wind over a far greater diversity of habitats, all fused together here on terrain fed by the heat and rain of the latitude, as far removed from the tourist's version of Florida as you can get. Just as Sewell Road is a relic of a real place, with bulldozers pushing up at its edges, so too is the Wekiva Swamp. Steve has studied the trends in growth and thinks what is left of this river system will one day become the Central Park of this region of Florida, gray buildings and roads and bustling people straining right up to the greenness of its boundary. It is heartbreaking to think he may be right.

Trails and firebreak roads snake back through the terrain here, but they are seldom marked and never interpreted. At the trailhead, there is a rudimentary map that omits all but the major roads. There are no rangers to patrol back here, and the implication is that if they don't make it easy, fewer visitors will come. This is management by inaccessibility, by default, really. Priorities set by elected officials at a state level are again changing, and this time not for the best. Paying the salary of a ranger or biologist is far less important than funding mechanisms that bring yet more growth.

We like our big queues in Florida, our pricey admissions, and advertising that promises a peak experience every moment of our visit. Some 40 miles away in Disney World, a "New Year's Eve" celebration happens every night, with champagne and fireworks. Visitors who sacrifice a lot of money to travel to Florida feel cheated unless they can deceive themselves into believing they are in the midst of an intense celebration every moment. Advertising validates the experience, giving them a template they can see on a billboard or a television commercial. It's a mighty spin we put on them, and in turn, they expect a mighty reward. There are no big signs leading to our trails back here—virtually no promotion of this experience—and the patience it might take to figure it all out seems such an enormous price to pay when you only have two weeks of vacation. And so, this low-profile "default" approach to natural resource management works. We seldom encounter others hikers on the trail.

Today, we will take a firebreak road we suspect will lead us to the edge of the big river, the St. Johns, some miles away. The last time we were here, it was too soggy to get close, swamp and marsh seeping back for a mile or so from the river's edge. Now, in the dry season, the swamp has retreated, moving closer to the main stem it filters and feeds. We plan to cover the nearly dry terrain it has left behind. Off we go down the trail, stopping just briefly by the old mobile home used by Deborah, the biologist who works in a field station here. We want to say hi because she is a friend, but the door is locked. A small travel trailer is nearby, with Tennessee plates, and from its open door someone is throwing out a basin's worth of water. A compact man comes out, gray, medium build, trimmed beard, watery eyes. His t-shirt says "Park Service Volunteer." He tells us Deborah is up in Tallahassee for a day or so, the state capital. We nod. The man's name is Bob, and he quickly tells us he is only there for a few days because the local campground is full, his presence justified by some sort of arrangement he made with Deborah. Neither Steve nor I care; I am sorry the man feels he has to explain himself at all. I look at him more closely. Bob is not so far from my age, and I wonder if I will end up like this, in a small trailer far from home, parked just for now in somebody else's woods, tossing out basin water through my open door.

We leave Bob and his tiny trailer and push on back into the forest. The trail is soft, the beach sand of 100,000 years ago still fresh just under a layer of wild grasses and moss. It sucks at my boots, just as the seashore would. I pick my way carefully, looking for the hard ground, rationing my strength for the day and the river. Remnant longleaf pines tower overhead and magnificent cones the size of large baguettes are scattered at the base of each trunk. We are up high now, at least for Florida, and the trail rolls with the lopping terrain, gradually up into pines and then down again into hardwoods, and finally to the dark margin of the swamp. On the upland trail, the crowns of the longleaf join, creating a foliage canopy overhead. The temperature is in the high seventies, but under the shade of the piney woods it is pleasant and cool.

The pines fall away and the wide, flat landscape opens, revealing a prairie of saw palmettos and gullberry bushes, stretching as far as I can see, right up to where they drop into the edge of the swamp. There they are replaced by sabal palms and then oaks and hickories and sweetgum, and finally, cypress, a primal tree left from the geological epoch when ferns were giving way to vascular plants, and mammals were only a glint in the eye of the cosmos. Steve, having left the lair of the academic medievalists, is far more given to Whitman and the transcendentalists now, nature's lessons of singularity and tolerance lingering from his own meditation on the human condition. Liturgy is no longer Latin and arcane, the dominion of aristocracy performed in the recitation of praise, but is now revealed in his immediate gratitude for the natural world. It is an awe we both share. "I think I could turn and live with the animals," says Steve, quoting Whitman, absently. "They are so placid and self-contained." On the firebreak trail under the warm Florida sun, the soil has dried and become as white as the silica in a child's sandbox, some patches so bright it hurts my eyes. It looks just like the fine sand I have seen on the beaches of the Florida panhandle.

It rained last night, and now I spot fresh, new tracks in the earth—the hoof print of deer, the skinny tripodlike feet of the wading birds, and a few times, the paw of a bear that looks for all the world like a fat human foot with claws. Ahead, we can see almost to the horizon, more saw palmettos and the occasional dead snag towering like some wondrous gray stick sculpture. There is an eagle's nest at the top of one, and Steve stops, lifts his binoculars, and looks more closely. "Mama's home," he says. I look, too, and see the large white head of a mature eagle in the nest, a bundle of twigs and branches almost 5 feet deep, a perennial treehouse that gets shored up and added to each season. The head turns to regard us, and then turns back, figuring we are neither predator nor prey, and thus of little use or concern to her.

To the west, a thick forest of hardwood trees parallels the spring-fed Wekiva, descending into the basin itself, and these woods seem shrouded not with mist but with an airy and moist light, a quality that makes them seem less corporeal than they are. Steve says it all resembles a nineteenth-century landscape painting, and it is as if we are on the other side of it, a work of river art framed, and us here deep in the oil dabs of its furrows, two tiny figures in the distance that could be trees or the dark stain of an ocher shadow. I think to myself that it is not unlike the stained-glass window moments of my childhood, a higher power radiating from the warm illumination of the divine light. We plod on, hardly talking, for this is how we usually go. Yet I am still enriched by knowing my friend is here beside me. It is the difference between sitting quietly in a pew by yourself and sitting next to someone dear to you. Words are seldom necessary. Hymns play, but only in our heads. Once Steve told me, of all of his religious training, he had most missed the wondrous, hypnotic prayer-chants, told in Latin, over and over in the early dawn. I thought then of human song as a rhythm of animal calls, for that is what it seems to be: A collective, unified poetry of voices from somewhere beyond conscious thought. Perhaps it rises out of a primal place that acknowledges a fuller sense of our selves. We sing because we are alive, and because we are in the world that gave us worth for so long, and now, having forgotten why, we still sing.

Our disputes on the trail are small, and they have mostly to do with where we are. Steve places great belief in topographical maps, used with a compass. I rely on them only as last resort, and instead try to pay attention to the sun and its movement across the sky as a directional reference. Dead reckoning— having a sense of where you are going based on where you have been—counts for a lot.

We have been deep in the forest before, hunting for one freshwater spring or another we think should be nearby. When we can't find it, Steve will stop, unfold his map from his backpack and put his head down into it, as if it holds the knowledge of the sacred screeds he once read. My reaction is to look for the higher areas, usually where the earth rises up into a mound of roots and detritus at the base of a sabal palm. If a tree is fallen or at least bent enough to climb, I will try to scramble as high up as I can for a view. I tell Steve that Bartram, when he came into Florida on the St. Johns River, was known to climb large cypresses trees to scout the landscape. "Yes," Steve has said in reminder, "and he nearly killed himself falling out of one."

Overhead today, a pair of sandhill cranes fly, wings stretched like tiny gliders, making that deep, throaty claack-claacking that sounds as if it comes from the twisting of a child's old wooden toy, the kind with a handle that allows the gadget to swing around itself. "When we hear his call," Aldo Leopold once wrote of this crane, "we hear the trumpet in the orchestra of evolution. He is the symbol of our untamable past, of that incredible sweep of millennia which underlies and conditions the daily affairs of birds and men." The cranes are so high that they can be barely seen. Sometimes they will reach a mile or more in altitude, cruising above the tiny ants of civilization below. No wonder the ancients called them the Birds of Heaven. Our Florida sandhills are mostly nonmigratory, and while they are heartbreakingly elegant in flight, I have also seen them feeding at the edges of golf courses. Like other birds here, they have learned to make do with what is left.

A strand of a creek, surging with tea-colored water, flows across a slight dip in the trail, and we stop to admire it. Next to it is a sprawling Carolina aster with its purple blooms climaxed out into white fluff. We figure the creek comes from a lake, upland near S.R. 46. We can jump the creek itself and continue northward on the path. But instead, we decide to follow its course and see if it leads to the Wekiva or the St. Johns. We have seen this creek several times before and have always wondered where it was headed. But the woods were too thick and the ground too wet to allow us to trace it for more than 20 yards or so. Today, with the dry winter landscape, we finally have the chance.

A thicket of vines, wild scrubs, and ferns next to the downstream creek edge make it hard at first to follow. But we pick our way around the thick green wall along the edge of the lush corridor back under the tall water oaks and old sabal palms. Finally the creek reemerges from its bunker of green and reveals itself. The ground back here is parched swamp, and each step I take is like stepping onto a dry sponge, just the slightest bit of give. Watermarks at the base of the trees provide a visual calendar of seasonal flood—the most distinct and recent one has left a line 2 feet above the forest floor. We step carefully, trying not to trip on thick roots or stumble over the buttressed arms of trees. Back here in the swamp, even the sweetgum reforms its base into the winglike buttresses, a nifty ploy to keep it upright in the soft substrate. I walk as I do through rainforests in Costa Rica and Nicaragua and Peru, looking down while still being aware of the direction I am traveling. But in those more tropical places, the tectonic landscape bulges up into real mountains. Here in Florida, I walk over land that is a prehistoric sea floor of shoals and terraces, tide permanently out since the last Ice Age, only the splayed out stumps of the palms rising into little islands formed by the entwined noodlelike lump of its roots.

It is easier, back here, to think of the past because the terrain around us resembles it. It is these swamps and the seepage slopes at their edges that have changed the least of all of our landscapes in Florida. The fire regime that burned through the upland forests and pastures over time—instigated first from the rich harvest of lightning strikes, and later maintained by Indians and Cracker settlers intent on clearing fields—is absent here. Even the routine "prescribed burns" used by park rangers to cull the building fuel of dead wood and to keep pinelands from climaxing out into hardwood forests seldom penetrate. The historic integrity of the place is enhanced by the primeval feel of it all, and the vines, mosses, ferns, and palms still rage, untended by civilization. Thoreau, in his recently discovered work Wild Fruits, writes of his reverence for such places: "as purely primitive and wild as they were a thousand years ago, which have escaped the plow and the axe and the scythe and the cranberry rake, little oases in the desert of civilization."

I know, rationally, that the modern Florida world is churning just outside the boundaries to this preserve. But it is distant enough to seem not even real, and that alone gives me comfort. It was not so long ago that the last brave warriors of the nation that whites called the "Seminoles" used places like the Wekiva Swamp as their refuge, retreating deeper inside as early Florida pioneers and their armies tried to hunt them down. As recently as the mid-nineteenth century, the Seminole chief Coacoochee and a band of two hundred hid out in this same swamp, fiercely resisting the encroachment of the white man's world. "I could live in peace with them but they first steal our cattle and horses, cheat us and take our land," Coacoochee said of the whites. "They come upon us thicker every year."

Deeper into the forest we go, and as we do, the cozy warmth of the winter sun fades, and the temperatures plummet. I am in only a sweatshirt and hiking pants, and I begin to shiver. The little creek, free of the confining foliage back on the trail, now carves itself clearly down into the deeply rich, dry muck, creating the false impression of the waterway as a northern stream, bounded on each side by faux banks that, really, are still only dry swampland. As the creek flows, it also sharply meanders, and when it does, it scoops out holes in the bottom of its outside edges that are deep enough to keep light from penetrating. As the forest continues to open, I see the tight switchback corners of the creek ahead of us, as if someone has drawn a series of giant U's into the ground, one right next to the other. I tell Steve we might cover more ground by walking from oxbow to oxbow, instead of following the stream along its shore, and he agrees. Now I welcome his compass as it lets us keep a straight course through the tangle of a subtropical woods.

Our new navigation technique allows us to move more quickly downstream, but we must guess where the next bend will appear without the comfort of having the creek in sight. As I am doing this, I see a thick hammock of stunted myrtles and palmettos in an unlikely direction, a wild grove that suggests the presence of more than just the flat, dry floor of the swamp. A shaft of sunlight shimmers on the grove, as if to remind me that if I missed the first clue, here is another. I push my way through the plants, bushwhacking with my arms, until finally I enter the center of the thicket. There at my feet is a tiny pool of springlike water, radiant in the faint traces of bronze light. It seems to be seeping out of an edge of its earthen bowl, and then creating its own run, trailing quietly away into the woods.

It reminds me of the other springs Steve and I have seen in the swamp, little miracles of water and light, usually found at the base of bluffs surging out of limestone alcoves, fresh, sweet rills that eventually find their way to the Blackwater or the Wekiva, and finally to the St. Johns and then to the sea. I call to Steve, and he answers from somewhere in the forest. Soon he arrives in a thrashing of bushes and is next to me in the hammock. We stand there and just watch, in awe. Finally, we turn and follow the run of this little spring, up for another hundred yards through more wild coppice, until it merges with the larger creek. From there, we continue north, oxbow to oxbow, for another hour until we find a great hickory tree growing laterally over the edge of the stream, and we stop there, mount its trunk and eat our lunch. We marvel at the configuration of this unmapped stream, happy to be alive and walking through a dry swamp, making our way ever toward the unknown, only the tiny movement of the compass point hinting at our true direction.

Finally, the light in the forest brightens, a signal we are approaching an opening, and as we get closer, I see it is a river. Too small to be the St. Johns, this is the lower Wekiva, a Creek name for flowing waters. In the dry season, it relies almost entirely on the energy of over twenty-five springs that feed it, surging timelessly north over its sandy bottom. It is late afternoon now, and we have a few moments left before we have to hike back. We sit on the edge of this river and silently admire it. I am as reverent as I have ever been, here on the verge of God's true invention. I remember Coacoochee, who was also called Wildcat, and for just now, I know something of the sanctity with which rivers like the Wekiva were once regarded. His nation lost, his land taken from him, Coacoochee still believed in the sacredness of the spring water. His twin sister, dead, had come to him in a dream and offered him a cup of pure spring water. "And if I should drink of it," he said, "I should return and live with her forever." The water promised myth, immortality, salvation, the hope of requiting every deep lost love of your entire life.

We have pushed our turnaround time so that when we walk back into the woods we do so at a more deliberate pace, trying to beat the impending darkness. It will be five o'clock soon, and for the first time, I think of the rest of the world and realize the traffic out on S.R. 46 will be fast and treacherous. Steve and I trudge back through the dry swamp, only yards apart now but hidden from the other by the dense foliage. Along the way, I take a detour by myself to the little pool of spring water we had found, still hidden inside its hammock. I hear Steve crashing dutifully ahead, his rustlings becoming more faint as he gains distance on me. It is nearly dark here under the canopy now, and by the time we finally reach the trailhead, it will be night. On my hands and knees, I put my face down to the clear water and sip it, immersing my face just under its surface. It is earthy, sweet, pure. And if I should drink of it, I should return and live with her forever. I hunch back up and take its taste with me, savoring it as long as I can. Off in the distance, I hear the faint sound of Steve yelling to me, and I fill my lungs with the strength of where I have been, and I yell back.

1. Shep next to the backyard pond I built.

2. Pine flatwoods in the Lower Wekiva River State Preserve, where we often hike. A storm is approaching.

3. Paddling my kayak on a local river. Photo by Michelle Thatcher.

4. The old Jones house just across the street, looking west on Sewell Road.

5. Looking south, there is a small coquina pond with marbles embedded on its edges. It was once fed by a (now dry) artesian well. Behind it is the arborlike structure that once held a swing. The pond was built in the mid-1940s.

6. Looking north, the concrete culvert and adjacent artesian piping for the well. The bush with flowers to the right is Turks-cap, or "sleeping hibiscus." Compare to the earlier archival photo (fig. 16).

7. Here I'm at a remote spring pool shaded by a sweetgum tree deep in the Seminole State Forest. Photo by Steve Phelan.

8. This brick barbecue pit was built around 1960.

9. The Cross Creek home of author Marjorie Kinnan Rawlings was built in the same era as my home on Sewell Road.

10. The camp of a homeless woman, Cheryl Ann Vantine, who later died. The camp was located in the woods that colonized the dead citrus grove directly south of my home.

11. Looking south at the house with the crepe myrtle in full bloom. A sugar hackberry is in full foliage next to the house.

12. A remote spring in the Seminole National Forest, not far from my home.

13. The concrete bench in the side yard, looking south. It is flanked by Turks-cap to the left, a tangerine tree to the right, bamboo in the background left, and a sabal palm to the right.

14. Zona Mathews Beckwith as a toddler outside the house that would become 201 Sewell Road as it was being built. Longleaf pines are in the background. The house was built with tongue-and-grove siding and had no electricity. Photo courtesy of Zona Beckwith.

15. Mike Durak as a young boy in the backyard, circa early 1940s. In the background, you can see the old chicken coop that was built before the bamboo was planted. Photo courtesy of Mike Durak.

16. Mike Durak as a small boy sitting on the lap of "Grandmother Synhoff" while his mother stands nearby, circa 1939. An old trellis built by John Mathews is to the right (it no longer stands). Note the plowed row-crop field that stretched between the property and State Road 46. Also note the concrete pipe in the ground next to the artesian well pipe. Both are still there. Zona Mathews Beckwith would play in the pipe as a young girl when it was filled with cool artesian water. Mike's mother's ashes were scattered there. Photo courtesy of Mike Durak.

17. Looking northeast toward the house, you can see the trellis at the entrance, the grassy "street" or lane, and the well-manicured bushes, circa 1950s. The Durak family, the second family to live here, bought the house from the Mathews and lived here until I bought it from them in 1990. Photo courtesy of Mike Durak.

18. Zona Mathews Beckwith on Easter Day in the front yard with her dog, circa 1938. Photo courtesy of Zona Beckwith.

19. This is the "before" shot of the woods adjacent to my house at the end of Sewell Road. The trunks were marked with spray paint so that trees could be inventoried—not to save them, but for the purposes of so-called "mitigation," or replacing them elsewhere, including in the landscaping of this site.

20. This is the "after" shot. The inventoried trees were cleared and turned into mulch. Sewell Road is in the background across the open field that was once colonized by the woods.

Chapter Four

Observed, as we passed over the same hills, the dens of the great land turtle called gopher.
William Bartram, Travels (1791)

Thoreau once wrote that a man is rich in proportion to the number of things he can afford to leave alone. That was likely true for the thousands of years before now. But to preserve the wildness of a place in Florida, you have to do more than simply leave it alone. The sprawl that first leapfrogged around Sanford for more hospitable interstate exits north of here—DeBary, Deltona—is now settling in. We are booming, driven not by birthrate but by incoming. It is a growth underwritten by our own local governments, all of which tirelessly busy themselves with giddy promotional hype in the name of economic development.

There are many laws intended to encourage private landowners to sustain the quality of the land and water to which they hold title and deed in Florida. But—outside of conservation easements that give tax relief to a landowner who agrees not to develop his or her property—edicts of this sort mean little when tested in the playing fields of a boomtown. While some landlords are wise stewards during their ephemeral reign, many do whatever they want in the antiquated belief that property rights enable the titleholder to have full, unrestricted dominion over the earth. I have heard elected officials publicly claim biblical prerogative when matters of landscape destiny are being considered. Their interpretation of Christianity unsettles me, as it seems to have to do less with equanimity and compassion than with cold-hearted, heavy-handed domination and short-term economic gain.

Despite protective decrees, the truth is that none of Florida is truly safe until it is purchased—or its development rights are acquired and it is taken out of the overcaffeinated loop of land development. Rawlings once asked, rhetorically: "Who owns Cross Creek? It belongs to the wind, to the sun, above all to the cosmic secrecy of seed. We are lovers and not masters, tenants and not possessors." All the supercilious legal documents transferring title from one person to another seem hopelessly trite in comparison.

The mall is finished now, and the incessant beeping of the heavy equipment from that job has finally come to an end. But the domino effect is underway, as predicted. Scads of freestanding plazas, restaurants, gas stations, and even a giant discount club are sprawling within a half mile of it. From the vantage point here inside my yard, I can't yet see the spanking new 151-store wonder that will one day transform us all. A smattering of Cracker houses, some remnant pine and oak, and a wide stretch of rolling pastureland hide the mall. It is a deception, because when I leave Sewell Road for the world, its presence is obvious. S.R. 46 has now doubled in width and been fitted with a fancy new grassy median. This now means that I can only turn right onto the highway, and then, to travel in the opposite direction, make a U-turn at the first median crossing. I call the Florida Department of Transportation and ask them why there is no median crossing opposite Sewell and am told the engineering algorithms don't allow it. Now the traffic noise that was once heard from I-4 only when the wind was blowing in the wrong direction booms routinely from the new and improved S.R. 46. On the other side of I-4, giant auto dealerships have arrived, including one that advertises itself as the largest Chevy dealer in the country. This new dealership sends powerful searchlights into the night sky, as if some wayward space traveler driven by the desire to consume will ride a beam down to Don Reid Chevrolet, trade in their extraterrestrial vehicle, and find themselves in a spanking new SUV with a sixty-month loan at 0 percent interest.

The sky has been diluted by light, and constellations that must have been comforting for ages have disappeared. The gopher tortoises that once lived in the prehistoric sand dunes and shoals where the mall now stands have either been destroyed or have made their way to the 20-acre woods-grove that, incredibly, still stands behind my home. The gopher, as natives refer to it, used to be eaten by Crackers, another entrée in their subsistence lifestyle, like heart of sabal palm, the root of the coontie, all manner of game and fish. The Seminoles and the Timucua and Mayaca before them ate the gopher too. But now it is disappearing not because of its role in local cuisine but because its habitat is vanishing. The higher sandhills where it likes to dig its 30- and 40-foot-deep burrows are being scraped, prodded, and paved. We are losing an average of 275 square miles of natural land a year in Florida to development, and an increasing amount of it is the dry uplands where the tortoise likes to live. In fact, wetland losses—which once characterized the growth of twentieth-century Florida and its "swampland for sale" schemes—have leveled off.

Wetlands, the benefactor of institutionalized caring, are now theoretically protected. You can still destroy them, of course. You simply have to re-create "new" wetlands to replace them, or agree not to destroy wetlands you own elsewhere, or have bartered using a trade-off system of "mitigation banking" points.

Human-engineered wetlands can work to filter and store water and even become a place for plants to grow and wildlife to live. But the catch is that they usually have to be fiddled with after creation, and that takes money, time, and earnestness. A Florida Department of Environmental Protection study that reviewed 119 new wetland sites created by 63 separate permits in 1990 found that only 12 percent of newly created marsh and swamps were ecologically successful. If wetlands are biologically complex, they are legally problematic. They are mired in laws, and, well, mire. Before being "protected" by law, well over half the wetlands in Florida were historically bled of their waters, frogs, fish larvae, wildflowers, and birdsong. Then they have been built up and enhanced and made suitable for modern habitation. In contrast, the naturally high and dry sandhills, with no protection at all and no need to drain or fill, have become the prize the wetlands were in the last century.

As for the gopher, it is considered a "species of special concern"—not as bad off as to be labeled threatened or endangered, but if trends continue, it will soon be. By law, it is a second-degree misdemeanor to kill one, with a maximum of sixty days in jail. But no one goes to jail for killing gophers. Laws require developers to protect suitable habitat on the property where the gophers can still burrow, or to relocate the reptiles somewhere else. Both options require a thoughtful approach to planning. Instead, what often happens is that the animal is simply plowed under—buried alive in its burrow— and the builder then pays the fee for an "incidental take permit." Real estate developers, who factor the cost of gopher interment into their equation, call this fee a "squash tax."

In my neighborhood, a Boy Scout leader was spearheading an effort to help relocate the mall tortoises, but the ultimate strategy from the developers was vague. Some 117 tortoises had been counted living on the site of the Seminole Towne Center. The developer, Melvin Simon and Associates, agreed to pay $15,000 to "relocate the tortoises"—which is about $128 per animal. But no one finally seemed to know if the tortoises were simply dozed under as they hid in their burrows, or if they were transported elsewhere. Either option was grim: Gophers are now showing signs of an infectious upper-respiratory ailment that leads to death. The cause is unknown, but human-induced stress is believed to be the culprit. As a result, managers of public parks and preserves don't want private-land tortoises moved to their natural habitats because the infections would spread to the healthy reptiles. I've stopped to pick up at least four tortoises who were crossing the road, because, despite their stress at being handled, it was likely preferable to being squashed. All were set loose in my backyard, and one has taken up residence there, burrowing down into the side of one of the sandy ditches that bracket my land. The implication for the future of gophers is clear. Sometimes I try to imagine how eighteenth-century Florida visitor William Bartram, who reveled in the equality of humans and animals and plants in God's greater world, would regard all of this.

If wildlife laws in Florida often give the appearance of affording protection, so too it is for what Bartram once reverently called the "vegetable kingdom"—our native plants and trees. Most cities here have a tree ordinance that prohibits taking of trees larger than six inches in diameter. But the laws, like most land planning decrees, can be circumvented with special approval permits. When developers have such a permit in hand, trees get discarded quicker than hanging chads in a Florida election. To the south, Casselberry—once a modest fern-growing hamlet—has tried its best to imitate the scorched-earth destiny of its neighbor Altamonte Springs. When Wal-Mart wanted to grow into a "Super Center" in Casselberry, it found seven hundred oak, pine, and camphor trees around the remnant creek of Howell Branch standing in its way. Little matter. Wal-Mart paid the summary fee to mow down the foliage and expanded its parking lot to where the trees used to be.

The City of Sanford, down on its heels for so long, has rediscovered Henry Sanford's imperialistic reverie and is growing like a Chia Pet with a good shot of Wagner's 20-20-20 Vegetable Grow. It has more than doubled its size over the last decade, extending its boundaries from its original historic core center at the edge of Lake Monroe all the way out here. The city has sprawled east, west, and south, leapfrogging in giant parcels, jumping over county land to annex new territories that promise a bounty in future property taxes. There were 23,176 residents living inside the far more modest municipal boundaries in 1980. By 2010, it is estimated there will be 45,259 people living inside the ever-expanding city limits. Trees are perhaps the most visible signs of this trend. One day, you drive by a wooded stretch of land; the next, there is open space. Less noticeable are the loss of all the tiny details that, together, once made Florida the lush, waterlogged paradise that Bartram found.

This is sprawl in its most efficient form, that is to say, poorly planned development that destroys green space, increases traffic, crowds schools, and drives up taxes. Worse, it is being subsidized by the government, with taxpayers funding road building, and even the development itself. Not only did the City of Sanford expand its boundaries out to I-4 to accommodate the Seminole Towne Center, it floated public bonds to help pay for it. When one last obstacle was in its way—the need for affordable housing for all the minimum-wage retail workers who would staff the mall—the state Department of Community Affairs (DCA) protested. DCA was first conceived as an agency that would oversee the integrity of county and city plans to make sure that real-life development was guided by such strategies. Theoretically, the plans, as required by the state's 1985 Growth Management Act, required that infrastructure be in place before new growth actually came on line. It was an honest attempt to control and manage the state's runaway growth. But exemptions, granted freely by local governments, effectively gutted this law, and the DCA became little more than a lapdog for whatever pro-growth governor was in office. When affordable housing wasn't forthcoming, the DCA simply caved in and approved the mall anyway.

And the "infrastructure" the new mall would need? Well, the city approved $6.2 million in municipal bonds that would pay for roads, sewer lines, and other improvements to bear the impacts the mall would generate. According to a report in the Orlando Sentinel: "City leaders had feared that developers of the $292 million Seminole Towne Center would not build in Sanford if the bond plan was not approved. Developer Melvin Simon & Associates will repay the bonds with up to half of the mall's annual property taxes over 14 years." In other words, they would "repay" the bonds by getting a $6.2 million tax break. Property taxes would help underwrite development—although the citizens themselves were given no referendum to decide if they wanted it to be so. It is a scenario being replayed throughout Florida.

When the city commission met to vote on the bond issue, publicity spin went to work to preempt the expression of common sense that normally would be associated with such duplicity. According to the Orlando Sentinel: "At least five public relations agents hired by the developer worked the crowd before the meeting, pinning bright orange 'Seminole Towne Center Supporter' buttons on about half the audience, the city manager and half a dozen city staff members. Community leaders praised the mall tax deal." Only one member of the Sanford City Commission objected. It was the (now late)

A. A. "Mac" McClanahan, a retired naval officer and longtime city leader. "The average citizens bank on their elected officials to look out for their welfare," McClanahan said. "Poor people." In order to float the bonds, the commission had to first declare 214 acres around the mall as "blighted" because it lacked the roads needed to support mall traffic. The vote designated the city commission a "Community Redevelopment Agency" that was placed in charge of resolving the "blight." An Orlando Sentinel reporter wrote, "Leaders hope the designation will bring economic bliss."

As the landscape has been heaved up and remolded around me, the character of the neighborhood itself changed, slowly at first, and then swiftly and profoundly. The effect was emotional whiplash, creating what could only be described as a sort of sociological meltdown. Like a ride on Disney's Space Mountain, it was full of twists and turns that have often left me in a breath-sucking three-G force awe of this new economic bliss.

Behind my backyard, there is a single Cracker house 500 to 600 feet away, a newer ranch home, and a couple of trailers, closer in. A developer has bought the ranch home and the trailers, and until he can figure out what to do with the land, he is renting them. There is a big husky man in the trailer closest to my back yard, right on the other side of the hog-wire fence next to the ditch there. Two orange trees, a queen palm, and a large ligustrum at the edge block most of what goes on there. But there is enough open space left so that I can see that he has hung a red punching bag from a low branch of a live oak. The punching bag, a big body-sized sack with the Everlast logo on it, is wrapped with duct tape to keep the stuffing in. I have seen him using the bag once, grunting heavily with each big ham-hocked wallop. Today I see movement through the foliage, and hear a voice yelling. Hey, it yells. Hey. Hey. Hey. Heeeeeey! It occurs to me that the Everlast man is trying to get my attention in the only way he knows. I ignore him. Finally, some tiny portion of self-awareness kicks in, and he says, loudly, Excuse me, Buddy. I look his way. And he yells, Hey!

I walk over to the hog fence, which he is leaning on. He tells me someone broke into his trailer. He wants to know if I saw the people doing it. I think briefly of the implication of this question and then tell him I haven't seen anyone. Then, to be conversational, I ask what was taken. He tells me, "they got my window air conditioner and my shotgun." I wonder why he keeps a shotgun in his trailer, and he goes "Awww. It's a gun, like anyone would have." Then he tells me, unbidden, that he "works concrete," as if that defines him in some way that nothing else possibly can. I nod in the direction of his duct-taped bag. "Training" he says, of his single encounter with the bag. "Tough Man contest coming up." I wish him well and back away carefully from the hog fence. The next day, I see his side door—where the entry had been made—has a large bull's-eye target fastened onto it with duct tape. Bullet holes are sprinkled over it like peppercorns, spreading out from the red center. A hand-lettered sign under it reads: "Enter At Youre Own Resk." Two more weeks and the man who worked concrete and his target were gone, only his duct-taped bag left behind. Later, when walking in the old grove, I found an abandoned window air conditioner, no more than 20 feet from the edge of the woods, near his trailer.

The developer who owns the trailer and three other dwellings on the 4 acres surrounding it has also bought the home at the easterly mouth of Sewell on S.R. 46 and has been renting it to a series of families. The current family seems sadly dysfunctional and purposeless. I have seen the children; there are alternatively three or five of them, running about in their underwear. When it rains, they sit in the puddles in the middle of the road and splash themselves with mud. Discarded cartons of Busch beer pile up in the metal garbage cans until they overflow. There is now a broken-down tractor in the yard and a small weathered gray boat, which wouldn't float if all the duct tape in the world was wrapped around it. My neighbor Mark has told me that he has seen both the man and woman at various times down in the county jail. The developer, by intent or coincidence, is becoming a suburban slumlord.

When I first moved here, the last house on the street directly across from mine was occupied by a single man in his thirties, a carpenter by trade. He wasn't unfriendly, but he did little around his property and was often out of town on construction jobs. One day when I was pulling weeds in my front yard, he came over and asked me if I wanted to buy his house. He had had enough of the local gridlock and was moving to North Carolina, where he could get some space; he would let the place go for just about whatever he could get for it. He had a soft country drawl. I told him I had all I could do to keep my own wits about me, and he said, "yeah, I know what you mean." A few weeks later, the tradesman packed up his truck full of most of his possessions and left. In his place was another single man.

He was also a tradesman of some kind, and I would see him coming and going in his pickup truck every day. Unlike the man who left, this fellow was not from here or elsewhere in the region. He was about the same age but somehow seemed more nervous, less centered. Once I ran into him in a local video store and, seeing he recognized me, I introduced myself. He was unkempt, and his eyes were bloodshot. He said he was from Arizona and was "renting to buy" the Cracker house he was in. He told me he was a hunter, a fisherman, and an archer, and I had no doubt that he might be. But in the couple years he lived here, I never saw him outfitted to hunt or fish, and only once caught a glimpse of him shooting arrows at a target in his backyard. A boom box was on, and it was playing Merle Haggard, loudly. The fact that the archer was so drunk he could barely stand up was disconcerting. But at least he was aiming in the right direction. Another time, I was out in my driveway when he drove home. It was a Friday night, around ten o'clock, and I could see the headlights bouncing off the trees the minute he turned onto Sewell. He slowly zigzagged his way from one side of the road to the next before finally pulling into his driveway, where he promptly crashed into a post supporting the carport. He fell from his truck and then, down on all fours, crawled into his house.

I write at home and usually keep to myself, so even before my neighborhood began to change, I didn't have the collegial relationship with my neighbors that Marjorie Kinnan Rawlings had with hers at Cross Creek. Then again, the Creek was far more remote, and, despite their legendary independence, Creek residents had a sort of unspoken pact to help others when in need. In fact, during my early years here, I was not sure how my neighbors viewed me. I didn't leave my home for a "real job" and came outside only to take a break and have a cup of coffee on the patio during weekdays. I thought of the poet of the Yukon, Robert Service, and how a reporter once came to interview him. Not finding the poet around, the reporter asked a neighborhood boy if he knew the man who lived there, or knew what he did. Sure, said the boy, we all know what he does. He comes outside and sits on the porch, then he goes back inside. Although Service's greatest work took place back inside, there was no understanding of this because it could not be seen by others. I was coming to expect that this was how my neighbors also viewed me. I sit on my patio, and then I go back inside.

But there were exceptions. The coquina pond I had restored had developed a series of leaks. If I looked out my window and saw the pond danger-ously low, I would stop what I was doing and go outside during my work day to perform some emergency plug-up work. The drunken archer apparently had taken notice of this, and not having a clue as to what it was I did inside my home, decided that I was unemployed. One late Friday afternoon, I heard him loudly proclaim to a visiting friend that his neighbor had finally found a job, and the job was "fixing up his fish pond." They drank their beer and got a good laugh at that, and then, later in the night, they got into a fistfight. I could hear them yelling and pounding each other against the walls, until finally it grew quiet. A few weeks later, the drunken archer found a woman, a big mannish-looking blonde nearly 50 pounds heavier than him and a good head taller. She moved in with him, and I saw them once in the Winn-Dixie, arguing over which direction they should push the grocery cart.

The drunken archer soon left, along with his girlfriend, and a young wom-an driving a beat-up Mercedes took his place. The woman's boyfriend was a big guy who "worked steel" and drove a big jacked-up pickup of the sort that is often navigated back and forth through mud holes for sport. With them were her young son and a pit bull they called "Gator." The couple took their partying seriously and had friends who did likewise. Guests came and went through the late afternoon, parking in their yard and into the road it-self. With nowhere left to park, the boyfriend began to leave his truck next to my vine-covered fence so that its tail end stuck out at the edge of my drive-way. My method of processing all this discordant information had been to emotionally shrug, not unlike the way Latin Americans in developing coun-tries shrug when asked if anything will ever change. I shrugged off everything but the tail end of the pickup, and one morning I walked over, knocked on the door, and asked the boyfriend to please move his vehicle and to keep it moved. Towering over me, he tried to glower, but I had caught him off guard and he genuinely looked surprised. He immediately moved his truck, and I thanked him. I came back and looked at myself in the mirror. My face was red and intense, and the muscles were straining in my forehead.

One Christmas evening, the couple took their truck out for a run in the mud in the woods north of here. The next day, a detective from the sheriff's department came to my door. They were looking for the boyfriend, who, af-ter what must have been a particularly ugly round of mudding, hit a guy in the head with an axe. When the police finally tracked him down, he was sent away for murder, and the young woman was left to entertain by herself. Gator died from an overdose of PCP, and a small lapdog named Ginger replaced him.

The house grew quieter, and its parties fewer. The young woman, having survived her extended adolescence, began to mature. I got to know her on friendly terms, and we settled into cordial conversations, usually by our mailboxes in the dirt street. She seemed straightforward and earthy to me now. She had a good sense of humor and a terrific smile. Once she locked herself out and I helped her get back in; another time she was short of food for a meal and I gave her some. I learned she had grown up around Lake Mary, the once-quiet community south of here that was busy turning itself into a linear shopping plaza along its main boulevard. With her new maturity, she was now anxious about the feral young renters the slumlord developer had been installing in the houses he had bought on our street. We now shared a legitimate commonality besides living at the end of the road, and it was a quiet fear of the ever-approaching sprawl and all its implications.

The disabled wife of the old man who kept yards died, and he followed not long after. The original Cracker house they first lived in had deteriorated into little more than a pile of wood, and the couple had moved into a new inexpensive Jim Walters home erected right next to it. When the man died, his twin brother came for a few days—which gave everyone a start because it seemed as if he had briefly returned to life. Then the surviving twin sold the Jim Walters home, the dilapidated Cracker house, and the lots they sat on to the same developer who was buying up the rest of the neighborhood. The developer promptly rented it out to an assortment of young men with Texas tags on their junkers. All were crack-gaunt with punked-out shaved heads. There were five or six of them, and they partied hard each and every night. One night I saw one of the men staggering down the middle of the road with a steering wheel in one hand and a beer in the other. On another, a young woman there pulled up her t-shirt and flashed me as I drove by. On a particularly troublesome full-moon Saturday night, the entire household erupted into a brawl. Ambulances and police cars poured onto Sewell, taking the injured to the hospital and the others to jail.

A family of new renters moved into the home at the east mouth of the road, and they were more surly than the others. There was a young girl and a boy, about thirteen. The boy was a mope, sullen and angry. When I would drive by, he would hang his head, and then I would look in my rear-view mirror and see him flashing the bird, with a grimace he meant to be a smile on his face. One day he appeared with a hybrid mohawk, skin on the sides but a tail hanging from the back of his head, punk-mullet style.

The Cracker home that flanks that one to the west has also been filled with renters, in this case, a couple with several young children. The couple are first cousins. The first thing they did was to mow the knee-high weeds, cutting the coontie that was there right down to the ground in the process. Afterward, they would leave children's toys strewn over the entire yard, swing sets overturned, and small kiddie pools deflated and full of leaves. When it rained, all of it flooded, of course. Instead of cleaning the ditches to allow the water to drain, they built little wooden makeshift bridges of scrap lumber and wooden pallets across the yard to the higher edge of Sewell. A particularly heavy downpour would have everything—deflated pools, plastic doll houses, beach balls, beer cartons, and the bridges themselves—floating. On one Friday afternoon, I drove into Sewell and saw that the renters and several friends had set up as a band, amplifiers and all, and were standing in the yard in 6 inches or so of water, pounding away at electrical guitars.

One day I was over on the old Durak property, poking around in the little pecky cypress shed there for some lumber I needed for a repair job. The shed was divided into two little rooms. One room with its dirt floor was full of the small logs, chopped and neatly stacked for the fireplace years ago. A rusty old shedding blade of the sort used on horses still hung on a hook, and a gallon can that once held Pepsi Cola syrup sat in one corner, full of nails. The adjacent room had large, thick, wood planks for a floor and a makeshift workbench. Farm and garden implements were strewn about—an old irrigation nozzle, a barrel of barbed wire, a bag of mole cricket bait. A window with its imperfect glass was covered with dust but still allowed some light in. Even though I knew this structure would never again be used as a working utility shed, I always felt like an intruder when I came here. Its original sense of purpose, even after all these years, was sound. People had worked here with great earnestness, and in doing so had established an honest and deep relationship with the land they lived on and the community that was around them.

As my eyes adjusted to the dim light, I saw a shiny metal container in the corner, hidden under an old bale of hog wire. It was a small child's metal lunch box with Scooby Doo cartoon characters on it. I picked it up and opened it carefully. Inside was a tiny measuring scale, a hash pipe, some wrapping papers, and an empty plastic Baggie with the distinct scent of marijuana.

I felt a sort of sacrilege had taken place, and my first inclination was to simply smash the box with a log. But another would come and take its place, and it would be hidden better the next time. There was nothing I could do or say that would make the reality of this little box go away. The sad, displaced lives that were surrounding me now would only continue to multiply. They were like Coachochee's white men. They come upon us thicker every year. I put it back, covering it again with the hog wire and tried hard to shrug.

The stranger life here becomes, the more I try to find things that make sense. I have a dog now, a little sheltie named Shep. He's a smart animal and makes a good companion. He particularly enjoys dashing around my big backyard at full tilt, chasing after squirrels, which seem to infuriate him. I have seen him trying to get at one who lives up in a nest in the crown of an old sabal palm. He circles madly and endlessly about the bare stalk of the tree, sometimes leaping straight up in the air next to it and barking. When particularly inspired, he will turn to the tree at the height of his leap and bite it, as if the tree and the squirrel are somehow allied as a single living being. The more he jumps, the better he gets at it. There are now small bite marks at my eye level on the soft, spongy palm trunk, so high they threaten to meet with the more precise dents of the red-bellied woodpeckers, which, having thoroughly pinged the trunk under its crown in search of insects, are now working their way downward.

I continue to take assignments and write articles and essays that often require me to be somewhere else. If I am away for two weeks at a time, the day-to-day changes here seem more sudden than ever when I return. Cheaply built freestanding buildings mushroom up from the old terrain nearly overnight. In a cubicle somewhere, an architect has created a template for constructing inexpensive structures that, rather than mediating with the local landscape, merely sit atop them as if grafted there. There is a Bennigans, a chain fern bar, across the street on S.R. 46 now. It is notable because it is the first neon of the new sprawl that I can actually see from the edge of my yard at night. Soon it will be joined by a Dunkin Donuts, a gas station, and an Office Max. The farm fields to the east, where underground terra-cotta tiles once irrigated rows of celery and later cabbage, have been covered with a shopping club and a low-rent apartment complex, Seminole Pointe.

Nonetheless, there is still a shard of the real alive here, and I find an increasingly urgent need to capture all I can of it. I don't want to have it disappear for good and have no one remember what it once was. I had once worked as a writer on a couple of short nature films with a local producer for a local PBS affiliate, and we have since become friends. I call him up and propose a more ambitious project: I want to make an hour-long documentary devoted to the Wekiva River, its ecology and history. I love the Wekiva and its swamp. But its existence, like that of my Cracker home, is in jeopardy because of the surrounding sprawl. Like my own property, it is a historic natural island bordered by swelling chaos.

My friend, Bob Giguere, thinks the film is a fine idea and suggests we actually produce it ourselves, using the affiliate station only to broadcast it. I am puzzled by this, and then I watch the programming on the affiliate more closely. Instead of constructing shows with thoughtful nature or ecopolitical themes, the local station relies almost entirely on what amounts to paid commercials to keep it running. That means that the local expressway authority only needs to pony up a couple hundred thousand bucks in order to find itself featured inside a faux documentary about the wondrous benefits of toll-road building. Such roads now cut arrow-straight swaths through rural landscapes, and growth around the swaths soon follows. The road builders are cheered on by developers who want to take advantage of the new access the roads provide to their property. For example, after Orlando's expressway system was built in Orange County, over 75 percent of new residential units, nearly 80 percent of new commercial space, and 73 percent of new hotel and motel rooms were constructed within one mile of that toll road. The ecological and cultural impacts of this road-related sprawl are devastating, but the infomercial funded by the Expressway Authority makes no mention of it. Certainly the editorial content of these programs is a slightly more sophisticated version of the late-night infomercials in which retailers like Ronco peddle food-prep hardware in front of audiences who are paid to be enthralled by the prospect of perfectly diced carrots. In this market, the three local major network affiliates are unlikely to devote more than a minute or so to environmental coverage. And without a functioning "educational television" channel to take up the slack, the growing metropolitan audience of Greater Orlando simply has fewer sources to help report, catalogue, and interpret what is really happening to the historic terrain here. The "vision" of the affiliate seems driven almost entirely by the need for à la carte funding. The good news for us is that if we find underwriting and produce a professional and thoughtful film, we can get it on the air.

And so we search for money for a documentary we can make without having to spin it to please an underwriter who is, in some way, addicted to sprawl. To do this in Florida is like hunting for a Gulf fritillary butterfly in an accountant's cubicle. Finally, we find a source of funding. With a state grant for "environmental education" in hand from the Florida Wildlife Commission, Bob and I head out to the Wekiva, where we will work on and off over the next six months on a film that we hope will capture some measure of its spirit. If I am excited about being able to fashion such a documentary, I am also looking forward to the simple redemptive joys the river and its wild lands can give. As much as I have shrugged, I cannot shake the grief of loss that was beginning to settle around me. The swamp, really, seemed my only hope.

I am maneuvering a small open fiberglass boat powered by a demonic outboard motor called a "Go-devil" to the middle of the Wekiva River, just north of the S.R. 46 bridge. Designed for shallow or shoaly waters, the Cuisinarting prop of the Go-devil spins menacingly at the end of a long steel shaft. To steer it, I must stand up in the stern of the boat and, with some force, jerk the handle on the motor one way or the other. If I loosen my grip, the Go-devil prop leaps from the surface and sprays everyone with water and bits of chewed water weed. Oddly enough, I have just returned from the narrow, winding tributaries of the Amazon upstream of Iquitos, Peru. There I saw rivers simmering with blackwater. The floating plant with the striking lavender flower, the water hyacinth, was in bloom, and several of the primitive air-breathing catfish known as the armored suckermouth were resting atop its leaves, up out of the water. Riverenos were paddling dugouts and sometimes driving larger handmade wooden boats powered by a Go-devil. The juxtaposition was complete, if somewhat jarring. If we have the same blackwater, we also have the non-native hyacinths and the suckermouths in profusion; like other exotics that have escaped, migrated, or been imported here, they are giving our native species a run for their money. If you just arrived here yesterday, you would have trouble distinguishing the native from the exotic, the real from the man-made. It is all alive, flamboyant, and mythic, as compelling to new visitors as Silver Springs and its celebrity once was to me when I first saw it and its underwater stage sets. Is it any wonder that Floridians have difficulty making wise choices about what is bona fide and what is not?

We are in the winter dry season now, and much of the rain-fed swamp around the river is bereft of the water that keeps it brimming with tea-colored tannins. The result is that, for these few precious months, the Wekiva is fueled almost entirely by the vents of the Floridan Aquifer, and the river now functions as a large spring run. Although almost all of its springs are on land, there is one here that is underwater, and we plan to dive into its cave to see how far we can get. With me are a topside camera operator, a sound man, and Bob. Bob came to Orlando from a PBS station in Maine a few years ago and is just now beginning to understand the eccentric biology of this place. A decade younger than me, he is a strapping fellow with short-cropped hair and clean, straightforward features. Although he has a good sense of humor, Bob projects a strong first impression of serious and earnest intent. Wearing a t-shirt and a baseball cap, he looks less like a PBS producer and more like a cop. But he is a good-hearted conscientious fellow who is also an accomplished scuba diver. Today he will shoot some underwater video, and I will accompany him to try to point out the natural features of the river-bottom spring. Bob is exactly the type of person I feel comfortable with underwater—someone who is dependable and cautious but also eager to explore. But this business of swamp-river diving is new for him, and despite his experience making films, he defers to me when it comes to planning the dive and locating the site.

There are several homes tucked away behind cypress and sweetgum on the east side of the river, but to the west, the thick woods of the Seminole State Forest push up to the water's edge. This vent we will dive has been charted as Island Spring, and its magnitude was once measured at 4.5 million gallons a day. The chloride content—a good measurement of salinity—was once found to be almost four times that of most freshwater springs. The implication is that Island bores down to somewhere much deeper in the aquifer, to that dark place where the ancient seawater that once covered Florida still languishes, locked away in the rock for all these years. The Wekiva is a major tributary of the St. Johns River, and on earlier travels to that main stem, I have explored a much larger river-bottom version of this vent in Little Lake George. There a salty spring mapped as Croaker Hole surges up out of a dark limestone abyss that is as round as a subway tunnel.

During the rainy season, Island Spring would be impossibly covered with the tea-colored swamp waters, but now we have a true "window" in which we can actually see down to the river bottom from the deck of our boat. I have spotted this spring during earlier paddling excursions, carefully watching for it with the sun to my back as I drifted over the surface. To find it now, I look for a landmark tree hammock in the middle of the river, and then, with the motor off, we use paddles to push our boat about 100 yards upstream from its midsection. The shallow bottom here is covered with thick filamentous algae, a man-induced river variable spiked by the heavy nutrients we humans spread around us. If we had entered from the other side of the spring and paddled downstream, we would have dislodged the algae, hopelessly murking up the visibility of the dive. But we approach warily, watching for the distinct place where the river bottom drops suddenly from 3 feet to almost 20. When I see this basin, I stop paddling and allow our boat to drift a few yards back downstream. Bob anchors, and we quickly suit up. We discuss the dive plan: We will flop over the side of the boat, sink into the shallow water, fin the few yards against the current, and then descend the sloping edge of the large limestone and earthen bowl surrounding the spring vent. From there, we will get our bearings, poke about at the edges of the cave in the light, and then enter the dark hole itself to see where it goes.

Once under the surface, I look up through the clear water to see our two-man crew back on the boat, their images vibrant and shimmering like an impressionistic painting. It is Monet on scuba. The temperature outside the spring, influenced by the air and the river, is a good 10 degrees cooler than the steady 72-degree upwelling. As I fin over the slope and down into the relative warmth of the basin, I more fully appreciate why manatees are seasonally drawn to other deeper springs along the larger St. Johns—compared with the cooler surface water, it seems toasty here. I adjust the way the tank rides on my back, check my air-pressure gauge, and look over to see Bob filming me with his camera. Here on the bottom, my depth gauge reads "18 Feet." A 5-pound largemouth bass hovers near me like a small torpedo, its ochre markings radiant in the sunlight. A school of hand-sized redbreasted bream scup about nearby, and a shiny metallic Atlantic needlefish—a saltwater species—darts across the surface, zigzagging like a wind-up toy. I glance over at Bob again. His image has been refracted by the halocline where the salt of the spring meets the freshwater. It is like looking out through the old, rippled glass in my house.

Finning to the cave mouth, I turn on my underwater light and shine it on the shadows just inside the entrance. I am looking for the sort of sea-bottom fossils that are often captured in the sedimentary limestone. It is this rock that holds the aquifer, the clear, cool water that historically has given life to

Florida. I wear no gloves because they are cumbersome and rob me of the use of my tactile senses. Like a sightless person feeling the encryption of Braille, I run my fingers lightly over the rock for any bas relief that rises, however slightly, from the limestone. Suddenly I stop. Next to my hand is a distinctive formation that faintly resembles the large portentous head of a primitive reptile. I am astounded by the completeness of it. I move closer, my mask just a few inches from the fossil, shining my light more carefully now. The fossil blinks, and then moves, nearly imperceptibly. A muffled whoooop bubbles from my regulator. I realize I have been looking at the very-much-alive snout of an immense softshell turtle that has somehow wedged its entire body into a lateral crevice in the rock. Turtles of this size were found throughout the Wekiva when I first begin to paddle it two decades ago. But like the big gar that once roamed here in schools, most have been harvested by fishermen and bow hunters for sport and for food. Survivors like this old animal have learned the tricks of hiding in unlikely places. Bob is still somewhere else behind me, and right now the knowledge that this animal exists is mine alone. I drift a couple feet back to admire the turtle in context with its rock. I think of how Bartram was just as surprised when he saw his first softshell in Florida during his own explorations here.

Calling it the "soft shell tortoise," Bartram described the animal as "flat and thin," 2 1/2 feet in length, and up to 40 pounds, with the rear of its shell being covered with "round horny warts or tubercles." As for its primitive head, "it is large and clubbed, of nearly an oval form, the upper mandible somewhat resembling a swine's snout. . . . The upper beak is hooked and sharp like a hawk's bill." Ever the astute observer, Bartram reported that the softshells "bury themselves in the slushy bottoms of rivers and ponds. . . . To such places they withdraw themselves when hungry, and there seize their prey by surprise, darting their heads as quick as lightning upon the unwary animal that unfortunately strolls within their reach."

The softshell has been here waiting, then, stoic in his determination and appetite, and I have interrupted his chance at a meal. I am in awe of its ability to veil itself so thoroughly inside the landscape in which it lives. Above, the modern world that is Florida swirls around us, and the vast woods that Bartram once saw are now diminished to relics, but the old boy still hides, so gloriously primeval that I can almost believe that this very animal has been here ever since Bartram last sailed away down the river over two centuries ago. Perhaps he is waiting for the gentle naturalist to come back. I feel some kinship with this notion, for that is what I also am doing, hiding and biding my time, and deluding myself with the sweet hope that the gentle spirit of Bartram might one day return and bless us all with some good sense. I move slowly away, silently wishing the turtle well—and thanking him for not seizing any part of me by surprise—and push deeper into the cave.

As I go, the cavern walls tighten so that my chest and the tank on my back alternatively scrape against the soft limestone. Amplified down here in the water, the scraping sounds like a child's sled being dragged across gravel. All is black now, illuminated only by the beam of my light. Suddenly, the gradual slope of the floor drops away, and the passageway plunges straight down into what cave divers call a "chimney." I shine my light into the juncture and see the energy of the upwelling is spinning tiny pieces of wood, sand, and dissolved limestone in the water column. The sediment churls furiously, suspended in a sort of eddy, and I pull my way through it, bend at the waist, and push downward into a shaft so narrow I can no longer turn around. At 37 feet, I come face to face with a well-worn log burnished smooth from the swirling sediment. At first I try to dislodge it. Then the picture of it coming loose and newly positioning itself between me and the cave mouth grips me, and I let go. I look deeper into the abyss beyond the log, following the beam of my light until finally it disappears into nothingness. Further exploration seems out of the question, so I settle for taking the regulator out of my mouth and tasting the water. It is slightly brackish, just a hint left of the Devonian sea that once covered the shoal and sandbar that would one day become Florida. I back out, gingerly, until I find a place large enough to turn around, and then, putting my hands to my side, I let the force of the antediluvian ocean push me out toward the light.

On the way, I pass the softshell turtle, who, this time, doesn't even bother to blink. Back on the boat, I take off my gear and run my hand through my hair. The sediment caught there scatters onto my lap, and under the bright afternoon sun I see that I have been wearing the detritus of Florida's geological history. Picking through it, I identify tiny sharks' teeth, fossilized animal bones, a freshwater snail shell barely larger than a pinhead, and scads of finely polished grains of quartz. Above, a swallow-tailed kite, newly back from Brazil, swoops low overhead, its scissorlike tail posed as if it is ready at any time to firmly clip itself around the moment. I finally allow myself to smile, free from the need to shrug, and fully awash in the wonder and glory of it all.

Chapter Five

What is a fundamental precept but one that serves all generations?
E. O. Wilson, biologist, The Diversity of Life

The realtors have been coming and going now, circling like wolves around a wounded calf. The first one arrived not long after the mall construction began. He sized up the fallout zone that would be afflicted by the development and saw Sewell Road was squarely inside of it. Taking the initiative, he called me on the phone, introduced himself, and told me that even though I had expressed no desire to sell my land, he knew that "all of Florida is for sale." It was a hard truth to argue with.

The realtor's name was Skip, and for a man with a dog's name, he had little sense of humor. He said he needed to come by to "walk the property," which is what realtors do when they want to sound serious to other realtors. Skip arrived with some contracts, wandered around in the yard a bit, planted a sign offering my property for sale commercially, and then went away. The sale price was determined not by the square footage of my home or by any existing cultural amenity, but simply by the size of the lot. I was curious about what might happen next. I cared for my place and its neighborhood, but its underpinnings were collapsing with great efficiency, and sometimes little changes revealed great truths. There had been a wood and concrete bench at a bus stop at the corner of Reinhart and S.R. 46 for several years now. The advertisement on the seatback of the bench showed two Florida black bears—a mother and her cub. Next to them was the plea: Leave Room for Us. It seemed a reasonable request, and although the real bears here had retreated into the Wekiva Swamp years ago, the bench struck me as an effigy, a symbol of what was once dominant and supreme. Last month, the bench was knocked over by a dump truck carrying fill debris from one construction site to another. Yesterday, it disappeared entirely and was replaced with a spanking new white bench advertising an insurance company.

I considered noble ideas like deed restrictions that would save the spirit of what had been here. But I knew no commercial buyer would give a whit about what was once here. The house, the garage, the barbecue pit, the old coquina pond, the night-blooming cactus, the bamboo. It would all go, just as the fields and woods and farm homes had gone before them, nothing left to remind anyone of the stories of the landscape. Skip kept his sign up for a while, and then one day I called and asked him to take it down. Another sign appeared next to where the dead grove fronted Reinhart Road just to the west, offering that 20-acre tract for sale. And then the owner of the grove appeared on our street. He was not a developer but rather the affluent, middle-aged son of the citrus farmer who once planted and cultivated the trees. He had pulled into my driveway and, standing next to his car, was leaning on his horn. I looked through the uneven glass in the window and knew who he was right away. He was driving a BMW and wearing white shoes. I debated whether or not I should even bother responding. His Beemer horn bleated some more, and then I went out simply to keep him quiet. Despite his wealth, the man's method of gaining my attention was really no different from that of the Everlast man who once "worked concrete" and lived in the trailer behind me. Hey! Hey!

I walked out the side door under the patio and marched with great purpose toward the uninvited visitor. "Do you own this property?" he asked, waving his free arm with one hand while continuing to honk in staccato bursts with the other. I walked right up to him until I was in his face. He stopped honking. I realized he was only trying to determine if I would be interested in selling my property, and if sanity had prevailed, I would have simply stood there and nodded my head and let him talk. But he had insulted me with his pitiable manners. I was in a mule-headed froth. Bargaining—indeed, civilized dialogue—seemed out of the question. Instead, I barked, "If you want to discuss business, give me a call and we'll set up an appointment." The veins in my forehead were again bulging, and my face was turning the color of the Turks-cap blossom. His eyes widened, and in one complete and fluid motion, he opened his car door, slid inside, and wordlessly backed out of my driveway.

Not long after that, the Duraks sold their remaining land between my property and S.R. 46 to a man named Carter Rucker, the developer who was buying up the other Cracker homes in the neighborhood and renting them out cheaply. The price of the land seemed to be low, but I understood they were well on their way to a new life and the sale of the 4 acres would help them get there. Nonetheless, the buyer seized upon that sale price as a way of defining what he would forever pay for other neighborhood property. Rucker begin a quiet campaign of bullying in which he offered me and my neighbors prices far below market for our land, hinting that we had no other choice but to sell to him. He intimated that if I did not wisely sell my land, I would end up with a retention pond next to it. Then, catching himself, he said: "Now, I don't mean that as a threat . . ." But what else could it have been? He had also repeated the same threat to my neighbor Kelly across the street. The fact that his threats were made in a syrupy, patronizing tone did not disguise his offensiveness. Not long afterwards, he dozed down the line of longleafs at the north edge of S.R. 46 and put in a freestanding plaza with a sub shop and a transmission-oil change business. At least once he tried very hard to scare another land speculator away from our property by telling her it was poorly suited for development—a tactic clearly aimed to dissuade competitive bidding for it. Rucker lived in a fancy upscale development with geometrically perfect lawns, insulated by walls and gates and protected by a guard house. All my conversations with him took place over the telephone, which, given the circumstances, was just as well.

By now, the county road department was finally planning to pave Sewell and had installed a sign on our road explaining this plan. But the paving has been inexplicably delayed. I call the Seminole County roads department to ask why. A man there by the name of Jim tells me that Rucker personally called to inform him there was no need to pave Sewell because he owned all of the property between Sewell and Elder. One day soon he would develop it and tear up their new county road, so paving it was unnecessary. "Imagine if we paved the road, and then the next day it was torn up for development!" Jim told me. "Channel six would have a field day with that!" I explained very clearly that Rucker did not own all the property here as he had claimed, and Jim seemed perplexed. I asked why he thought the developer had called him about this issue at all. "Well, I imagine he's a good taxpayer who doesn't want to see us waste money." I asked if any other developers had been "good taxpayers" and called, thusly, when such a road paving was planned—even one in which they owned all the property that lined it. "Well . . . no. No one's ever called before." I was angry when the deceitfulness of this sunk in, but I was yet unsure as to what I could do. The developer, despite all his prosperity, was a smarmy manipulator. The situation would continue to devolve, I was sure of it, but for now I turned back more completely than I ever had to the past.

There is a large water oak between my house and my garage. Its trunk is at least 4 feet in diameter, and its bark distressed as if it had endured centuries of weathering. A clump of mistletoe grows at the top, and its limbs are spiked with bromeliads. Squirrels build nests there every season and chatter nervously over the limbs, sending Shep into a rage. Twisted boughs stretch nearly horizontally over the garage and patio and well out into the yard. I guessed the oak to be at least two hundred years old, but during a long-distance conversation I once had with Mike Durak in Tennessee, he told me the tree was planted when he was a boy. That's the thing about Florida—sun, rain, and chlorophyll have an enthusiastic partnership here.

One day I was out tending to the wedelia, the dandelionlike wildflowers that were growing at the base of the oak. Antillean in origin, the little wedelia has been growing in Florida long enough to be considered a native plant. As I poked about, I found little bits of white rock and shell just under the surface. The water oak had been churning the earth like a tiller in slow motion, painstakingly uplifting what was buried below with the unhurried movement of its giant roots. There is even a name for this dynamic—bioturbulence. I got a magnifying glass from the house and began to examine the white shards. There were a dozen or so of the freshwater snail, Viviparus, the species that makes up the bulk of midden mounds in the basin of the St. Johns River. There were other relics, too, and looking closer at a single thin gray disc, I discovered it was a fragment of a turtle or tortoise shell. There were pieces of rock that were limestone, the soft karst of our aquifer. Lime rock of this type is associated with the springs farther to the north and west of here but is virtually absent in these dark loamy bottomland soils. I took out one triangular piece shaped like a small modern iron with a flat bottom. As I grasped it in my hand, my fingers went easily into the indents on its side, gifting me with a flat-bottom abrasive tool. Holding it in my right hand I moved it across my left forearm, gently at first and then with more vigor. It struck me that this chunk of lime rock would have been of great service in scraping the inside of animal skins clean of flesh. If I were a roaming Timucua or Mayacan, I would have wanted it in my tool kit. I dug some more at the base of the water oak, but all I turned up were more bleached white snail shells.

Elder Creek, before it was ditched, once meandered through the land that is my backyard. Over the years, it roamed nearly anywhere it wanted as it made its way down to the St. Johns from the southerly uplands, perhaps even flowing here where the water oak now grows. Mike Durak had told me that Elder collected the seepage waters from the uplands to the south and had once flowed as clear as a spring run. This newly churned-up cache is likely the remnant of a seasonal camp, a place where the Timucua and the people before them visited to hunt and to fish on the bank of a pure little stream, away from the others. Topographical maps show the flatwoods falling away not long after the terrain slopes north toward the river from here. This is the last high land at the edge of river's historic wetlands. It would have been reasonably dry here, safe to camp. It was not hard to imagine that one day the people who had used the seasonal camp had disappeared into the horizon, perhaps tracking a bear or an ivory-billed woodpecker or a panther, stepping lightly through the thick palmetto and pine, following a narrow animal trail. And here—after a thousand, two thousand years?—the residue of their life is tossed up before me.

Trees, in Timucua legend, were the "one-legged ones" created by the gods as so complete that they had no need to move or to speak, except through the sound of the wind in their leaves. They were protectors because they held fast to the land and, with their canopy, provided shelter. Now this one-legged one has finally spoken, allowing its roots to till up the language of others who lived in this same place so long ago. I sit on my haunches under its wide boughs and roll the shells and stone over and over again in my fingers. If I had been moving too quickly, I would have missed it all, but I am now learning to listen more closely to the whisperings in the landscape. Who gathered this snail, this shell, this piece of lime rock? Was it a small child, a woman, a young man? Once these tiny murmurs are sealed under layers of concrete, neither bioturbulence nor myth will do them much good.

When I first moved to Sewell, I would use my home as a retreat to hunker down between journeys, to write, and to prepare for the next assignment or trip. Physically, I am traveling less now. But in other ways I am on a very distinct journey, disking up the historic memories of place, not unlike what the roots of my water oak have done. I am just not sure where the shards I uncover will ultimately take me.

I know the homestead will go, and there are still many things I want to know about it before it does. I think of what I would like to ask the Duraks as they are the only ones I know who have lived here. As I am sifting through this process in my mind, I get a call from a woman with the unlikely first name of Zona. She had seen my name in a story about my new book in the local Sanford paper. In the article, I had mentioned living in a "Cracker house" on Sewell Road. Zona took note of this because, as a young girl, she had also lived on what would become Sewell Road. She looked up my address in the phone book and found that, indeed, I lived in the same home. She wondered if I would mind if she and her husband, Art, came out to see her old house. Zona had a soft southern accent and a gentility that had been forged in another time. She was a member of the Mathews family, the first occupants of my home, and her father sold it to the Duraks. "I am not sure what a 'Cracker house' is," said Zona, "but my daddy was a Cracker and he built it, so I guess that makes it a Cracker house!" I was struck by the absolute completeness of that moment, of how I began to ask for information, and how that information in turn made itself available to me, like ancient artifacts newly upturned from the ground. I couldn't wait to meet her.

We set up a time for Zona and her husband, Art Beckwith, to visit. Meanwhile, she sent me several old sepia-tinted photos of the homestead. The earliest was of her as a little girl standing next to the house as it was being constructed. In the photograph, she was a toddler, maybe one or so, and was standing by herself in a yard that was full of lumber. Long planks of heart wood cypress were variously leaning against the house or, as tongue-and-groove siding, had already been nailed onto it. There was a small house or large shed standing nearby. Tall pines, which looked like longleafs, towered in the background. The roof was not yet on, and the doors and windows and even parts of the walls were unfinished. Both the house and the shed were up a foot or so from the ground atop concrete blocks. There were no electrical or telephone lines or any signs of power tools or other modern conveniences. Zona the little girl stood, legs apart and lips pursed, a little child's peaked hat on her head and a bow under her chin, an outfit with long sleeves and short pants. She had a chubby, contented toddler's face. It was 1928, but it easily could have been a hundred years earlier.

Another photo was taken maybe six or eight months later. Zona was in a white dress, with socks and sandal-like shoes. The house was finished, and she was standing next to the front porch with her father. She held one tiny chubby arm up in the air, and her father reached to grab it, rather than pulling her to him. He looked like a strong young man, sharp, clear features and a full head of jet black hair, slicked back. He wasn't smiling, but he wasn't frowning either. He was dressed in tight black pants with a watch bob chain from one pocket, and white shirt with tie. He had taken off his boater-style hat for the photo and was holding it in his left hand. He looked like a man to be reckoned with. Sewell Road was in the background, and it was only a one-lane rut in the sand then, and behind it, to the west, there was nothing but forests of tall pines.

A third had the words "Zona at Easter" written on the borders. In it, Zona was standing in the front yard next to a white husky-type dog. She is dressed in her finest Easter clothes, and is now a striking young woman with the dark features of her father. A final photo is of "Mommy and Daddy," taken perhaps the same day. They are both dressed up in their Sunday best, an attractive couple entirely at home in the isolated countryside that was then Sewell Road. Unlike the caricature of slack-jawed backwoods "Crackers," this family is fully resolute, learned, elegant even—people who have met the harsh demands of their time and, having risen gracefully above them, have prevailed.

When the photographs were taken, on the single-lane "hard road" that would one day become S.R. 46, you could expect to see a vehicle pass every half hour or so. Six miles of traveling west on the hard road took you first to Paola, and then across the Wekiva River and its great swamp, to Glenn Ethel. Both communities, which prospered at the end of the nineteenth century, relied on turpentine stills and sawmills—industries that drew directly from the sap of the pines and the forests themselves. Each village had its own railroad depot, school, and post office. As fields were cleared of timber, citrus was planted.

Both villages could have grown into prosperous modern Florida towns. Instead they were devastated after back-to-back freezes in 1894 and 1895 wiped out the early citrus business in and around Seminole County. The cold froze the sap and snapped the trunks in great, sickening cracks. The link between people and the place where they lived was unambiguous then. Those who were less than steadfast left in droves. When Zona was a little girl, only the names of those communities were left on the map. Today only the graveyards remain.

If you traveled a few hundred yards east, and then north up Monroe Road, you could walk through the heart of the village of Lake Monroe, the farming community that had taken root in the rich alluvial soils of the river delta. Lake Monroe farmers had planted citrus, too, but instead of abandoning the land after the freezes, they dug in their heels and switched to row crops. Fields were plumbed with terra-cotta pipes fueled by the wealth of artesian waters that flowed freely here, fed by rainfall onto the porous sand hills to the south. Perhaps the settlers at Lake Monroe were more motivated, and able to respond more flexibly to the environmental conditions. Having a reservoir of readily available artesian water to keep the new crops moist certainly must have helped. Geography and the hydrology it hides beneath it simply weren't as generous to the settlers of Glen Ethel and Paola. There was an ultimate disconnect between people and place, and it had been brutal, sudden, and final.

In Lake Monroe, you could continue toward the St. Johns to the railroad tracks and the busy "Rand Yard," where open gondola rail cars and boxcars of celery were iced for transport to the north. In the 1920s, Sanford was variously "The Celery Capital of the World" and "Celery City," and everyone was proud of this. (Indeed, the slogan lingered until the early 1970s, long after celery had been dethroned as the economic mainstay.) The "Roaring Twenties" of the North had spilled over into the peninsula by coaxing in a new wave of tourists, some of whom were lured into buying property here during another of Florida's land booms. In 1925, a couple of years before Zona was born, the grand rambling brick and stucco Hotel Forrest Lake opened on the riverfront of Sanford. Large luxury steamships were still running the St. Johns, and Sanford was the southernmost port for them. The Spanish Mediterranean–style hotel was the centerpiece that could revitalize the city, reclaiming the grandiose ambition of Henry Sanford for his "Gateway to South Florida." But the ambition had run out of time: Not long after, Forrest Lake himself—an entrepreneur, a banker, a former mayor and state legislator—was caught embezzling funds. His bank collapsed, citizens lost their life savings, and Lake went to jail for six years. The Great Depression arrived with a vengeance, and, bereft of tourists, the hotel soon went bankrupt.

Henry Sanford had ridden the first Florida boom in the 1880s, and in the early years of Zona's life, Sanford's second boom had arrived, followed by its very own bust. A spat of substantial new "winter cottages" had been built in the 1920s in downtown Sanford, but those who lived in the fields and woods outside of town existed in a little sphere of their own, enduring and embodying the ethics of hard work beyond the seasonal influence of tourism. Florida's free ride, brief as it had been, was over, at least for now, and Sanford pulled into itself. Up in Cross Creek, writer Marjorie Kinnan Rawlings and her husband, Charles, bought a 74-acre tract of orange grove and settled into their own Cracker house. The experience split them apart as a couple, but it brought a new awareness to Marjorie, who came to quietly revel in the gift of place, absorbing the intimacies of the landscape in her own little Cracker world.

In Cross Creek, she observed: "In the lakeside hammock there is a constant stirring in the treetops, as though on the stillest days the breathing of the earth is yet audible. The Spanish moss sways a little always. . . . A covey of quail passed me often so that I came to know their trail into the blackberry thicket where they gathered in a circle for the night, making small soft cries. This was the cosmic life, with suns and moons to make it lovely. It was important only to feel close enough to the pulse to feel its rhythm, to be comforted by its steadiness, to know that life is vital, and one's own minute living a torn fragment of the larger cloth."

After she first contacted me, Zona wrote a note about her own place, the one she knew as a child: "Our road had no name and the house no number. We had no electricity at first. Daddy built the house and cut the wood with a hand saw. He was pretty adept with that, even able to make music with it, and it was great fun for us girls. All the children in the neighborhood gathered on the road in front of our house after school to play ball (usually Daddy was out there with us), hopscotch, hide-and-seek around the house and garage, and various other childhood games. He was a great father. He taught me how to read music and to play the piano.

"When we moved into town and left the house, Mama cried. She loved it, too, as we all did. I would love to see the house and see the changes and improvements over the years. And to meet you, another happy occupant."

Before Zona's visit, a terrible drought began to descend on us. Some claim that central Florida is in an extended drought and has been ever since the groundwater level began to drop back in 1935. We had another bad drought in 2000, and that, combined with the excessive withdrawals from the aquifer, caused the shallow sandy-bottomed lakes that characterize the landscape of Florida to begin to dry up. In Lake Pithlachocco near Gainesville, the receding shoreline exposed an incredible discovery: ancient dugout canoes, some dating back five thousand years, were uncovered for the first time since they went under.

In the basin of Orange Creek—which included Rawlings's beloved Cross Creek, as well as Orange Lake and Lake Lochloosa—water quality had begun to deteriorate in the mid 1980s. Construction of homes and roads in the basin, along with an increased demand for groundwater and repeated droughts, caused it. All of those lakes were now becoming eutrophic, which is to say, nutrient-rich and more shallow, which is to say, approaching death. Rawlings's home at Cross Creek, celebrated as a state historic site, would remain as a physical icon, but the landscape was steadily leaking away, draining off through the faucets and the ditches and canals of contemporary Florida.

With the drought, sinkholes have begun to open up again. One formed last week under an entrance ramp to I-4 near Lake Mary. I have watched sinks form ever since I first arrived in Florida, and like everything else here— Bike Week, Spring Break, Oktoberfest—they have a distinct "season." The sink season is usually that special time of the late spring and early summer. Warming weather spikes a use in groundwater, and without rain to replenish that underground reservoir, the terrain begins to collapse. This has happened in Florida even before it was heavily settled as most of our lakes were first created as sinks. Now, though, the land-use practices of hyperdevelopment have accelerated the process. In 1986, hydrologist J. G. Newton reported that "construction practices often set the stage for sinkhole occurrence." Newton's claim is modest, considering the cause-and-effect data on record: Near St. Petersburg, the pumping rate in a well field tripled during the single month of April. Groundwater levels dropped 10 feet, and within a month, sixty-four sinkholes formed nearby. A well being drilled near Tampa in 1975 actually turned back onto itself, creating a 300-foot-deep sink that gobbled up the well-drilling rig, a water truck, and a trailer loaded with pipe—all within ten minutes. In 1981, a sink in downtown Winter Park performed likewise, although without the aggravation of well drilling atop it. The sudden-collapse sink there imploded with no warning, and within a day had consumed a home, a municipal swimming pool, and an imported car dealership, along with its pricey Porsches.

Rainfall, our source of aquifer recharge, now stands little chance of ever evening up the odds. Pavements, roofs, and storm-drainage systems dramatically decrease the rate at which a natural landscape can rehydrate itself. For example, a University of South Florida report showed that down in Orange County the recharge capacity of the Floridan Aquifer was estimated to be 210 million gallons a day—but 228 million gallons a day were being pumped out. As more recharge is lost as more water used, the deficit will only continue to grow. Demand for potable water here is satisfied almost totally by pumping from the aquifer. A study by hydrologist B. E. McGurk with the regional water management district has revealed that total withdraw from Lake, Orange, and Seminole counties—which cradle the Wekiva basin—increased from 150 million gallons a day in 1970 to 350 million gallons a day by 1995. If the trends continue, the rate will increase to 602 million gallons a day by 2020.

McGurk writes, with great restraint: "The concern exists that decreased Floridan aquifer potentiometric levels, in response to increased pumping, will result in lower spring discharges within the Wekiva River basin." To address this, the district McGurk works for has set "minimum flows" for the eight largest springs feeding the river system. Reduction of spring discharge rates below these "minimum flows" may result in "significant harm to wetlands within the basin," McGurk reports. Yet pro-growth politicians who allow the district to exist have covered all their options: The district does not have statutory power to deny water consumption permits, regardless of the loss in spring magnitudes.

I have been asked if I take the decline of spring flow personally, and I say, well, my artesian wells are dry and my yard is sinking, gradually settling down in shallow pockets, as if hit by a large ball-peen hammer. The springs, to me the most magical of places in the Florida landscape, are disappearing before my eyes. If nothing changes in regard to how they are "managed," they will one day cease to flow. The single natural feature that has inspired enchantment in my heart since my very first childhood visit would forever vanish. How much more personal can it get? On one particularly bad day of considering this, I go out in a fit of madness and jump up and down in one of the tiny yard sinks, trying to make the depression go deeper. But it is clearly determined to settle in its own good time, and it doesn't budge. I know there is a newly drained cave lurking down there, somewhere in the karst. Maybe after I leave it will continue to burgeon, and perhaps someday it will even reveal itself, siphoning all the new slabs of concrete and asphalt down into it.

Today's water deficit was forecast decades ago. In the 1920s, a renowned botanist from the New York Botanical Garden was startled by what he saw happening here, even then. His name was John Kunkel Small, and in various collecting trips to the peninsula during the early decades of the twentieth century, Small became heartbroken that his favorite tropical hammocks—rich habitats bristling with orchids and rare wildflowers—had been cut to the ground for development. Elsewhere, wetlands had been drained by canalization. Small, who had "described," or discovered, hundreds of new species of plants in Florida, railed against this deforestation in his nonfictional *From Eden to Sahara: Florida's Tragedy*, published in 1929.

"Florida is being drained and burned to such an extent that it will soon become a desert!" he warned. "Yesterday a botanical paradise. Tomorrow, the desert!" Later in the twentieth century, a soft-spoken agricultural agent for Orange County by the name of Henry Swanson echoed Small's warning. In the 1970s, as the Disney meteor was inspiring another Florida land boom, Swanson looked around and saw lakes and springs beginning to dry. Florida, said Swanson, was on a latitude with all the great deserts of the world. It is only the wetlands and their plants that keep us green. When they go, and when the groundwater under it goes, the surface itself will change. Politicians ridiculed Swanson, describing him as a Chicken Little. And now, thirty years after Swanson's alert—and seventy after Small's first warning—there are more sinks dropping into the landscape than ever before. Nonetheless, those precious high chunks of uplands that recharge the springs with rain still have no protection, and deforestation of natural lands continues, unabated. Ironically, a law passed in 1996 called the Swanson-McEwan Bluebelt Act provided tax relief for property owners who did not develop land that was in a high recharge area. Prime recharge lands for local springs were identified as those that deliver at least 7 inches of pure rainwater to the aquifer each year and that have "rapid soil permeabilities." Despite the appeal the law had for landowners, as of today no county in Florida has implemented the law because they fear the loss of tax revenue.

"We try hard to preserve the old furniture that our ancestors sat and slept in," Small once wrote, "but neglect the things that can never be replaced or even imitated."

Zona and her husband, Art, are in my driveway this afternoon. I go out to greet them. They are both dressed neatly, almost as if ready for church. Now retired, Art was once clerk of the circuit court in Seminole County. Zona raised their family. They are healthy, slender, but somewhat stiff from age, walking cautiously now. Although they look younger, I figure they are close to eighty. Both are wearing glasses. Zona is smiling broadly, and it is a nice, open smile, as if she were a friend and we were meeting again, after many years away. This is the first time she has been on the property since she left almost sixty-five years ago. They are both clearly happy to be here. Right away I ask Zona why her family had moved. "We were way out in the country then," she said. "And I was a young girl getting ready to start high school. So we moved into town so I could have more extracurricular activities and such. There just wasn't much out here at the Lake Monroe School for that sort of thing." When Zona says moving into "town," she means Sanford. And despite the scant 4-mile distance between here and there, in her time, that was a lot of territory to cover.

I take them inside the house, and Zona stops in the kitchen and looks around. She is trying to find something she remembers. "I was so little then. It was so long ago." We walk into the living room. "It was turned around," she said, meaning the room and most of the bottom floor of the house itself. "After Daddy built it, in the early 1930s, he added on to it, and then had it picked up off the blocks and turned around." The side that now faces the driveway once faced the road itself. An upper floor had since been added, and the Duraks had put in a fine hardwood floor over the planked pine that was first here. Zona remembers playing with her sister in a closet here, back when all the walls and ceiling were covered with the narrow batten board. I open the door to the closet under the stairway. Inside it is still lined with batten. She looks at it silently and shakes her head, as if the remembrance were settling in. We walk outside and Zona takes in the back porch, now enclosed and partially fitted with the jalousie windows. "The porch used to be open. My sister, Evelyn, and I used to play on it for hours. We had big chairs there and we would prop up our teddy bears in them. We had a great time." I look more closely at her now and see the little girl there in the early photos, still bright-eyed, intense, still room for some wonder left to be found in her world.

We circle the house, slowly. "I remember as a little girl playing in a big ol' concrete culvert or something of the sort. It was almost like a kiddie pool for me, I was so little. Daddy would fill it up with the well that was next to it. It felt so cool in the summertime." I know the culvert she means, and we walk to the cactus, and I pull back the thick bush of privet there. Under it is the mouth of the culvert, nearly a yard wide, and sticking a few feet up out of the ground like a concrete barrel. Next to it is the now-dry artesian well encased in a smaller metal pipe. When I first moved here, the culvert was empty. I couldn't figure out a use for it, so I filled it with dirt and planted the seeds I had gathered from rain lilies there. Art and Zona look on at the little "pool," and she smiles now in a different way, more pensive, seeing something as intact as it used to be.

I feel an instant kinship with Zona, almost as if I had known her before, perhaps in another lifetime. But I know it is really because she is here and expressing her quiet delight and reverence for a place that I have also come to love. Her experiences here were vastly different from mine—she was a pretty, young, independent-minded girl in the remote countryside of Florida coming to know the world for the first time, and I am a middle-aged man. But we have both found solace and peace here in our own ways, and the affection we both feel for it can't be any more actualized than it is at this very moment. We sit for a while on the concrete bench. It is cool now, and pleasant to be out. A pair of cardinals flits and chirps sharply nearby from the privet. A zebra longwing drifts through as if following an unseen trail of infinitesimal updrafts, heat rises too slight even to be felt by the birds.

"Daddy had a garden right over here . . . a garden of zemias—the butterflies just loved them! And there was a Turks-cap just like you have—we would take the blossoms and suck the nectar out of them. And there was a fish pond with goldfish in it." She pauses. "And the nights. I vaguely remember the kerosene lights before the electricity. I loved to read and I would read by it."

"Well, let's see, what else? Mama would wash our clothes, and boil them. And we didn't have any plumbing—we had an outhouse, of course. Our neighbors were the Draas, the Fredericks, and two Dunn brothers across the street, and Daddy's brother Dewey, just to the south of us. Mrs. Frederick was my Aunt Thelma, Daddy's sister. Daddy came here as a young man from north Florida and worked for the Atlantic Coast Line railroad. So did Mr. Frederick. That's all anybody did—farmed or worked for the railroad. We had two passenger trains going each way, every day, and of course, there was all the celery and citrus to be shipped and all that. And here on the road, we had chickens and a food garden and shared a cow with Dewey. We'd take turns milking it every day."

There are so many subtle updrafts that have risen and fallen in Zona's life here that I feel nearly overwhelmed by the pretense of trying to grasp it in so brief a time. And how bright were the stars in that pure night, and how sweet was the scent of the wisteria with no automobile exhaust to diminish it, and how complete in its quiet was an early Sunday morning in those few precious moments of a false dawn?

I can't ask these questions with any sense of confidence, and instead I wonder how far the sense of community stretched then. "Well, we were outside the edge of the 'town' of Lake Monroe. We were probably more associated with Paola. Up on the 'hard road' at the corner there was a little general store with a barber shop. We called it 'Monroe Corner.' Everyone would go up there; it was a big social place to gather. And the hard road was just one lane, you know. If another car or truck was coming, you'd have to pull over to let it pass."

The old grove was not yet planted, but instead was an open "flatland pasture," left after the longleafs had been logged. "On the other end of that field was the canal—is it still there?" I tell Zona that it is, and that it still flows down to the St. Johns, draining the historic pine flatwoods as diligently as it always did. "It was cut down deep into the ground, and Evelyn and I would go there and gather clay from the sides of it. We'd bring it back. It was a great treat because you could mold it into things. It was a whole different way of life, we just made do with what we had. And we were never afraid of anything, even out here in the woods." Zona pauses, then reconsiders. "Well, there was never anything to be afraid of!"

From somewhere down the street comes a long, loud string of profanity, a mindless bray from one of the slumlord's feral renters. Zona looks up at me, less embarrassed than I by the outburst, and turns back to the past. "And we had a whip-poor-will. It sang to us at night. Do you still hear it?"

Chapter Six

We are a remnant people in a remnant country. . . . We have come, or are coming fast, to the end of what we were given.

Wendell Berry

I am out in the side yard this morning giving Shep a run with the Frisbee when I hear Mark calling from across the street. I walk over to the edge of my fence, and he leaves his property and walks across Sewell. We talk, me with arms spread out and gripping the top of the fence, and him pacing on the dirt-shell road like a very large caged bear. We have joked before about being increasingly surrounded on all sides by sprawl, but we know that soon we must strike some sort of reasonable negotiation with buyers that will allow us to leave here with enough of a profit so we can at least replace what we now own elsewhere.

O. P. Jones's wife has died, and not long after, he moved away to Deltona, just up the interstate. He returns nearly weekly to check on his yard and house and keeps both up so well it is hard to tell that the house is not occupied. But the fact is that he has left Sewell after living here since 1970—"longer than anywhere else I ever lived in my life," he once told me. It is now down to Mark and his family, Kelly and her new husband, and me. I have suggested that everyone list as one contiguous block with a single realtor, and everyone, including the newly absent Jones, has agreed. But the realtor, a perpetually tan blonde, has not turned up any leads and seldom contacts us to let us know of any progress. She is a residential specialist and may be in over her head with this commercial business, but if so, she is not letting on. The shadow of the nearby slumlord developer hangs over us all, as we know he is waiting us out. "That boy wants something for nothing," says Mark of the developer, dismissively. "Hell, he can go on and make those dumb-ass offers all he wants. Sylvia's been ready to leave. But I can wait until the right time. I can take an early retirement and get my pension money when the time comes, and we can move and go on up to Carolina where it's quieter. Leave Clay here with the house, and he can stay till he can't stand it anymore. By then, it'll all be developed, and then maybe he'll get a fair price for it." Mark moves back a few paces, looks both ways up and down the street.

"Yeah, we got 'civil-i-zation' all around us now—so what? One good thing about it is I can go and get anything I want about 200 yards from right here, don't need to put but 1,000 miles a year on my truck. I can go up to the buyers' club and get myself 100-pound bags of dog chow for the beagles, and go right across the street and get myself a bag of donuts, and then go another little ways more to the Eckerds and get my drugs. Where else you gonna be able to do that?" He laughs, and I laugh, and we know that is exactly what sprawl does bring, scads of consumptive opportunities for everyone, all spread out along one anonymous road or another. It is just when relic neighborhoods are left in the middle of it that the irony becomes more crisp.

"Hell, I get forty-eight hours a month of vacation time, and I take it and go hunting with my dogs—they're good dogs." Shep wanders out onto the dirt-shell road, lifts a leg, and urinates on Mark's fence. Mark looks at him more closely. "How old is Shep now?" I tell him, and he wonders how long shelties can live, and I say, maybe another six or seven years, maybe longer if he gets good care.

"I don't believe in taking 'em to the vet, none of that stuff. The best hunt dog I ever had was thirteen. His teeth were coming out, and he was falling down. That's no way to live. I took him out back and shot him. Stacie was crying, said, 'you had that dog longer than you had me.' And it was true. But there was just no other way to do it." I ask about the kids—I see the boy bagging groceries up at the new Publix, but seldom see Stacie any more. I tell him what good kids they are, and in my heart, I still think of them as the age they were when I first met them. But Clay's old enough to have bought his own new truck now, and Stacie is going to community college and working nearby at the national AAA headquarters down in Lake Mary. I figure she must be in her early twenties by now.

"Well," says Mark, stretching out the word as if it is a prelude to something that could be worth considering. "Stacie's getting married, you know." A longer pause, a shaking of the head sideways, and then the punch line: "Marrying a . . . Yankee." A true look of distaste now, as if biting into a pork rind that went sour weeks ago. "Boy calls me 'Mark' and says 'yeah.'" Mark steps back and then forward, the color in his face rising. "I tell him: 'Listen here, we might not do things all slick like you do up in the Bronx, but we got manners. You call me "Mr. Metts" and say "yes, sir" and "no, sir." And I tell you one more thing: If you hurt that little girl, I'm going to come looking for you and kill you, and no one will ever know the difference. You understand that, don't you?'" Mark pauses again, a good southern storyteller, knowing just when to lend effect. "'Yes, SIR, Mr. Metts.'" "Weeeelllll. She's twenty-three . . . I told her to wait till she's thirty. But me and Sylvia were already married for three years when we were that age. What can you do?"

Mark is a southerner, true and unreconstructed, and proud, every bit as much relic as this little neighborhood. It is an identity where good manners and respect count for a lot. I had just read a study from Vanderbilt University showing that regional self-identity in the South was gradually eroding thanks to urbanization, which is a form of sprawl. The study found that the number of people who are fiercely proud to be called southerners was being noticeably diluted by newcomers. From 1991 to 2001, those who identified themselves as "southerners" declined from 78 to 70 percent. Moreover, a new book is trying its best to link sprawl to discourtesy. Douglas E. Morris, the author of It's a Sprawl World After All has written: "Sprawl isolates people in their own homes . . . turning America into a society of strangers. [And] because no one knows anyone else, it has helped to create a culture of incivility. People realize that if they're never going to see anybody again, they can be rude and uncivil."

A loud crashing noise, as if someone dropped a very large platter of glass, comes from somewhere up the street, where the young renters live. We both look in that direction. There is a little outdoor lean-to made out of old plywood, and it shelters a ratty couch next to the Jim Walters home. Someone has written with spray paint on the plywood in red: "Pimps R Us." I have seen the skinheads sitting there, swilling from cheap wine bottles and passing around a joint in late afternoon. When they first moved in, they would play rap and hip hop, sometimes late into the night. The more buzzed they got, the louder the music would become, until finally the bass would thunder through the few remaining trees between them and us and rattle the windows of our bedrooms. I have called the county's code enforcement board several times to make the slumlord clean up the property, and I was ready to call the police when the music stopped one night and never started up again. I tell Mark this.

"Well, yeah. I stopped by there one night on the way home from work, with my uniform on. I told em: 'Don't you boys go playing that Af-ri-can music all hours of the night, with all that drumming and everything. Because we don't like it.'" I try to imagine the specter of Mark, at 350-plus pounds, standing at the door in his sheriff's uniform, no casual visit but come to lay down the law, red-faced and sober. I then picture a room full of besotted and stoned skinheads, the worst paranoiac nightmare of their young and pitiful lives materializing before them. It is an image that gives me far more pleasure than it should.

I met the chairman of the local county commission yesterday. He came to a talk I gave on a new book at an annual meeting for Seminole County Library volunteers, and then attended a banquet that same evening for the Friends of the Wekiva River, the grassroots environmental group working to save the best of what's left of that system. The banquet was in a fancy hotel down in Lake Mary, and we were all dressed up in ties and coats. Developers and politicians who feed off of them were invited because there was the hope that political fellowship might somehow transcend the vast unroaded territory between them and us. It seemed that it did at the time, but in retrospect I realize it was only because I drank two Vodka Collins down very fast, and then the evening became pleasant and fuzzy enough to endure.

In one odd and surreal moment, I found myself washing my hands in the men's room as the Seminole County Commission chairman, with his cowboy hat and boots on, entered. Despite his macho accessories, he was an unlikely cowboy—a thin, bespectacled, and mustachioed insurance salesman. But he grew up here and when younger had been a roper in a local rodeo, and he hung onto that image, playing it as far as it would go. We made small talk, and he let me know that he also "goes on expeditions." The comment was in direct reference to my new book, which was full of stories about various water-themed adventures I had been on around the world—two months on an oceanographic mission to Cuba, a month diving with archaeologists in a deep cenote in the dry tropical forest of the Dominican Republic, a 120-mile paddle through the Everglades, and so on. In at least two of these journeys, I had come close to losing my life during complicated technical dives. While I do not consider myself an extreme adventurer, and, in fact, only use diving and other outdoor experiences to access information about people and place, when put in perspective with most conventional trips, I guess these could be considered challenging explorations.

I then wondered what sort of "expeditions" he went on, and the chairman told me that once he and some guys took a motorboat for five days down the Suwannee River. I was about ready to ask him if he really thought having a motorboat on the Suwannee with a cooler full of cold beer was a true adventure, but instead I shook my head and, bidding him good-bye, went and got one last drink. I am certainly no stranger to reverie. But the grandiose quality of the chairman's self-image was startling, even to me.

It struck me that self-deception and delusion likely affects how we manage our landscape. The state Wekiva River Protection Act, enacted in 1988, directed the three counties that share management of the Wekiva River watershed to devise plans that would stress settlement of a "rural" character on private lands there. In the decade before that law was enacted, Seminole County approved 2,000 homes in the protected area; in the decade since, they sanctioned 2,400 homes—with an estimated increase of another 8,000 people. More recently, Seminole planned to allow a county-owned regional sewage treatment plant to extend its lines under the Wekiva into Lake County to allow more settlement on the western shore of the river. The Friends of the Wekiva River and others took legal action when Seminole attempted to permit more than four units per acre inside the protective "rural" boundary as part of an upscale development called Astor Farms. When thwarted, county commissioners proposed a Wekiva River Protection Act II, which would weaken the existing act by opening the state statute up to political maneuvering via continual reassessment of its boundaries. Although they promised not to push the scheme as a state law, they did exactly that only months later.

Although such growth is promoted in the name of economic prosperity, none of this sprawl pays for itself. According to the Florida Hometown Democracy coalition, for every $100 in tax revenue generated by new development, it costs $130 in government services, including roads, schools, law enforcement, sewage treatment, and so on. And beyond those tangible costs, there are other debts yet to be fully factored: the loss of groundwater, of trees and habitat, of wildlife, of clean air and surface water. The cost for all of this is passed along to the consumer, and it comes not at the beginning of a project, but somewhere between then and the very end.

I finally decided that if a five-day motorboat trip on the Suwannee was a demanding expedition, then growth is a free good, and four units an acre could be considered "rural" density.

There's a one-eyed bunny in the yard today, an eastern cottontail. There've been rabbits here over the years, grazing on the remnant lawn that, increasingly, has become dominated by wildflowers. The transformation from St.

Augustine grass to native plants doesn't seem to bother the rabbits. In fact, I've seen as many as a half dozen out there chomping vegetation at once. Feral cats pick them off or wound them when they get the chance. Once, when I was lying in bed nearly asleep, I heard a rabbit get grabbed under the house. The rabbit screamed loud and shrill like a young child being mortally wounded. I lay awake a long time after that, wondering what I could have done to have saved it.

The renters up the road bring cats with them, let them breed at random, and when they move, they leave them. There are an estimated 10 million feral cats in Florida now—killing millions of birds and small mammals—and the population may partially be explained by the transience of the place. Unlike Mark and Sylvia's children, who have grown up around me with a strong family grounding and an old-fashioned civility, the new children are hardly here long enough for me to even tell them apart. I am now only aware of their presence when an adult is yelling or cursing at them. They are the human counterparts to feral cats, unwanted spawn. If I feel remorseful for them, in my gut I also dread the day they will grow up to do the same to their own children.

Of all the rabbits that have roamed through my yard, only this one-eyed bunny is left. He just keeps coming back, despite a handicap that leaves one entire side of his body blind to predators. I usually see him early in the morning and just before twilight. He just sits there and chomps fresh new wildflowers and shiny blades of grass. Shep has given up trying to chase him, as he has finally learned that the energy efficiency of pursuing a rabbit—even a half blind one—is far too great for his aging sheltie body. Maybe the bunny's blindness has forced him to rely more completely on his remaining senses, which have become more finely tuned than those of his fully sighted counterparts ever were. In the land of the unsighted and the feral and the unwanted, the one-eyed bunny may, after all, be king.

Last year I saw a juvenile rabbit hiding under the large bush of Turks-cap near the stand of bamboo. He was about the size of a softball—a brown, furry softball. His ruse was simply to freeze when I walked by, as he was too small to even be much of a runner. That decoy behavior probably served him well. But, two weeks later, for him or one of his brethren, it didn't. I was cutting the montage of grass and weeds behind the garage, trimming it down from midcalf level. Back and forth I went with my internal combustion–powered mower, chomping greenery as efficiently as any rabbit ever had. Suddenly

I heard a crunch, and the exit hole on the mower begin spitting out fur. I stopped the mower and looked closely onto the ground and saw tiny parts of what had been a very small rabbit. He had heard me and my mower roaring and had frozen, thinking it would save him. It didn't. I stopped mowing and went inside and put my head in my hands. I felt awful for the bunny, and my grief was so great it did not go away for the rest of the day. Finally it occurred to me that I was feeling for all of us who think we can just freeze and dodge the blaze of meanness and spite and sprawl of the world, to ignore all the forgotten offspring that now gather on the landscape, and that it will pass us by without harm, when in fact, it is just narrowing its range.

A week later, I was in remote Cat Island in the southern Bahamas, sitting on the wooden stoop of the back door of a one-room restaurant, drinking a cold Kalik and watching the sun go down over the water. Freshly shucked queen conch was being cooked up in the kitchen nearby, and the sweet, rich smell of butter and conch meat was in the air. Fat white cumulus were re-forming themselves over the shallow lime-green sea, and the edges of vapor billowed in crimson and burnt umber. In the midst of it, unmistakably, I saw the little bunny. The cloud image changed as I watched, and his legs stretched out in front of him in great, free abandon. He was running.

I woke with a start last night at 2 a.m. for no good reason, and it took me a while to get back to sleep. It's quiet at that time, the early morning noise from S.R. 46 muffled by the buffer of young pines in between me and that road, and I relished the solitude. The predominant sound was the sweet call of the chuck-will's-widow coming from the old grove. It was so enchanting that I went outside and sat quietly in a chair on the patio in the dark and listened to it. It went on for another half hour, and by then, I was so relaxed that I could have slept the rest of the morning in the chair.

Yesterday evening, an unexpected cold front sullied the skies and dropped the thermometer by a good 10 degrees. The plants are already beginning to show signs of seasonal change. There are two bald cypress trees I planted as saplings around the little pond I built in the backyard, and like their wild counterparts, their needles are turning an auburn color with the season. Up in the front yard, the leaves of the sweetgum have become yellow and brown and are nearly ready to drop. The blooming cycle of the giant cereus cactus on the north side of the house seems to have peaked.

Lisa stopped over yesterday for dinner. She brought me a square, flat stone paperweight with an inscription incised in gold letters. The inscription read: "Nature Never Did Betray the Heart That Loved Her." Lisa is a beauty, leggy with strawberry blond hair and exquisite natural features. A talented editor and writer, she is modest and unassuming, more steady in her disposition than I could ever be. She grew up as one of seven kids in Orlando, before Disney arrived. Her dad captained a houseboat, and the family spent many weekends on the St. Johns, cruising and fishing and swimming, back before corporate theme parks reshaped the idea of family fun into something that must cost a lot of money. Like me, she has a sort of angst about the sudden growth and the loss of natural places in the region but seems somehow less susceptible to the distress that it causes me. And she looks forward as much as I to the time we can spend together outdoors, as that affords a spiritual nourishment and bond so profound it seems to be woven into our souls. Perhaps we secretly relive our childhoods when we are together this way, sharing in the true wonder that natural experiences can still deliver. If so, our immersion in nature must transcend intellect, resonating with a pure innocence that still lives, tucked away deep in our hearts.

By the time she arrived it was pleasant out, the bugs knocked back by the cold snap. I cooked up half a chicken in the smoker grill I had put out in the old brick barbecue pit, tossing on a few asparagus spears just at the end, and sprinkling it all with generous dashes of soy sauce and olive oil with freshly minced garlic. I took off the grill lid and put a long slender loaf of Italian bread atop the sizzling food, just long enough to warm it. A few minutes later, the bread came out mildly scented with the flavors of the chicken and asparagus and garlic, and with the meat and vegetables, it all made a great feast. Afterwards, we walked around the great, ever-changing, half-wild field of a yard, seeing what nature might reveal. To my surprise, there were a half dozen new buds on the night-blooming cactus, the grand finale for the fading tropical season. I steered Lisa to the front of the house so she could see the fretwork of climbing flowers there. She expressed surprise and quiet excitement at how they were all blazing away—the pink coral flower, the blue plumbago, and the lantana. She asked if I did anything to encourage the blooming, and I said I cut back the hardy fast-growing weeds that might overwhelm the flowering plants, but that was about it. A zebra longwing trembled by, and a cloudless sulfur rested on the tiny blossom of a coral plant. A Gulf fritillary flew in, bouncing from bloom to bloom, its wings the intense ginger color of the cypress needles.

Lisa grows flowers as well, roses and lilies and such, but she lives in a more conventional neighborhood with symmetrical well-tended lawns and sees few butterflies. There is much written now about butterfly gardens, and how a homeowner can cultivate selectively to draw in those flamboyant winged insects. But truly, if your flower garden is isolated in the suburbs, surrounded by other yards and roads, all zealously sanitized, a butterfly will have to work pretty damn hard to flutter in from some place more natural just for a few sips of nectar. They come to this yard, I am sure, not just because of this cluster of flowers but because there are still acres of land around me that are not poisoned. There is the old grove, of course, with delectable leaves for a caterpillar to eat, and behind me, there's another 3 or 4 acres with a house and a trailer where the yards are not unlike my own. For the most part, the lawns here are Darwinian. The grass that survives does so at its own peril, and there is little attempt to kill insects with poisons. I recently read a newsletter from the Florida Native Plant Society, a loosely knit group of folks concerned with returning some degree of sanity to our landscape by excising high-maintenance hothouse plants in favor of those requiring no chemicals or excessive watering. The Society defined a lawn as "anything you can walk on."

The only exception I make to this horticultural Darwinism is with lubber grasshoppers. When they are juveniles and barely longer than the nail on my pinky, they seem harmless and even quite striking, given that the pitch black of their bodies is scored with splats of bright yellow. But as fat, stocky adults, they grow to 3 and more inches in length and chomp their way through everything in sight. When I see them, I pull them off the leaves and squash them underfoot.

I went outside this afternoon and tried to read, but the infernal high-pitched bulldozer alarms from a nearby strip development made it hard to concentrate. Then a helicopter began to fly low patterns over the neighborhood, twack-twacking its way back and forth, likely transporting a land speculator casing out the terrain. I allowed myself to briefly reminisce on the quiet of the place, even until the early 1990s. There was no cable out here then, nor any garbage collection. All five houses on the road were occupied by the owners, and there was a sense of intimacy afforded by the sheer act of living on a dead-end dirt and shell street. When I first met Mark's wife, she told me she reveled in it, too. "We're so far out of it on the road here that the Jehovah Witnesses don't even come by!" I recycled everything then, bringing in cans and bottles and paper to a junkyard at the edge of town, tossing most of the organic waste into a compost pile; the little that was left, I burned in an open pit. The compost pile spiked the growth of the hibiscus nearby so that it stayed in bloom nearly year-round, and the rich humus of the pile made fine potting soil for habanero seedlings. Having a fire pit in the backyard was standard out here then, and it was not unusual to see patches of smoke smudge up every week or so from other little rural roads as homeowners combusted the waste that they otherwise couldn't recycle or compost.

The helicopter finally left, but the jangle of bulldozer alarms continued. There's a certain anxiety that repetitive sounds like this engender. The human response seems to be reactive movement, although I can't figure if it is the creation of a nervous energy to match the harsh staccato noise, or simply a need to get up and flee. Perhaps it is a traditional fight-or-flight response to a potential threat. Whatever the reason, the noise will only get worse. A 2004 University of Florida study showed that the state's population, now just more than 16 million, will grow to 24.4 million by 2025. Orlando—sloganized as "The City Beautiful"—is distinguished as the "most threatened by sprawl" among regions with 500,000 to one million population in all of Florida.

A reporter specializing in growth and development at the Tampa Tribune, Mike Salinero, recently offered a definition of sprawl as "haphazard development that consumes rural land far away from city centers, costing taxpayers extra money and harming natural resources." Up to now, wrote Salinero, "Florida's official response to this overwhelming surge of humanity has been either resignation or denial." Florida's theoretically sound growth-management laws, first passed in the 1970s, "have largely failed." The dilemma is deeply rooted in the political-economic system itself, an institution that grew out of the welcome-wagon mentality that marked the early settlement of Florida. The book I am reading here in the backyard is The New History of Florida, edited by Michael Gannon. In it, historians Gary Mormino and Raymond Mohl have written, "[Growth is] magnified by a weakly developed public sector—a political and economic system that routinely avoids important action addressing the state's social problems." And they add, as if addressing the immediate bulldozing moment that surrounds me: "In Central Florida, periodic freezes have damaged citrus crops and forced orange growers to move farther south, leaving abandoned grove lands to suburban Orlando developers."

I put down my book and thread my way through the old grove, under crab orb webs and around thorny cat briar vines that grow up into the trees. By the time I reached the other side of the woods next to Smith Canal where Zona used to go as a young girl to collect clay, it is relatively quiet. I am stunned by the amount of trash just inside the edge of the woods—an old TV, two huge wooden boxes with little compartments in them, a broken lawn mower, some useless chairs, a mattress, piles of clothes, and scads of garbage bags. Clearly, the woods is now being used as a temporary dump for those too confused or hurried to actually find the real one. I picked up a crumpled piece of paper, an assignment from high school, maybe tossed there by a student living in the apartments nearby. Along the open space between the woods and the canal, wild bladderpod weeds had grown 6 and 7 feet tall and were full of fat green seed pods. I pulled down the frilly limb of one, snatched off a pod and opened it. It contained three perfectly formed little peas. But there was a light slime on the seeds, and its odor wasn't particularly pleasant, so I decided not to try to taste it as I usually do. I counted two new gopher tortoise burrows, fresh sand piled up at the entrances. Trash had been tossed on one, but the tortoise was still able to burrow out with no trouble. I spooked a large raptor, and while it flew away quickly, I got enough of a look at it to see that it was a barred owl. Maybe it was passing through, crowded out of some other clear-cut woods and looking for solace wherever it could be found.

I walked to the edge of the canal, pulled back some chest-high dog fennel to get a view below and to see how high the water was. It was half full, a good 5 feet or so deep, and was loaded with hydrilla and flowing with a good 1-knot current to the west. It would cross under the Reinhart Road bridge and then angle north, finally streaming north down to the St. Johns River. I find it remarkable that anything can live in these ditches, and yet I have seen fair-size bream and tilapia here. Several times I came with a net to seine just out of curiosity. During one of my seining excursions, I recovered grass shrimp, crayfish, a Seminole killifish, and a clear chub, along with many gambusia.

My biggest find in the canal was an apple snail, a mollusk that usually confines itself to clear and healthy water. Indeed, on the Wekiva, Pomeaus—the largest of all our North American snails—is regarded as an indicator of water quality. When sediment muddles its world, eel grass and the algae that grows on it die off. Apple snails, which favor this algae, vanish. So too does the wading bird with the fawn-colored plumage known as the limpkin since the apple snail is a mainstay of its forage. Limpkins are already in noticeable decline on the Wakulla Springs run in north Florida because of excess nutrients leaking into the spring from the wastewater effluent of a sprayfield operated by the City of Tallahassee. Now a new study shows they are declining on the Wekiva as well because the ecology feeding apple snails has changed. The snail in Smith Canal must have been a real adventurer, wandering upstream looking for new territory or whatever it is that snails in distress seek. I brought it back to my aquarium, where it joined other native plants and fish, and started feeding it fish flake food. It responded well, and then I begin to give it bits of lettuce, which it promptly ate. One day I dropped a tiny chunk of Polish sausage in for the crayfish, and the apple snail went for it. By the time the crayfish got there, her soft black mantle was nearly wrapped entirely around the sausage. He went in with claws outstretched, determined to pry it from her clutch, and he did. He stalked off like some miniature sci-fi creature, a Terminator squeezed down to the size of a 2-inch-long crustacean, the sausage prize grasped firmly in his claws. The snail went back to eating algae off hydrilla, which was also in the aquarium. One day I picked up the plastic lid to scatter fish food and discovered she had begun to lay little patches of pink eggs, each the size of a fat BB. Before she was done, there were six patches of them, each spat with a dozen or more eggs. I did some research on this gastropod then and found that each egg would release a fully formed miniature apple snail, usually within two weeks of being deposited. After three weeks in the aquarium, she also had a growth spurt that added a half inch to her shell, marked by a sharp line like a tree ring delineating the end of her old shell and the beginning of the new addition. I figured she must like it here. But if her snail appetites were satisfied in some ways, her life was incomplete sexually. The little pink eggs, unfertilized, never hatched, instead hanging to the aquarium lid until they finally lost their natural adhesiveness and fell into the water, where they were promptly consumed by the crayfish.

I was thinking this morning about my earliest visits to Florida from the Eastern Shore of Maryland, where I had grown up. The shore was a peninsula, too, of course, and it was every bit as flat as Florida, which is an old sandbar, stacked atop other old sandbars, dead coral, and soft lime rock. But unlike Florida, Maryland was temperate, and the rock that underlay it was solid and dense, with few of the hidden grottos that karst promises.

My grandfather had begun traveling here from the Shore in the 1920s to buy and ship produce back up north from the southern interior of towns like Wauchula. He specialized in the strawberry, a winter Florida fruit that was ineffably sweet and succulent and, during the colder months of the northern states, a delicacy that was almost impossible to find. At first he used the railroads since the highways were rudimentary and couldn't yet promise anything resembling efficiency. But the railroads, recognizing the power of their monopoly, began to raise their shipping costs. My grandfather, said to be a brilliant, impatient man, devised a way to cool the box of a mid-sized truck by using ice and a circulating fan—creating the first of what would be refrigerated vehicles. An extra day or two on the road didn't matter as much if the product could be kept chilled. There likely were other inventors trying to do the same thing at the time, but his gimmick was cheap and low-tech, and it worked. My grandfather soon had a fleet of sixteen refrigerated trucks—a truly ambitious feat in the Depression years—and was making money hand over fist. He began to live here seasonally, and my mom went to high school down near Wauchula, and then for a brief time to an art school in Lakeland. Despite his time in the Florida interior, my grandfather was an outsider—but he was a welcome outsider as he came with money and bought the products of hard labor, all based on the local resource. In one letter he once wrote to a fellow produce buyer, he said: "I guess we'll all do pretty good as long as these Cracker farmers keep growing all those wonderful strawberries." I found a box full of old photographs from that time. Most were black-and-white, although some were in sepia, like those Zona had brought me. In one, my grandfather posed in front of a tented display at the Hardee County Strawberry Festival in Bowling Green with crates full of fresh berries, all with his signature label on the wooden boxes. He is wearing dark pants, a white shirt and tie, and spectacles, an otherwise serious-looking man who seemed distinguished primarily by the pride of what he had accomplished here. His brilliance was not just in transportation innovation but in understanding the regional landscape and how to access the wealth that was cultivated in its sandy, well-drained furrows. In several less formal photos, my mom, as a very pretty, young, vivacious brunette, was with a group of friends at the edge of Lake Arbuckle down in Polk County. Large cypress trees with moss towered at the shore of the clear, sandy-bottomed lake. In one wide-angle shot, my uncle Hurst, my mother's brother, was behind the wheel of an old wooden Chris Craft run-about on the lake. He had on a white t-shirt with a pack of cigarettes rolled up in one sleeve. He was good-looking, rakish. The lake seemed wild, naturally intact. There were no signs of structures anywhere, and the only hint of things human-made were the vintage cars and the boat. Other photos showed picnics and wading in the water and more boat rides.

Everyone seemed always to be smiling and in high spirits. In one, my mother was laughing with great delight, and the expression on her face was one of joy.

Of all the photos, there are three small ones printed in color, and I find them the most astonishing: They show a home my grandfather once owned in Lakeland. The similarities between the yard of that home and the yard of mine were breathtaking: There was a solid brick barbecue, a concrete bird-bath, a hedge of thick foliage, and a white wooden arbor crowned with a vine so thick it looked like a hedge itself. The home was wooden, with two stories. In one photo, I could see four or five people sitting in lawn chairs in the background, enjoying the Florida outdoors. I had not yet been born, but if I had been, I could have been there with them. In fact, I sometimes question whether I might have been there in some way, given how closely my Sewell Road homestead matched the one of my mother's own youth. I wonder about collective memory, and unconscious memory, and what it all passes along to our own spirits when the time is right for it. What do we really know about the energy that draws us to a place and gives us peace there? Is it nature alone, or is it the affection and bond others have long had for it?

Lisa and I load the kayaks for a visit to the headwaters of the Blackwater Creek this morning. It is Sunday and early, and most other potential motorists are either sleeping or getting ready for church. It is my favorite time to be anywhere here because I can pretend that Florida is no longer overrun with millions of people. The roads are open and free of the horn-blowing, tailgating road-raging that marks a typical day's drive on the filled-to-capacity roads in the heart of central Florida.

I know from thumbing through a guidebook that the St. Johns River Water Management District owns over 2,000 acres of shoreline here, mostly on the upper Blackwater Creek and on the western shore of Lake Norris, the lake that feeds the creek. There is also a huge chunk of land managed by the Boy Scouts of America on the north shore, with a slice of the Ocala National Forest squeezed in between. As a result, the Creek itself and its riverine habitats form a very real corridor for the movement of the black bear between the Wekiva and the national forest. In fact, the intent of the land purchase in 1996 was to help create that corridor. A small spring on Boy Scout land, Camp Le No Che Springs, is mapped here, a designation that sounds like one of those made-up Indian names Boy Scouts invent around a campfire. Like

the spring, Lake Norris itself once had an authentic indigenous name, beyond that given by some more recent mapmaker, and I briefly consider what
that might had been. But I don't linger on this. I am excited about visiting
a superbly retro Florida lake that—despite a few homes tucked away on the
eastern shore—is mostly surrounded and buffered by natural land.

This conservation land is only 20 miles or so from my house, and really,
it is part of the larger Wekiva River system, although it is too far afield to be
included in most river-management plans. We park near a deserted trailhead,
look under the shade of a live oak at a large map showing a nearby put-in
for paddlers and a short trail for hikers, and then begin unloading our kayaks from my jeep. The landscape rolls more here, a muted reflection of the
karst terrain found in northern Florida. As we unload, two young women
approach over a hill on horses, a galloping Australian sheepdog ranging out
in front of them. The dog reaches our shady spot before the horses, and he
immediately sits and pants loudly, sounding like the soundtrack for the little
engine that thought he could. My neighbor Mark has a dog like this, and
they are clever animals, with little faces that seem almost human in their sen-
sitivity and responses. The women draw closer, and Lisa, who has kept and
ridden horses for years, talks with them about trail riding and horse business
as they pass. By the time the horses and dog are gone, our gear and kayaks are
unloaded and ready to be shouldered to the creek nearby.

I lift one of the little boats—not a problem, it's barely more than 40
pounds and just 9 1/2-feet-long worth of space-age plastic—and walk it
down to where a posted brown icon sign of a stick person in a canoe indi-
cates a launching point. The launch is a skinny puddle of tea-colored water
a few feet down from a narrow wooden bulkhead. I drop the one kayak in,
retrieve the other and do the same, and soon we are both situated and—with
our sandwiches and water and binoculars and bug spray stored behind our
seats—ready for whatever comes our way. It's by now midmorning, not much
more than 10:30 a.m., and we are the only humans on the creek.

We have paddled a lot on the lower Blackwater, about 20 or so miles
downstream, where the river becomes wider and deeper and at one point
cuts through a higher terrain of pine flatwoods. Here, the creek is narrow,
shallow, and not much more than a single-lane water route through a low
hardwood swamp. But it is more than enough, and the thick canopy of cypress and sweetgum above shelters us from the new sun, and the cool water
under us keeps us comfortable. There are as yet no bugs, and that is always an

unexpected bonus. We paddle a half mile, past some spectacular stumps of logged first-growth cypress—far more here than we usually find on the lower river. Several are the diameter of a generous-sized living room table. They must have been at least two thousand years old when girdled and cut.

Great spats of apple snail eggs have created little pink perforated lines on the dark cypress knees and trunks, a contrast from how we usually see them on aquatic plant stems like pickerel weed downstream. Not surprisingly, we see no actual snails at all. After having laid its brood—using an air sac that allows it to creep up out of the water and to breathe—the snail beats a hasty retreat below, down to where it can hide from the sharp talons or bill of a wading bird or kite. There it quietly lives out its life, thinking thoughts known only to other apple snails, rising up above the sky of its aquatic world only when it is driven to propagate again.

We paddle on, Lisa moving ahead with strong, even strokes. I admire the way she navigates her little craft with such effortless poise, the way in which the behavior seems to be more fully actualizing her. I have seen many other paddlers in swamps, and few have the sort of composure really needed to make the experience work for them. Most are anticipating or reacting to imagined dangers, and in doing so, have emotionally removed themselves from the behavior almost entirely. But this is not so for her, and I find myself in awe of her grace, and grateful she is here to share this place and this time in my life. Lisa spots a thick-leafed, dark-green leather fern, rare elsewhere but predominant here in the understory. She remarks how the swamp will soon brighten up when winter drops the leaves and the cypress needles from its canopy. Our vista into it is limited now to a only a few dozen feet, and it is a dark and moody vision, a primeval petri dish left from some distant Paleozoic era, a place dominated by mosses and ferns and odd gnarly vascular plants trying to be trees.

Soon our dark swamp brightens noticeably as we approach the lake, and the cypress become silhouetted with a golden morning light. We paddle out of the river mouth into the lake and are astounded at its size—it is well over 2 miles across to the northern shore. At this end of the lake, cypress are growing several hundred yards from land, and we can navigate between them, just as we paddle through the lower river's swamp during the wet season. But these are not ordinary cypress. They are like giant bonsais, stunted and distorted, trees that seem to be sculpted rather than grown. The tallest is no more than 20 feet—compared to 150 feet or more for an adult cypress—and they are crowned in creative foliage flows of slopes and dips and swells as if some Zen bonsai master has been carefully pruning the boughs for effect. Nearly all are partially hollow, the energy of the roots down in the sand and mud flowing up through the outer cambrus layer to the featherlike needles of the crown, still sending it nutrients and renewal and life.

Clearly, given the amount of fiber in the trunks and the way it has entwined and twisted upon itself, these are ancient trees—easily hundreds and hundreds of years old. Yet they escaped the wholesale logging that removed nearly all the old-growth cypress from Florida swamps, beginning in the 1880s. Their stunted hollowness likely made them worthless to timbermen. Yet it is that same characteristic that makes these trees enthralling to us today. There are large bundles of gray twigs on the crowns of the bonsais, nests of some kind. In the distance, I see ospreys gliding, and remember that the guidebook had reported over one hundred active osprey nests on this lake. That is a wondrous sign in itself for the act of nurturing young raptors requires the sorts of fodder only a healthy lake can deliver.

As we paddle, a light wind builds from the north shore of the lake and moves the water toward us in small wavelets, which splash inside the trees. The sound that echoes from the trunks is not unlike that of someone gently sloshing water in a wooden bucket. I think of the Timucua Indians who once paddled this lake in their dugouts, how the reverberations we hear might even imitate the slosh against the sideboards of their own hollow crafts. From where we sit, the entire shore appears natural. With the blue, cloudless sky overhead and the solitude of the lake broken only by the splashing of the water in the cypress, we seem to have drifted back into time, the concurrence of sound and place as aligned as it ever was.

Near one shore we spot wildflowers in bloom. I know the yellow primrose willow and the tight, butter-colored bud of the spadderdock lily and the purple rod of the pickerel weed. But I must look up this one in a wildflower guide, and when I do, I find that the great white-blue bushes we see growing from the rotting half-submerged stumps are hemp weed, a prosaic name for a remarkable flower. Best of all, at least ecologically, there are few of the exotic hyacinths that sometimes dominate other lakes and rivers, especially those disturbed by human manipulation.

There are so many reasons to be grateful now, to be fully in this moment: It is Sunday morning, a traditional day of Christian worship, and Lisa is 20 yards away on the other side of a stand of cypress, and the sun is warm on my head, and the water is sloshing inside its time tunnels. I look up and thank God for a lake that has kept its heart intact. And then I express gratitude for having a companion who has the spirit to feel as passionately as I about places that matter to the soul. When I am done with my little silent prayer, I realize that tears are brimming in the creases of my eyes. I wipe them away and smile, unashamed. I think now of the gentle Quaker naturalist Bartram, my spiritual guide on so many trips on the St. Johns River and its tributaries. He wrote in 1791 that all of the outdoors was a cathedral for him, a place where we "learn wisdom and understanding in the economy of nature, and be seriously attentive to the divine monitor within."

The wind is picking up now, and a big fetch from the broad side of the lake molds the water into whitecaps and sends them rolling toward us. I settle back in my seat, steady against the expected swell of the waterscape, and paddle toward Lisa. The cypress are booming now with loud cracks and muffled explosions from the building waves. It is as if a Bach prelude has risen in crescendo, and the horns are sounding, and a choir of angels is singing, all in the water and in the deep blue sky that cradles us from above, and in the divine monitor within.

And hope for wild Florida places, a hope that has been so badly wounded in my life, is rekindled once again. I think then of old Lake Arbuckle, of the joy once expressed there, and imagine that, just for a moment, I hear my mother's sweet, lost laughter in the sway of the light autumn wind.

Chapter Seven

We saw a single pair of the rare Ivorybills. They were very shy, relentlessly swinging from tree to tree, and taking good care to keep beyond gun range. . . . Shortly afterwards, a troop of Carolina Parroquets came darting through the trees, each individual screaming as if determined to outdo his neighbor. . . . Once six Swallow tailed Kites came in sight together. When at length they left us, the scene seemed to lose something and we hurried on.

William Brewster's account of a birding trip on the Wekiva River (March 1877)

I drive out to Rick Roberts's house this morning to pick up some tie-down straps for the kayaks. I have traded in my thirteen-year-old Pathfinder now for a new Mazda and rather than jamming the 'yaks in the back and securing the hatch lid, I now need to mount them on the roof. I am going more for the new-car scent instead of wet dog, which is how the old SUV was beginning to smell. While most are in a frenzy to grow, I stubbornly cling to the notion of minimizing. The Pathfinder was a gas hog, and while it was not even close to the fuel consumption of the ridiculous SUVs known as Hummers, it was wasteful and expensive to maintain. Right before I traded in the Pathfinder, a woman in a black Hummer actually ran me off the road as she chatted happily away on her cell phone. It was an obtuse act, one I shouldn't have taken personally for anyone who owns a solid black vehicle in sunny Florida clearly is disconnected from the reality of the place. As I struggled to take control of my vehicle, I looked up to see the Hummer's vanity license plate as it sped off. It read: "Choose Life." The intent of the plate was to preach to abortionists. But at that moment, when I was being edged off the road by a vehicle three times the size of mine, it simply left me with one thought: That's easy for you to say.

Rick's an outfitter who lives right on the Wekiva, just off a road that for a mile or so parallels the river at the top of the high and wooded easterly bank. It is the same road that once led to Katie's Landing, a campground and outfitting service once run by Katie and Russ Moncrief. I have known Katie and Russ for over three decades now, first driving up to the Landing from the suburban sprawl of southern Seminole County in a muddled attempt to better understand the river and the place years ago. During my early visits, experiencing river and place meant loading up a canoe with large amounts of cold beer and, with like-minded friends, blundering up and down the river with little regard for what I was actually seeing. I am not particularly proud of all that now. But I am comforted somewhat that I had enough sense to allow the energy of the river to eventually quiet me. As in most of the rest of my life, opening my senses to nature has been a trial-and-error experience.

Katie's Landing was a 5-acre campground and canoe-rental service with a little general store. While there were a few smaller camps and outfitters who rented canoes and sold supplies on the river, Katie's was the largest and perhaps the most reliable. It was also distinguished by the fact that both Katie and Russ Moncrief helped found an environmental group called the Friends of the Wekiva River in the early 1980s. They had a very real conservation ethic, even back then when it was a less popular concept than it is now. Russ and Katie were, and still are, singular individuals who are vitally alive and ebullient with life, even now as they move into their eighties. Their Landing sat atop a 5-acre pre-Columbian midden mound, the largest of its sort along the river. When the smaller steamboats made semiweekly trips on the Wekiva to the village of Clay Springs at its headwaters in the nineteenth century, they stopped here at a real "landing" to drop off or pick up supplies, usually oranges, turpentine, wood fuel, or other products from the local resources.

But the steamboats were long gone by the early 1980s. The landing had been replaced by an old Florida-style fish camp, and then, after the Moncriefs bought it, it had been upgraded a few notches to accommodate Katie's hobby of paddling. "Love me, love my canoe," Katie once told me with a big smile when I first met her. She was in her fifties then, and she is in her seventies now, and like all radiant women with a big heart, she remains forever radiant. "I don't think Russ ever had much of a choice," she says, not of her personal allure, but of her obsession for paddling.

Katie's Landing and the other little outfitters shared the Wekiva with some seventy squatter shacks that had been built atop the islands of the river. The distance between the day-trip paddlers and the squatters was a mighty one, indeed. The squatters, taking advantage of the fact that the river was a border between three counties and waging no single county would have jurisdiction over the midstream islands, had built all manner of Deliverance-style shanties there over the last several decades. I found most of them clannish and unsociable, driving beat-up old motorboats back and forth with supplies, seldom looking up to acknowledge anyone who was not part of their subculture in a supreme act of reverse snobbery. Some of the shack owners lived there full time, and they were perhaps the most menacing, as they assumed full territorial rights over what they considered to be their river. Large amounts of alcohol, loaded weapons, and crossbows—which they used to shoot large garfish or softshell turtles for sport—only added to this air of intimidation. One could argue that these were the authentic heirs to the landscape, as they were here first. But in comparison with the more genteel behaviors of the original Sewell Road families, these folks were clearly a breed apart, truculent and defiant and raw. They reminded me John Muir's description of the timbermen he encountered when he first visited the lower St. Johns River during his "Thousand-Mile Walk" in 1867: "They were the wildest of all the white savages I have met. The long-haired ex-guerrillas of the mountains of Tennessee and North Carolina are uncivilized fellows, but for downright barbarism, these Florida loggers exceed."

State officials finally worked up the nerve to lay down the law as the shanties were not just illegally built, they were all adding great streams of pollutants to a river that itself was becoming endangered. The squatters and their shacks were finally removed by the early 1990s, and the islands again reverted to their original state—the higher shell middens with their cypress and sweetgum, and the lower natural hammocks with palms and muscadine vines, ferns, and mud. Odd, but now that they are gone, I miss the peculiar and unexpected experiences an encounter with any of the squatters might have provided. I guess it's a lot easier to romanticize such events when you are not paddling a narrow channel next to a surly drunk with a crossbow and an angry pit bull in a battered aluminum row boat. There are Jet Skis that sometimes zoom about on the Wekiva now because the boating lobby in Florida is powerful and rich and works hard to allow the owners of their products to go most anywhere, despite their lack of navigational skills and etiquette. The damage these skiers cause to the shoreline and the disruption to the habitat is likely equal to if not greater than that of the old squatters. And whatever else they might have been, the squatters were at least aware of the distinction of place. The Jet Skiers, in contrast, usually don't know the difference between a natural river and a retention pond. Like all of central Florida, the Wekiva is being threatened not just by development and upland storm water but by the direct impact of affluent and clueless boaters. Not too long ago, a wildlife biologist surveying the river for macroinvertebrates had his little craft swamped by mindless Jet Skiers, and he lost the results of a day's worth of careful science. I sometimes wish the ghosts of the squatters would return for just one afternoon and, finding themselves afflicted by a fleet of Jet Skiers, would unleash a politically incorrect dose of responsibility on them.

Katie's Landing was finally removed itself after the Moncriefs sold it to the state in 2000. The structures that had once been there—the trailers without wheels, the little store, the concrete bath house—were all removed, and the mound itself has now reclaimed its five-thousand-year-old preeminence as a high, culturally accrued bluff of soil and snail shells and ancient pot shards, studded with magnolias and oaks and cypress. The Board of County Commissioners of Seminole County, which only chipped in about one-sixth of the cost, almost derailed the sale because the Moncriefs had publicly endorsed opposing commission candidates in earlier elections.

Driving S.R. 46 these days can be a dangerous chore unto itself because of the increasing swarm of speeding, tailgating motorists, intent not on a relaxing ride through the countryside but on getting somewhere else as quickly as possible. Thankfully, this is Sunday morning, well before noon, and the road is sparsely traveled. I pull into Rick's lane, a dirt road he shares with a dozen other homes tucked away back here in the woods, and follow the path as it winds down the bank toward the river, finally crossing an old jerry-rigged earthen bridge that spans a branch of the river. Once across, I drive next to a 20-foot-wide sliver of the branch back to where the sabal palm fronds push in over the path, brushing across my windshield and hood as I go. Shep is with me, and he grows excited as we drive through Rick's gate, and we see that his two corgis are in the yard. Dogs, finally, smaller than him—what a delight it must be! I park and let him out, and the three go off romping together in some tiny-dog bacchanal of heads and tails and fur.

Rick comes out in shorts and bare feet, baseball hat and t-shirt—his uniform. He has a big smile on his face. He's an old surfer dude, chronologically aged but still a kid. We dig some straps out of a utility shed and talk some about tie-down techniques. He tells me that a 12-foot gator living on the other side of the riverbank had recently become more cantankerous, and a licensed trapper came out to remove it. "He only had three legs," said Rick, of the big reptile. "Maybe he lost one in a fight with a bigger gator. So I guess he had to be meaner than the others to compete for food. . . . But one day, he came out of the water after the dogs. It was his time to go." I tell Rick the gators were here first, and he says, "yeah, but the lame ones didn't live long enough to get mean. They were toast, buddy. Someone's been feeding them. And now, they just don't know any better."

It is time to leave so I call Shep, and when I open the door and ask him if he wants to "go for a ride," his head tilts, his ears perk, and he is in the car within seconds. Rick picks a bouquet of larger wildflowers that look like black-eyed susans, and says Lisa might like them, and I stow them in the back seat. And with that we are off, back across the crumbling river bridge and onto S.R. 46, which is still quiet enough so that making a left against traffic is not a problem. The sun is out now, and it is a gorgeous day to be alive, and I can't wait to get home and sit in my camp chair next to the brick barbecue, maybe with a Sunday paper and a muffin and a freshly brewed cup of cappuccino.

I pull into the driveway and open the car door, and Shep bounds out as if he had been gone from his home for years, and not just an hour, hot on the trail of an unseen squirrel. In the backyard, I turn on the pump to the little pond I built here a decade ago, and water trickles down a pile of small limestone boulders like a tiny grotto. Leopard frogs squeak and jump and then settle back into their frog routine, hiding, only their bulging frog eyes exposed, down there between the leaves of the floating hyacinth. The pickerel weed is blooming now, tiny little purple orchidlike blossoms lined up on each organic rod tip. I see something large move on the ground out of the corner of my eye, and as I turn, it freezes. It is a yellow rat snake, and he had been making his way through the tall grass until he saw me. He is almost 6 feet long and big around, as a constrictor should be. While I know that snakes of his nature are harmless and beneficial, it still gives me a start to see one. I watch him carefully, and his body in its freeze-frame moment has stopped so thoroughly that his back has a series of ripples on it, as water surging down a stream might if caught by a quick-lens camera. I turn my head away, and when I look back, he is long gone, happy not to be eyeballed by a large, fleshy predator who is so genetically new that he barely fits into the ecological equation. I may be at the top of the food chain for now, but it is a precarious perch, and given all the mayhem humans are inflicting on the terrain that sustains us, time is not on our side.

There is no heavy-equipment work going on today, and the traffic noise from S.R. 46 is slight. Back here, surrounded by queen palms and bamboo and remnant longleaf, between my freshwater pond edged with moss-covered coquina and limestone and the enclosed porch of my old Cracker house, I allow myself the luxury of feeling alone and unthreatened and safe, just for now. Here, in my delusionary little world, there is no loss of lands, no need to think about moving, there are no duplicitous developers looking to make deals, just me and my dog and my place here on earth. I move in my chair, and as I do, I see a 4-inch-long anole scamper across a bare leafless twig, all brown now and headed into a cluster of green leaves. Inside the leaves, he stops and cocks his head to watch me. When he sees I am watching in return, he begins turning green, first his tiny legs and eyelids and then the top of his head. The initial burst of color camouflages him from any avian predator from above, rather than any threat from below. In a few more seconds, though, his entire body is lightly dusted with green, and then he blinks his eyes as if winking at me—he knows he is changing, and that I know it, too. But he will do it anyway because that is what anoles do to survive.

I think of the powers I possibly could have, and the ability to transform into something else that might shield my soul's core is not among them. Not too long ago, I went back to my high school reunion. I had been an all-conference athlete then, and the name tag I wore at the reunion used a photo taken from my yearbook. Several people made a point to tell me that I had changed less than anyone there, and I knew that was both my comfort and my doom. If I could change at will, I would be less susceptible to the scorn of those who have compromised their lives as chameleons, hiding under a façade to protect themselves from their bosses, their spouses, their children, the great stresses born of our hyperactive, consumptive society. No wonder the whole notion of environmental advocacy in this strange place is such a foreign, exotic idea—why align yourself with those who are preordained to lose, why bring yourself down with them, when it is far easier to move a few squares over and blend in with the prevailing public sentiment? Go along and get along; don't rock the boat. Alter your eyelids first, then the rest of your body. Soon you are indistinguishable from all else around you. Honestly, sometimes I get so weary that I wish I could change. But my ragged mortal soul has made its own commitment now, and it feels as if all the rest of me is just along for the ride.

Above in the sugar hackberry tree, two Carolina wrens flick about, just like the ones that each spring build a nest inside the patio overhang by the side door. They emit a low-grade buzzing sound of a chirp, a song that makes them sound vaguely electronic. The wrens scatter, replaced by a set of seasonal visitors, the tiny black-and-white warbler, which vaguely resembles a dwarf ladder-backed woodpecker. They hop between the branches, nibbling at the BB-sized fruit of the hackberry, sometimes hanging upside down to do so. The warbler's presence is also a cue that other migrants will be moving through soon, headed down from the North, every bit as dependable as the migrating "snowbirds," the retirees who overwinter here from Michigan and Ohio, some later deciding to stay forever when the turmoil of annual round-trip travel becomes too much. It is warm here in Florida, always warm, and despite the ravages of everything else, it always will be. For those who settle in the self-contained little retirement communities with scant trace of the natural landscape, the real Florida will always be perpetually out of reach. When they die, they are sent home to be buried, back to where their hearts have always remained. And did you know the second leading air-freight item out of Florida is dead bodies, all flying home to roost for the big sleep, no connection ever made here stronger than the call to the distant place they will always know as home?

Although I was not born here, Florida is my homeland now, and always will be. There is a family grave plot back on the Eastern Shore of Maryland with my name on it, but I won't be going there. I'll be put to the earth right here, in the place that didn't create my heart but that fully captured it, a place bursting with the indelible seed of natural romance, dreams cleft from the stamen of a rare wildflower, the way a swallow-tailed kite glides across the sky at sunset, the spring water that is the color of my father's eyes. My grand-dad died here, and later, my dad. My cousin, the one closest to me in all my life, met her husband here when they were both fine-looking and young, and brought two children into the world down in south Florida. Her dad—my uncle who once boated Lake Arbuckle in his wooden run-about—started drinking here as a young man, and never really stopped. He became careless, drifting, and sad. But once, in a lawn chair in his backyard, I saw him place a homegrown string bean on his white t-shirt, and when the bean grabbed ahold with all its little filia and held fast, he laughed at that. A nice healthy laugh, despite himself. Little bean, defying gravity. Like he had once tried to do. But he wasn't able to hold on that tight, and he had tumbled downhill with little grace. And it was Florida that launched him on that roll, this place in which nearly anything could happen. Although my uncle's grip on this dream never left him, his real-life ability to realize it surely did.

I talked to my friend Sandy on the phone today. She used to live here, not far from Lake Jesup, in a soggy, wild, wooded area locals call the Black Ham-mock. She's worked for Florida Audubon and now works as the director of an environmental learning center in St. Lucie County down on the coast. I tell her I am working on a project about sprawl. She hesitates. "Everyone talks about how private property owners lose the value of their property if they can't develop—or lose their property to eminent domain. The taking of property. Well, you know, there's a whole other kind of taking, too." Sandy is a pretty woman with a vague resemblance to the actress Sandra Bullock, big brown eyes, and a cheerful air. She laughs a lot and deeply. But she doesn't laugh now. "It's the taking of the starry night. The taking of the birdsong. The taking of the sunsets. The taking of my groundwater. No one's put a price on that." After our conversation, I take Shep outside for a run on the north side of the house, near the night-blooming cactus. Rains have started again, and the artesian well there has miraculously responded by renewing its flow. It is as if I have my own little spring coursing out of a metal pipe stuck in the ground. The faucet has rusted off, and the shallow upwelling flows freely now. I have dug a little furrow so the water runs away from the house and into one of the shallow, grassy ditches the Duraks dug years ago to help keep these old flatwoods drained.

The water settles into its own little run, spring-clear and cool and slightly sulphurous, and continues downhill until it reaches the back of my property, and then leaks into a larger ditch, one that will transport it out to S.R. 46. I am listening to the sound of my flowing well when Shep spooks the one-eyed bunny. The rabbit runs a zigzag pattern until it reaches me, and then it sits only a foot or so away from my feet, its bad eye turned to me. The eye is bluish, forever unseeing. If I wanted, I could reach down and touch it. When I was a little boy, my grandfather told me that if I could put salt on the tail of a wild rabbit in my neighborhood, I could catch it. I chased that rabbit day after day, salt shaker in my little five-year-old hand, with no success. But now the rabbit has come to me, and I didn't even need the salt at all. The bunny twitches once, turns his good eye in my direction, quivers in fear, and then speeds off again.

Shep wanders about some more, and I let him go where he wants. He follows his nose, a good dog on a scent trail, and heads for the old grove, jumping in one tiny sheltie leap across the ditch that separates it from my backyard. I follow several yards behind, curious as to where his unseen path will finally lead him. Every time I visit the grove, I am always astonished at how well it has been colonized by new growth since a freeze took out the original citrus trees in 1986. All of the trees, save for a half dozen at the distant southwest corner, were frozen to the ground. Even after its demise, the grove managers tried to "manage" their land by tilling each row with a tractor to keep the weeds under control, as if they might someday replant. They did that right up until the year I moved into my home; by then, newly colonized native trees had already begun to grow around the base of each dead citrus trunk, so the effect was to grade earthen aisles in a newly birthed native woods.

I ask a friend, a former grove owner, about all of this. His name is Joe, and he is a well-educated man whose own family business was once growing and processing citrus. They produced their juice under the name of a brand with a little bluebird for a logo, and had done so for several decades. Joe told me the grove owners here likely saw the future not in citrus but in real estate, and as the "business corridor" around I-4 began to grow, they would most likely allow the last pretense of citrus to go as well. Plowing the grove at least made the land seem agricultural, and thus eligible for a lower property tax than if it were primed for commercial speculation. A half dozen trees do not make a grove; yet replanting this far north, where killer freezes could hit again, just wasn't worth it anymore. Growing citrus was what they did because the land, before sprawl was endorsed and encouraged by local governments, wasn't valuable for much else. Since Joe's family business has dissolved, he has tried many things but has never hit on a winner. Even his personal relationships have begun to suffer. Recently, he went bankrupt. Can I argue that the conversion of the landscape has also changed him inextricably, that it has forever thrown off his timing?

Earlier in the twentieth century, few wanted to spread out into the countryside—aside from those hardy souls like the former occupants of Sewell Road, and their counterparts who lived in other remote enclaves, such as Cross Creek. Like elsewhere in the country, Floridians of that era grouped around cities and towns. In one way, then, one might say these folks who lived away from cities were the archetypes of modern sprawl. Yet there is a distance so great in this definition that it can only be described as celestial: These settlers were self-sufficient and independent, taking nothing and wanting nothing. And their rugged spirit was self-regulating in terms of population overload. The carrying capacity of an environmental system, even a fragile one, could bear a smattering of low-tech homesteads on it, especially when a "commute" was not required.

The settlement patterns of Florida didn't much change until speculators went out into the countryside and bought farmland and woods and swamp, dirt cheap, and created the illusion of a city when, really, none existed. I thought of Golden Gate Estates South, the General Development fiasco that sprawled east of Naples into the Big Cypress. All manner of canals were built to drain the land, and roads with signs were constructed to show that this was a place to be reckoned with. The plan, even then, was illegal—its canals and berms interrupted the sheet flow of water moving overland, and no matter how hard they tried, the developers never quite grew the critical mass needed to settle the land. The ambitious project was only realized in their let's-pretend brochures and flyers and advertisements—which has always been a peculiarly Floridian method of maneuvering reality, even in the nineteenth century. In all fairness, the developer's Orwellian marketing is the natural descendent of the spring resorts of the 1800s, which were promoted to early tourists as "salubrious"—capable of curing nearly all ills known to humankind. Lawsuits and bankruptcy put General Development out of business, and the only thing that really kept southern Golden Gate Estates from eventual development was that the landscape was still so remote and swampy that even most starry-eyed buyers regarded it not as a primary home site but as an investment.

With few structures, the land was easier to reclaim and to ecologically re-attach to the Big Cypress. But there were exceptions: I drove down there a few years ago to write a magazine article on the remnants of Golden Gate South, which was situated between Belle Meade and the Fakahatcheee Strand. There I found a dozen or so ramshackle trailers and oddly constructed huts tucked away in the undergrowth where the luxury homes were once to have been built. These were the property owners who, half-crazed with the failure of speculative promise, moved onto their land anyway. It was a futile effort as the land still flooded seasonally, and the state was busy buying back as much of the property as it could. I remember walking down the middle of one of the abandoned asphalt streets—marked with a sign as 10233 St. NW—and finding panther scat in the middle of the road. I was hoping to talk to someone who lived here, and to do so, I walked over a narrow jeep path inside a thick swatch of woods that seemed to lead to a structure. Halfway there, I saw homemade greenhouses of clear plastic tarp sheltering healthy 5-foot-tall marijuana plants and heard several very large dogs barking with malice in their canine hearts. I beat a quick retreat.

Although the 20 acres of woods south of my property are neither vast nor remote, if you knew nothing of its brief history, it would seem like it had been here forever. Florida is good at erasing its past with its climate. Wood rots, and rain and warm sun reclaim any landscape ripe for the reclaiming. Perhaps that's why so many renegades and reprobates have come here, half-expecting Florida to weave vines and weeds over their own sordid pasts, covering it with a patina of sun-washed soil, brand-new real estate for a brand-new life, Rust Belt madness hidden just centimeters below. No wonder serial killers with rattletrap old cars are routinely burying their prey under our terrain, figuring it will hide their sins just as the anonymity of this place, its sheer lack of community, has briefly hidden their own.

Animals have been traveling through this old grove since it died, depositing a variety of seeds in handy self-fertilizing piles of scat, a natural colonization augmented by the climate. As the original citrus trunks rotted, sabal palms—encouraged by the heavy fertilizers applied around each cultivated tree—grew in great profusion, four and five to each citrus stump, all competing for space. They were later joined by slower-growing trees—laurel oaks, southern red cedars, even sugar hackberry. Gopher tortoises now live back in here, and one of the things I do when I walk this woods is to see if their burrows are still active. Gophers learned long ago to burrow deep—30 and 40 feet—down into the sandy soil. The tunnels help regulate their body temperature, keeping them cooler in summer and warmer in winter, and even insulating against the periodic lightning-driven wildfires that were once a part of seasonal life here on this waterlogged peninsula. Up to three hundred animals and insects share these same holes—from walking sticks to indigo snakes and armadillos—so having the gopher around is a good way to help remind ourselves that there's as much under the terrain as atop it. But these gophers are cut from a strange cloth. Certainly, in the years when this grove was active, they weren't living in it. Topographical maps show higher terrain just to the south, and there must have been some superb sandhills in the uplands there. Now that malls and box retailers over on Reinhart occupy the uplands, the reptiles are seeking refuge anyplace they can. There is no way to ask them where they came from with any certainty; we speak a different language. Regardless of their origins, they are here, and today I count six burrows, each with a mound of dirt nearly a foot high at each entrance. As usual, I see no tortoises, but the portals to the burrows seem well-used, shaped by the coming and going of their shells, dorsal-round on top and plastron-flat on the bottom. Perhaps, like the chuck-will's-widow I hear at night, the gophers have returned home to reclaim an ancient territory. But the territory is under duress now, and it's missing a lot of essential things that once bound it—not the least of which are the Crackers who once lived here.

The gopher was sometimes an ancillary Cracker food group, and for those who ate them, the animal was felicitously called the "Hoover Chicken." This old grove is a strange no-man's land now, and those who live nearby think the ancient reptile is something to hassle or to kill, pointlessly. I saw two burrows once that were caved in by some dim-witted human trying to capture a reptile by digging 4 or 5 feet back. The diggers had no clue that the holes were actually eight or nine times that long. Another time I picked up the dry, empty shell of a juvenile that had been shot with a pellet gun. I brought it home to join my other natural treasures on an old table on the back porch— the pot shards, the sharks' teeth from the springs. I've only once seen an actual gopher out of its burrow back here. When it saw me, it hunkered down motionless, as freeze-framed as the rat snake, genetically fixed in a reptilian endurance born of distant millennia.

It finally occurs to me that all that lives in these woods has been chased here by the loss of wetlands and uplands around us. As a historic forest, it may not be much, but as a 20-acre chunk of protective foliaged habitat, it's a sanctuary. Its trees allow a valuable oxygen exchange and help keep the immediate area cooler than if it were rooftop and asphalt. When these trees go, I wonder what will become of the wildlife and birds. And of course, as I always do, I wonder what will become of us all.

I have contacted the City of Sanford about the development that will one day replace these woods. When I do, I tell an official there of the existence of the gopher tortoise burrows, and of the many trees that seem to be larger than six inches in diameter and so are, theoretically, protected by the city's tree ordinance. The chief planner there is a courteous and patient man who has promised to keep me informed of all pending changes. Until a preliminary site plan for the development is submitted, there's not much I can do. And, of course, I am skeptical about the intent: There are few developers in this region who really care about the idea of sustainability, and of balancing use with preservation. Many are abrasive, wealthy bullies who attend public city and county hearings only to make cases for the prosperity their work will bring. One big man with a self-righteous air likes to present himself as a God-fearing "Christian," and I have heard others on various councils and commissions refer to him as such as if this gives him tacit permission to annihilate the terrain for his use. The notion of a natural landscape and the animals it sustains means little. Not long ago, he carelessly drew up an incorrect engineering plan that ended up destroying wetlands and flooding an adjacent neighborhood near the Econlockhatchee River in east Orange County, all in the name of expediency. What of the biblical concern for all of God's creatures, of His heaven and the sacred earth that He created? What of this man's self-professed Christianity?

But there is more than just a natural reforestation of the old grove land going on here. Many new residents are pushing up against the woods now—apartment renters and those poor lost souls who inhabit the run-down houses and trailers now owned by the developer-turned-slumlord. There is no investment, fiscal or emotional, for them in this place, and the result is a disconnect between their lives here and the remnant woods nearby.

We cross through the forest to the south side, where Smith Canal runs parallel to the edge of the old grove. Deep and straight, the blackwater canal is now also full of hydrilla, the non-native import from Sri Lanka sold for the freshwater aquarium trade. The underwater plant has been quietly moving out of the St. Johns and growing its way upstream. It is so healthy that tiny white blossoms break the surface from its frilly green whorls. I see a great blue heron a few hundred yards downstream, and it is motionless in its classic wading-bird pose, nothing mattering except the tiny fish it has sighted, waiting with generous persistence for its dinner to swim another millimeter closer. I call to Shep so he doesn't spook the heron, and we turn and walk back into the woods, past the oak and sabal palms, turning at the air conditioners to the little path that leads finally to the edge of my property, where my own shallow ditch creates the boundary. Shep and I leap across it to my backyard. He looks up at me—small dogs must always look up—and wags his tail. It was a good walk for him.

Seminole County, despite its fierce Indian name, is a bedroom community with 70 percent of its residents working outside its boundaries. That means some developers found cheap rural land well outside the range of urban service centers—clearly violating or exempting the rules that county comprehensive plans, by state mandate, require. Underpinned by the Growth Management Act of 1986, the rules are precise and simple: Infrastructure such as roads, sewer, and services like police and fire should be up and running by the time the development itself is ready for business. Urban, rural, and green space would be mapped out in each "comp plan," and future land users would, ideally, have to locate in the area zoned for each. "Urban service areas" would be targeted for growth because, well, they can bear up to it better than the rural countryside. The problem is that every year, these local governments pass thousands of "amendments" that allow exemptions to the plan and permit "leapfrogging" out into the country. When a particularly aggressive pro-growth governor, such as former developer Jeb Bush, comes into office, the Department of Community Affairs—the state agency entrusted with monitoring and approving these amendments—defaults to rubber-stamping exemptions. In 2001, the DCA filed only 4 challenges to 100,000 amendments statewide; in 2002, they challenged 9 out of 8,000 amendments. The examples of community dysfunction that follow this sprawl are many but perhaps can be simply explained by charting how long it takes firefighters to respond to fire alarms. By mid 2004, Orange County needed a dozen new fire stations in order to service the newer outlying developments. "You're seeing rural areas turn to suburban areas and with that comes a greater need for fire service," a deputy chief of the county's fire rescue operations told a reporter in 2004. Response times in the formerly rural areas can be twice as long as those older neighborhoods that were traditionally outfitted for such services.

A report published by the Healthy Community Initiative of Greater Orlando in 2002 evaluated all the many "indicators" that together help qualify a livable and sustainable community. The broad-based HCI included civic leaders, businesspeople, and technical experts, and the resulting report seemed fair and balanced, if a bit cheery. However, of the thirty different indicators, the issue of "sprawl" seems most troublesome. The HCI defined sprawl as "unnecessary land consumption—repetitive one-story commercial buildings surrounded by acres of parking, and a lack of public spaces and common centers. It is poorly managed growth with a disregard for a sustainable balance of nature, economy, society and well-being." At current rates of growth, in thirty years there will be no land left to build on in Orange County, and the only natural terrain left will be in parks.

As the soil is covered with impervious surfaces, it not only loses the capacity to recharge the aquifer, but the once-valuable rainfall becomes a quandary unto itself. A study in the Water Resources Bulletin shows that when 25 percent of natural terrain is covered with asphalt, concrete, and rooftops, a once-in-one-hundred-year flood could occur every five years. Another analysis by the National Oceanic and Atmospheric Administration has found the impervious surface area of the lower forty-eight states has now become larger in area than that of our existing wetlands, and it will continue to expand as we continue to grow. Once impervious areas cover only 10 percent of a watershed, they alter the shape of channels, raise the water temperature, and sweep urban debris and pollutants into aquatic environments. Ultimately, the impacts also diminish the variety and populations of fish and aquatic insects.

Sprawling means other things, too. In 1990, central Florida families averaged 46.6 miles a day driving to work, school, and shopping. In 2002, the average was 54.2 miles. That means more fuel burned, more money spent, more land paved, more pollution emitted. And there are the intangibles: "Sprawl spreads us out, leaving neighbors farther apart and reducing community connections." Another indicator, "Community Stability," shows that 100,000 people either move in or leave Orange County each year, creating a discordant "population churn." That means an average of 45 percent of elementary school children change schools midyear. The "churn" then, becomes a measure of "our highly mobile and relatively unstable population base."

Nonetheless, despite the increase in sprawl, traffic congestion, energy use, pollution, and lack of connection, there is one last indicator that in central Florida seems to contradict nearly all others. Under the category of "Perceived Quality of Life," the report notes that polls show "We are an optimistic community." In 1999, 86 percent of those surveyed believed their personal quality of life was good—which was a 10 percent increase from 1986. To its great credit, the HCI reports notes: "We emphasize the word 'perceived' because how people experience their lives may or may not be related to objective trends in the community." In other words, the salubrious marketing spin inspired by the first promoters and repeated by the modern developers is everywhere pervasive.

Advertising and marketing seem to mold our self-image more than any single aspect of reality here in Florida. Within the context of this highly delusional community mindset, developing an ethic for the land and an appreciation for sense of place has little meaning. We are a community that is—despite all the happy-face sloganeering to the contrary—disconnected from place. Image-creating has become an art form here; it is as if the just-pretend atmosphere of the theme worlds has spilled over into real life.

Poor planning has also turned us into one giant, sprawling city of commuters. Using a federal government standard for reimbursement for miles traveled to and from work, school, shopping, and church, the average family here spends $7,194 yearly on travel. And in a 2000 study, drivers lost an average of sixty-six hours in traveling increasingly congested roads—a 600 percent increase over 1982. Collectively, idling in traffic wasted 335 million gallons of gas. This waste can be clearly linked to a decline in air quality. We have a flat landscape and prevailing winds, and that helps distribute our exhaust better than in, say, Los Angeles. Nonetheless, air pollution, driven largely by auto emissions, was measured by 1.2 million pounds of toxins released into the air in the year 2000 in central Florida alone.

Longer and more tedious commutes aren't just harder on the pocketbooks and the air quality. It results in a stream of angry and hostile people, mostly from somewhere else, cutting off each other, tailgating, even pulling over for the occasional fist fight at roadside. Mike Durak told me that when he lived here as a boy and drove out on S.R. 46, if you passed a car you didn't know, you waved and they waved back. They still do that in remote communities in northern Florida. But hereabouts, hand waves take a different form today, and are often practiced by extending the middle finger and pushing it forcibly toward a fellow driver.

I think of how sprawl isolates habitats and realize that paradoxically we are detached from the world here on Sewell Road, too. The word "isolation" sounds odd, especially now that I can see neon from the extruded chain restaurants and fern bars a few hundred yards away. Nonetheless, despite their cheery come-ons, these restaurants aren't culturally authentic or even very friendly, except in an institutionalized manner, and I find the excruciatingly perky automatons who staff them simply tiring. One of the latest additions to the extruded chains is "Joe's Crab Shack," and despite its contrived funkiness and its fake weathered sign and its name, it is not run by Joe and is not a shack, and the crabs—instead of being local blues—are frozen Alaskan king crabs. I visited a friend in Southern California two years ago and saw an exact replica of Joe's Crab Shack there. Despite its invitation to adventure, it was about as risky as going on Disney's Pirates of the Caribbean boat ride thirty times. Nothing changes, and the pirates, which are manufactured and safe, all raise their arms and plastic rum bottles at the same time, and drink deeply, of nothing at all. Or, as Mormino and Mohl have written in The New History of Florida: "Theme park attractions have created artificial worlds of elaborately contrived environments where tourists 'experience' Thunder Mountains but rarely appreciate the real Florida."

Because the native culture has been displaced by a society of newcomers, regions like central Florida are blank slates for restaurants to introduce new themed eateries. There is scant allegiance here to a shared cultural ideal, except to the faint-but-undying memory of how it used to be in Ohio or Michigan or New York. The effect is not unlike how the many plant and animal exotics are able to easily colonize Florida—because the natural systems are in such disarray. As a result, all of central Florida serves as a testing ground for pilot restaurants by Darden and others that would wish us a Red Lobster or Olive Garden or Bahama Breeze on every corner. If it works here, it'll work anywhere. Demographers dictate everything from menus to newspaper content not by common sense, but by focus groups and surveys.

Author and poet Jim Harrison once wrote that "the danger of civilization, of course, is that we piss away our lives on nonsense." We are considered civilized now, yet our actions are increasingly uncivil, and our values determined not by sustainable worth, but by marketing. Eat at Joes? I would rather graze on roadkill.

Chapter Eight

We are just emerging from a technological entrancement. During this period, the human mind has been placed within the narrowest confines it has experienced since consciousness emerged from its Paleolithic phase. Even the most primitive tribes have a larger vision of the universe, or our place and function within it.

Fr. Thomas Berry, The Dream of the Earth

Lisa came over this afternoon after spending the morning riding her thoroughbred, Ben. She reported a great ride, for after all he is a champion, a chestnut-colored, tightly muscled animal, and she is one of those rare athletes who understands the gradations of finesse. Usually she practices dressage with Ben, an intricate, highly challenging exercise in which the animal is encouraged to trot, canter, gallop and do various in-ride shift changes around an outdoor arena. But Ben and his owner are, at heart, trail riders, and on some days, Lisa takes Ben out through the remaining forest that surrounds his paddock, another pine flatwoods with enough upland scrub to support a few gophers. Ben lives way out in east Orlando now, in a place that used to be all country. Houses now push in on all sides. The most recent assault came from an adjoining "neighborhood" that, like so much built in Florida, had to be raised above the natural landscape to keep it out of the floodplain. There's no way in the world an elevated terrain like that won't have storm water draining off its edges. And so now there are great puddles in Ben's paddock where once there was dry grass. Nearby, the remnant pine flatwoods are being clear-cut for more homes. The owner of the pasture where Ben lives has just signed a contract with another developer, and soon Ben's paddock will also be leveled and tons of fill dirt brought in to raise the land up to a suitable height so it can also be covered with roads and manicured lawns and rooftops and driveways. If Lisa is to keep him, Ben will have to go somewhere else, somewhere deeper into the country.

There is symmetry here for I will soon have to go somewhere else, too. For now, we go to sit on the white stone bench at the north side of my yard, between the home and the cereus, which now has its last season-end bloom of five blossoms. The Turks-cap, which spent most of the summer putting its energy into growing long, green, leafy steams 6 and 7 feet high, is today full of the bright-red hibiscuslike blossoms that never quite open, the terrestrial version of the tight yellow bloom of the spatterdock water lily. When Lisa sees it she says it looks like someone made little crepe paper flowers and hung them all over the giant bush. No fewer than four cloudless sulfur butterflies are bouncing about the blossoms, and a zebra longwing is making low, lazy swoops over it all. The zebra, narrow wings and striped yellow over black, is our official state butterfly, and breeds nearly year around on the peninsula. Bartram reported it when he first came into Florida in the 1760s. Lepidopterists have speculated that the butterfly was blown here from the wider Caribbean. Still subtropic by nature, they seldom range much father north than Tallahassee.

We approach the Turks-caps, and I pinch off the trumpet of one of the flowers and suck the sweet nectar from the bottom of its natural vase, just like the Duraks once showed me. It is still intact, no bee or hummer had yet taken it. I pinch off another and hand it to Lisa, who does the same. I have brought a copy of a guide to Florida wildflowers with me because we want to try to identify a blossom Lisa saw out at the paddock today. We thumb through the pages until we come to a member of the willow family—likely the primrose willow with its tiny green cross in the center of the leafy yellow petals. But her flower was smaller and slightly different. There are over four hundred plants in this state found nowhere else, and the book, while ambitious, just can't portray them all. The longer we sit on the stone bench, the more our senses open to the wildflowers that surround us. The simple act of sitting still to more fully see is revealing a new world, hidden down in the ragged green macramé of a lawn.

I don't fertilize or poison this "lawn." In fact, it is not a lawn in the traditional sense at all—although the word "traditional" is hardly appropriate since Florida historically had no natural lawns. When we cover our sandy terrain with coifed "turf grass" we do so in rank imitation of English Tudor estates—and what finally is the point of all that?

The field guide we use is divided by colors of the flowers, a handy visual method to make a quick identification. "Oh," says Lisa, stopping at a page coded to white. "Here he is." She bends over at the waist and picks up a tiny white flower, six petals, but the whole no bigger than one-eighth of an inch across its face. "It's Mexican clover." She holds it next to a picture of the same, and the match is accurate. We look down into the green macramé some more. A bluish little glimmer of a blossom comes into focus. It is only slightly larger than the Mexican clover, and in the late afternoon autumn sun it has partially closed its petals. Still there is enough of it open to see it is a member of the snapdragon family, one with no common name—Agalinis setecea. As I look around, I see we are surrounded by hundreds of these tiny snapdragons. Lisa also identifies a plant studded with light-green buds called hairy spurge and another with a diminutive burgundy flower named milk purslane. We thumb some more through the book, and I find the creeping cucumber, a tiny member of the gourd family with a half-inch-long fruit that looks for all the world like a miniature cucumber. I tell Lisa it grows in a vine and hangs from a corner of my patio roof, rooted in the leaf detritus there. Lisa tells me with a yard like this, we can do most of our wildflower identification without having to move more than just a few feet in any direction.

But we do move. "There's a morning glory of some kind here, too," I say. We get up to look, and sure enough, there it is dangling from the top of the sugar hackberry, still open and light purple under the coolness of the tree's canopy. Once up from the bench, we scout the ground behind the garage, in the sunny place where the Duraks once planted their garden. Here we stumble on several false poinsettia, a bouquet of wood sorrel, three types of exotic house plants that now thrive on their own, along with a clutch of elephant ears, and two trailing vines, one a Virginia creeper and another the southern fox grape.

There is a third vine here, too, one far more noxious and invasive than the others. It is the air potato, and, at its peak, it nearly obscures the terrain under it. From a distance, it looks like kudzu, but it bears a grayish potatolike bulb on its vine, and that tuber is the reason it is here. Imported from West Africa, where it had been grown as a food, it was soon found that—left to drape itself at random across the landscape without the deft hand of cultivation— the air potato became something else entirely. The tuber, both the one in the ground and the one growing on its vine, can be bitter and even poisonous if not properly cultivated and prepared. In Florida, it was once thought that hogs might like it, but hogs aren't senseless, and without a value as livestock food, the air potato was left to its own natural devices. Now it has become one more of the many non-native "exotics" that have spread over the state. In this way, it is the botanical version of the tilapia, the Amazonian herbivorous fish the Florida Fish and Game imported in the 1960s simply to give anglers another sport quarry. It wasn't until fishermen reported the tilapia would seldom take a hook that they discovered their import was a herbivore. Later they found that tilapia would grow stout and hearty and would move in great droves across the streambeds and spring runs, crowding out other native fish, and living long, healthy lives uninterrupted by the intervention of a fisherman's creel. "They come in here like a herd of buffalo," a fisheries biologist once told me, describing the tilapias' arrival in a local spring run. And that is what the air potato has done, moving across the disturbed landscape with the force of a vegetable cyclone, smothering everything that doesn't move in a great quilt of exotic chlorophyll.

There are, in fact, more exotic plants and animals in Florida than anywhere in the United States except Hawaii, and the disruption of natural ecosystems have made it so. Like all else in the disturbed landscape of this state, it is both a source of torment as well as a satirical delight. Indeed, on February 3, 2001, the Second Great Air Potato Roundup took place in Gainesville. Volunteers were urged to "take back their natural area, one potato at a time." Some eight hundred air potato wranglers showed up and harvested nearly 8 tons of the tuber. Contests were held and prizes awarded for the most collected, the largest (the size of a cannonball), and the oddest, which, one volunteer noted, bore a strong resemblance to the profile of former U.S. vice president Dan Quayle, although that the name of the tuber was spelled without an additional "e" at the end. Like the aquatic hydrilla, the air potato has been outlawed and placed on the Florida Noxious Weed List, which means it cannot be introduced, possessed, moved, or released without a permit. Which makes perfect sense in a Catch 22 sort of way: When something is so out of control in Florida that nothing much can be done, the logical step is to pass a law against it.

As we wander around my yard, we take a closer look at this outlaw vine. While it does sport a stunning clutch of large heart-shaped green leaves, it otherwise has no purpose except to smother all it touches. I pull at one of the longer vines trailing down from a tree canopy, holding on to a stem that is as strong as thick twine. It resists at first and then gives way, and down come a half dozen potatoes, none thankfully as large as a cannonball, but one hits me squarely in the head, bounces into a ditch, and rolls into a gopher tortoise burrow there. Lisa seems happy that she has been spared from a head-bopping tuber but finds it ironic that I have just brought them raining down on us. "Sir," Lisa says, in mock officiousness, "step away from the air potato vine." She also tells me that my gopher tortoise is now in violation of state statute by "possessing" an outlaw tuber in its burrow. I tell her it is not my gopher tortoise, but was an escapee from when the mall was being built and its brethren were being buried alive in burrows there. She asks me what I will do with it when I leave, and I said I didn't know, and the truth is that I don't. There are many questions to be answered still about this leaving business. The gopher tortoise and the air potato are the least of my worries.

I have been out in the world today, and on the way home, I drive past the entrance to the Seminole Towne Center on S.R. 46. There at the side of road, back behind a sidewalk no one uses because it goes nowhere, were three homeless people. I had seen them before, individually begging at this and other intersections nearby. Sprawl has created seven lights on a quarter mile of road where previously there was only one. For a panhandler, that is a good thing as cars simply must stop more often. The homeless people were rugged and beat-looking, not that old really, maybe in their thirties or so—a sturdy blond woman with short cropped hair and two slender men with long hair and beards. I had seen one of the men crossing the road one day, and he had a decided limp, as if a broken leg had healed poorly. He also seemed somehow to have lost his equilibrium, as if not drunk just for this day, but forever. With them next to the sidewalk to nowhere was a shopping cart from Eckerds and a dog, which was lying on its back in the little patch of grass. The homeless woman was scratching its belly. A dog on the world's longest walk, no home to return to. They all looked so forlorn. I drove into the mall to find a bracelet for Lisa's birthday, got disoriented by the sensory overload of the place, and beat a quick retreat back out to the parking lot as soon as I could. As I drove toward home, the man I had seen limping was standing by a stoplight holding a handmade cardboard sign. Homeless. Please. God Bless. I wanted to give him money, although I had so little I couldn't even afford the bracelet I had planned to buy. I considered emptying my pockets of change, perhaps a dollar or so. Then the light changed, and I followed the cars in front of me, driving on beyond the personal misery just as I would drive on beyond a car wreck.

Earlier, on S.R. 46, I had traveled past what was a large swatch of thick woods on the other side of the interstate. Bulldozers have been grinding away here just beyond the northern edge of the road over the last several weeks. They have been very thorough, and as a result, the once-thick forest of pine and oak has now been cleared to the ground. The newly denuded landscape is all black wetland soil, pocketed with pools of water and piles of burning stumps, nothing else, except for the feeling of loss, of great apocalyptic loss. And then I saw the new sign advertising the lame development that would go there: The Park at Dunwoody Commons, a condo complex named to sound like some fancy English estate. Next, tons of new clay and sand would be brought in to raise the Park at Dunwoody Commons several feet above the floodplain, and it would be covered with exotic trees and grass. There would be two general types of condo design, named "Siesta" and "Biscayne," designations that have nothing to do with central Florida. A preconstruction brochure for these homes shows a photograph of a happy young couple sitting on a floor and together looking at an object, an experience that seems to be affording them nothing less than total bliss. And when it is complete, this new "neighborhood" would be entirely reborn from the embers of a pine flatwoods, and no one who came to live here would know this was a fertile river delta of the St. Johns, a place with a luxuriance of soil and water so commanding it had once shaped a culture.

I realized, of course, that our bioregion was losing its own natural equilibrium at an alarming rate. Unless some natural disaster cleaned the earth of our mistakes and gave us a chance to rethink our behavior, it would likely stay lost, inebriated and off balance forever like the poor forlorn homeless.

A cold snap is finally headed our way this evening. It was so warm last night that I had the windows open and the ceiling fans on. But this morning when I was making cappuccino, I tapped my finger on the glass pane over the barometer and the needle there dropped almost half an inch. It is December now, and winds are building out of the northeast, and the first freeze is forecast for tonight. This used to really mean something in Florida when a freeze could affect your entire livelihood by killing your citrus crop. Until the early twentieth century—even when Rawlings arrived to tend her 74-acre grove in Cross Creek—the standard method of reacting to an impending freeze was to stack dry wood in piles in the groves and to burn and tend it during the coldest hours of the night. Later the wood piles were replaced with kerosene-fired grove heaters. When I moved into Sewell, there were a couple of old grove heaters still left from when the Duraks actively cultivated the dozen or so trees on the land here. Preparing for a freeze was a very utilitarian behavior; having your crop destroyed was like letting money pour out of your bank account. Now it means losing some exotic tropical ornamentals like philodendrons and dieffenbachia that don't belong this far north anyway. Still, there is something unique about the typical Florida reaction to a coming freeze, and it usually has to do with laying old blankets and comforters atop "cold-sensitive plants." Newcomers are perplexed by this, as if homeowners are literally putting their plants to bed by tucking them in for the night. Yet, this thirsty, fragile flora could not survive without the kindness of human intervention. Sure, citrus trees need intervention, too, but they supplied fruit and juice and economy. Exotic landscape plants supply one thing, and that is décor.

Sometimes water is left running all night just to protect these décor plants. When that happens, the aquifer continues to diminish, and the terrain sinks just a little more. There are various regional chapters of the Florida Native Plant Society to encourage locals to think locally when landscaping. They point out, quite accurately, that native plants don't have the high-maintenance needs—fertilizer, water, and energy—of exotics, not to mention the need for labor-intensive cultivation. But new real estate developments set the tone, erecting grand porticos with exotic plants, sodding the property end-to-end with replicas of an English Tudor lawn, and then proclaiming themselves "nature retreats." Overall, Floridians use an average of 175 gallons of water a day—about 65 gallons more than the national average. About half of this potable freshwater goes into landscape irrigation. Our springs are drying, and our potable aquifer is diminishing. Yet the regional water management district continues to permit large developments and golf courses, allowing ravenous gulps from our declining groundwater. In contrast, a recent survey by the Florida Water Services showed that 80 percent of Floridians believe "water conservation is critical." The distance between what the average citizen wants and what their government practices is vast. We have insulated ourselves so thoroughly from reality that the logic of cause and effect has been removed from the rule-making equation.

As I walk my yard today, I feel the new places where the earth continues to sink into the soft terrain of rock and soil. The intricate filigree of soft limestone under me holds our reservoir of life-giving water, but it is not as easily seen—or realized—as it would be if it were on the surface. Maps made by cave-diving cartographers may cover miles of diveable cave that stretch away from the sink or spring that provides a "karst window." Yet, these charts are limited to what the mapmaker can physically experience. The smaller crevices and fractures that snake from the main stem of any cave await some yet-uninvented technique to fully make themselves known to the air-breathing world. Despite the fragility of it all, we romp like modern cowboys over this landscape, taking all the water we want—and much we don't even need—without a clue as to how it will affect the aquifer it has been drawn from. Our insensate use of this water has been compared to writing checks on a bank account without any clue as to what the balance may be. When the checks start to bounce, wells are simply sunk deeper into the aquifer, the awls of the well-drillers searching for the caves that, for now, are still liquid-filled.

I have been into these caves before as a diver and, floating there in solution, have felt a kinship with the earth I seldom know in any other place. In those moments, it seems as if I am flowing through the veins and capillaries of a living being, accessing the circulatory system through an incision in the soft tissues of karst. The experience easily becomes spiritual to me, and it is made so not just by the visceral sense of connection it affords but by the majesty of the proportion, a tiny human alone in a dark and powerful abyss. Perhaps this spirituality is informed by an innate human fear of the earth's true natural powers. This same healthy foreboding was woven into the greater appreciation that the Paleo-Indians—and those who followed—had for the universe that surrounded them. I worry that our intellectual jump-start on technology and science has exceeded our human capacity to feel, to respect, and to worship. Our conceit that we can continue to break the earth and then to put it back together again with impunity is a peculiarly modern one.

I went out today and half-heartedly did a little Christmas shopping, bought a new electric space heater, and then came home. Shep's starting to show his age now, and he sleeps a lot in the day, often curled up on the comforter of my bed. But today he was at the door, tail wagging, ears up, bursting with energy for a walk. I stashed my new purchase, changed into jeans, a sweatshirt, and a ball cap, and we headed out through the backyard and into the old grove for a little hike. It was nearly 4 p.m. With the winter sun low in the sky, it was cold enough in the shade canopy of oak and palms to give me a chill. We ducked under some catbrier, broke through some low-growing blackberry vine, and walked to where I knew two gopher tortoises were living. I wanted to see if they were keeping their burrows open, and they were.

We walked toward the Smith Canal, and as we did I picked up the distinct scent of burning wood, not the fireplace kind, but the kind of scrap you toss in an outdoor bonfire. At the canal, the woods opened, and we walked west along the edge of the deep ditch toward Reinhart. Halfway there, I saw the smoke I had been smelling and stopped to look more carefully back into the woods. About 100 yards inside, two shadowy figures were hunkering down around a fire, fiddling with some things. It was the camp of some of the homeless I had seen back out on S.R. 46. I clipped the lease of the tether onto Shep, and we walked in. One man sat in an old wheelchair, bundled up with so many clothes that he looked like the Michelin Man. His face was dirty, and he had a wild beard, and as I approached, I looked into his eyes; he seemed as if he were looking back at me through the surface of water, as if he were drowning. Over a year ago, I had walked back here to this same spot and found a mongrel dog, almost dead. He was sleeping, and when I approached he woke up and looked at me with those same eyes, compounded by the complete inability to save himself, to get up and to run; that's how this guy looked. His companion was older, maybe my age, but thin, tall, wiry, and he was busy cutting the top off a can of Progresso soup with a cheap metal can opener. I said hi, and he said hi, and the other guy said nothing. I told the thin guy there were about a dozen or so oranges on the trees left at the edge of the old grove, out by Reinhart. "Sweet oranges," I said, as if to make it sound better. "You guys ought to take them; they'll just drop off and rot." "Thanks, mister," the old guy said, and I realized he was actually a decade younger than me. And then: "That's a real nice dog . . . colored really well." "Yeah," I said, "a miniature collie, his whole litter colored just like that." "Yes, sir, a really pretty dog." I stood there for half a minute and stated the obvious. "It's going to get cold tonight," and the thin guy said, "yep, it sure is," and I told them to keep the fire burning and turned to leave. The thin guy wished me a Merry Christmas, and the other guy finally moved, just enough to toss a small branch on the fire.

I walked Shep back toward home, following the trail next to the canal until I reached the wild black cherry tree, leafless now, the only green on its scrawny limbs the clump of mistletoe at the very top. There we ducked into the woods, weaving through the thick muscadine and catbrier, the latter of which clawed like its namesake with its thorns, looking for a firm hold on my clothes. The image of the panhandlers had gripped me more surely than the catbrier, though, and I promised myself I would come back on Christmas and bring them provisions. There was no remedy I could offer, no real panacea. They were also brought here by sprawl, hopping off the interstate onto an exit so congested with traffic that cars backed up at lights every 50 yards or so. But they were also here because sprawl had happened so quickly that there were still large predevelopment swaths of land on which to camp—the pasture behind the drugstore with its small herd of goats, the larger pasture just to the south with its smattering of cows, and the grove-turned-woods behind my own home.

Although planners had once promised that all would be "built out" on S.R. 46 between the interstate and the original city of Sanford within five years of the mall's grand opening, the economy has been sluggish. And how many malls, really, could one metro area truly support? Most of the business comes from the novelty of the new retail megaplex, but shoppers with short attention spans soon lose interest. Retailers are then stuck with enormous square-foot rental costs—all based on the projection that the initial burst of shopping would last forever. In the long haul, the only ones who usually benefit are the construction companies and the developers themselves—in this case, the mall-building specialists of Mel Simon and Associates. The company's founder lives not in Florida but in the safety of his upscale neighborhood somewhere in Indiana. By the 1980s, his company was opening three enclosed malls every year. According to the Indianapolis Star, "the Simons are also known for their lavish parties, which benefit charitable and political causes," usually Democrats. This mall has certainly created local jobs, but they are mostly the minimum-wage sort that characterizes the great bulk of the service workforce down at Disney and elsewhere in the region.

Despite the very obvious downside of poorly planned growth, I increasingly worry about the media not getting it. The daily newspaper, the Orlando Sentinel, seems to be wallowing in some outdated paradigm that doesn't allow for integrated thinking and decision making, as stuck as the now-extinct animals in the La Brea Tar Pits ever were. Departments—news, features, sports, and so on—are tightly compartmentalized and even territorial, without much communication between the editors of each. Stories are reported for news value, followed up a couple times, and then dropped when the timeliness wanes. There is scant interpretation of what is covered from a perspective of more than a few days at a time. Worst of all, there is no way for the paper to report on how it has played a major role in impacting the environment by endorsing political candidates who champion growth at all costs.

The logic is breathtakingly artificial and doesn't much allow for the reflection and analyzing that comes with considering the rhythms of life and of nature. Impending real estate developments aren't truly evaluated for long-term sustainability of people and place but are merely reported as news events in the business section. Despite the occasional special reports that heroically tackle our impending water shortage, or that earnestly cover the never-ending attempts to develop the Wekiva basin, the paper's mission is muddled. It seems to be heavily conflicted between the ethical obligation to the public's right to know and the growing need for corporate shareholders to realize a quarterly profit. The creation of occasional civic-minded projects seems less driven by a journalistic passion than by a need to win awards to use as a marketing tool in the media marketplace. The appearance of being politically correct has become more important than the actual practice, a dysfunction that mimics the doublespeak of private corporations everywhere. There is no particular conspiracy behind all this; it is simply what happens when large corporations attempt to package the news. Independently owned Florida papers, like the St. Petersburg Times and the Daytona Beach News Journal—while also bound by profit-making standards—do not seem nearly as obsessed by them.

The historic mission of the daily newspaper, as A. J. Leibling once described it—to afflict the comfortable and comfort the afflicted—is no longer a consideration when top editors, publishers, and advertising minions are among the comfortable. The newspaper's conflicts keep its own readers from fully realizing how each bit of news impacts the land, the water, the air, the wildlife habitat, and the ultimate quality of life. When the paper stretches for a civic-minded compassion, the effect is disingenuous. A touted literacy mission that would have all children "Reading by Nine" is contradicted by a territorial editorial tone that censors rather than celebrates diversity. Clearly, no one but the paper itself has the self-appointed authority to arbitrate taste. Nonstaff contributors who might be able to provide an original voice are discouraged by draconian contracts demanding all rights to their work. Otherwise thoughtful staff writers who might be able to help interpret the puzzling sociology of the community are kept on a short leash. There seems to be a near-total disconnect between how the newspaper reports on the community and what the community is truly about.

Today is Christmas. I stayed over at Lisa's last night, and we had Christmas early this morning and then went to her folks' place for a great extended celebration dinner with her brothers and sisters and their families. It is sunny and cloudless, a nearly perfect Florida winter day, temperatures edging up to the high sixties by noon. I get back to my place by late afternoon. On the street, only the Metts family has put up decorations. They do so each season, for Halloween and Thanksgiving and Easter. Even though their kids are nearly grown now, I figure it's a way to sustain a tradition. It is memory, made real by the simple act of doing. There are large plastic red-and-white striped candy canes lining the pavement leading to their front door, a wreath and oversized stockings on and around the door itself. There are no other signs of Christmas on Sewell, except that the Jim Walters home with its seven or eight renters has trash cans that now overflow with Bud Lite cans.

I pick tangerines from one of my trees, and begin packing several bags for the people living in the woods. I put in pieces of two fried chickens, a large loaf of French bread, a couple dozen tangerines, several red paper plates of Christmas cookies Lisa had baked—snowmen and Santas and holiday trees. I thought about this for a minute, then added a pint of vodka. It gets cold in the woods, and political correctness aside, if I were homeless and could only afford to numb myself with 12-packs of cheap beer, and the liquor store were too far away, and the East Indian man there would not serve me anyway because I was soiled, vodka would be a welcome treat. I pulled out a couple of old coats and three sweaters from the closet, and by the time I had finished, I had quite a pile of stuff. It was too unwieldy to carry, so instead of hiking over with it, I decided to drive.

The open, weedy space next to the canal was wide enough for my jeep, and so I turned onto it from Reinhart, carefully navigating several deep ruts at the entrance that was full of water. I saw their camp from the jeep path by the fire smoke, parked, and got out with the one large bag of food. It was twilight now, and starting to get cold. They were sitting around the open fire on cheap plastic patio chairs. There were two men and a woman, and as I approached, one of the men—the tall, thin guy who had commented on Shep the other day—got up to leave. I called to him, but he didn't recognize me and kept moving away with great purpose, as if fleeing. I realized that driving in likely made me seem far more threatening than when I had walked in with Shep the other day. My SUV back at the edge of the woods looked shiny and official, and I could have been anyone, from the owner of the property come to evict them to some mean-spirited redneck come to harass them. I had talked to the people who staffed a homeless medical team, and they told me the police of the City of Sanford would routinely drive out here to scare and intimidate these sorry, lonely souls. I wondered if, when off duty, they later go to church with delusions of Christianity in their hearts?

The remaining man staggered to his feet as I got closer. He was muttering something, and I finally realized he was warning me to stay away. Beaten and broken, he wanted to stand his little piece of ground, here on Christmas afternoon. Then he began to grope inside his coat, as if trying to find some sort of weapon, maybe a knife. But he was so drunk he couldn't figure out where it was. I had frightened them, clearly. The woman remained seated, and I recognized her as the blonde I had seen at the intersection before. She was wearing a heavy plaid jacket, a cast-off. I tried to put them at ease by wishing them a cheery sort of Merry Christmas. The man stopped groping, paused, and looked at me stunned. "I've brought you some food," I said, and put down the bag. "There's some chicken here and some bread and some cookies."

The man tried to focus with little success, and the physical effect was that his eyes widened. "God bless you, brother," he said earnestly. The songwriter Shawn Mullins once wrote about meeting a benevolent wino on the Pacific cliffs of Oregon, a man who looked far older than his years, sort of a look-alike for the dead hippie poet Richard Brautigan. He was a nice old guy for a younger man, Mullins wrote. And that was how I thought of this person, bearded, wizened, weary, clothes so dirty they were gray, a spirit crushed down hard. And at the same time, he was also gentle and docile and scared, like the old dog. I finally pulled out the bottle of vodka from the bottom of the bag, and when he saw it, his face lit up like he was a little kid again, just for this one brief moment, and he smiled, and the years melted away for a few seconds there. It was a real Christmas for him, and he had the joy of a real surprise that would not scare him. The woman finally stood up and asked me if I was from the "church in Sanford," and I told her, no, I was from another church. I was really from no church at all, of course, but didn't want to confuse them with that information, since they seemed comfortable with the idea that people connected to a church might actually help them in some way. "They came out here the other night," said the woman, of some local church people. She was a female version of the man, still young enough to be a natural blonde, but weathered hard and smooth like the old pieces of cypress I see lying at the edges of the Blackwater Creek. I thought of William Kennedy's tenacious hobos in Ironweed. I asked what the people from the church did. "They sang us Christmas carols. And they gave us some cans of food."

I had seen these people by the roadside before, of course, and I had safely objectified them all by their condition. They were homeless, and that was that. Perhaps what was most jarring was that they existed here in the midst of all this apparent prosperity, a stark reminder of our society's failures, juxtaposed next to the hypermaterial wealth of a giant shopping mall. While this had disturbed me, the full impact of their existence had never sunk in. Now here, in their camp in the woods behind my house, I could no longer objectify them, and I saw them finally as humans—sad, tortured, bedraggled human souls, down so low on their luck they will never get back up again. The woman touched the sweaters I had brought, running her fingers over the soft wool like a little girl who had just received her first nice party dress. And then she put her arms around my neck and hugged me hard. She said, "Pray for me." And then, "Pray for us all." I hugged her back. She had a mild scent of wood smoke and perspiration. I held her, still, and she said: "It's so hard. You just don't know. So hard." She could have been a cousin, an aunt, a relative long lost and never ever found again. A real person with an ineffably damaged heart, made numb by the incidental mercilessness of the world, collateral damage in our obsessive western quest for material satisfaction. Finally, I released her and backed slowly away. I wished them Merry Christmas again, and then told them to take care of themselves, although the moment I said it, it sounded trite. And then I begin to choke up and turned quickly so they wouldn't see me do so, and walked hurriedly back to my vehicle. By the time I reached it, my eyes were moist and I had a lump in my throat.

As I drove home, I thought that if sprawl had lured the homeless here with its promise, it would soon obliterate the temporary place where they lived, forcing them to move on. It would, of course, do no less to me, because all of the landscape in central Florida was temporary, no permanent sanctuary to be had. We would all have to move, sooner or later. There was some money that distanced me and the homeless, but really, not that much. The Hungarian writer Frigyes Karinthy wrote a short story in 1929 introducing the concept of "six degrees of separation," a theory in which everyone on earth is separated by only six acquaintances from one another. John Guare later used that idea for a play that was named for the phenomenon. There were surely degrees of separation between myself and these homeless people even before our meeting, and they were far fewer than six. We all were at the mercy of the steamrolling momentum of all the Dunwoody Commons sprouting around us, and ultimately, we were equally powerless to stop it. I went into my old Cracker house, turned on the little electric heater next to the couch, and poured a tumbler a third full of dark Haitian rum. In the corner was a small southern red-cedar that I had cut from the woods and decorated with Christmas ornaments from my own childhood. When it has been closed up for hours, my home still has that old-house smell, a sensory reminder of all the lives that had once charged it by their long-gone dreams and exhalations. The rum was of good quality, one I save for special occasions. I intended to sip at it and to reflect on the day and on the conditions that bound us all—what had been here seventy-five years ago, and what was here now, and maybe to try to make some sense of it. Instead, I drank the glass in several long gulps, until finally I was numb enough that the tears stopped rolling down my cheeks.

Chapter Nine

We are going through a dark evergreen tunnel. At each side, solid as a wall,
the thick black-green mass of impenetrable mass of foliage rises.
One begins to realize a task of engineering. Dynamite will do no good here.

Into Tropical Florida (1887)

There is a break between hunts in the Seminole State Forest, and so I plan to hike into it today. Like the rest of the historic Wekiva basin, the forest is a fertile warren of habitats—as many as thirteen diverse types from upland sandhills and scrub to blackwater stream. Wildlife here has responded in kind. Unlike publicly owned land designated as a "park," the forest is open to hunts from tree stands—small, temporary platforms attached to the trunks of high trees. Since it supports one of the thickest populations of Virginia white-tailed deer in the state, the competition to get a hunt permit every year is fierce. The deer, said to be bigger and fatter than in most other regions in Florida, stroll around, nibbling acorns and the tender ends of saw palmetto fronds—except on certain days, they get shot. I have no complaint with this because it is a sustainable hunt, helps thin the wild herd, and keeps the animals from overgrazing the natural food available for them. And for the hunters, it allows them their own wilderness experience, which must be every bit as profound as my hikes and paddles are for me.

But there is a deep and terminal irony in it for the animal. Lisa is hiking with me today, and as we drive out to the forest, she considers the quirk of it all: "That's so strange when you think about it," she says. "You're just minding your own business, living your life, and then one day, people start firing guns at you." Yeah, I say, sort of like a drive-by shooting in south Florida, except there the season doesn't have an official beginning and end.

Wild hogs are fair game here, too—a 261-pounder was pulled out of the forest last year, fanglike teeth so long it could barely close its mouth. I sometimes see the ruts the hogs leave in the floor of the woods when they snout around, looking for tender roots and tubers. The Spanish originally brought in these swine and long ago allowed them to go feral, and now they are lean and sinewy and humpbacked, mean enough to bite off a human appendage if they could get hold of it.

On a recent hike by myself, I saw a half-grown boar, brown-pelted and wary, and he stood motionless under the low frond of a sabal palm and eyed me with great caution, perhaps thinking that if he didn't move, I wouldn't see him. He was about 100 feet away, young and timid and offering no threat. I sat down cross-legged on the ground for a half hour, waiting to see what he would do next. He stood there, looking back, and did nothing, not moving a muscle. Finally, in appreciation of his determination, I slowly got up and walked away.

The state forest is meant to be part of a larger corridor of public land between the Wekiva watershed and the Ocala National Forest, a portal to allow bears and other animals to roam back and forth between those two vital rangelands instead of isolating them inside each. Acquisition of that corridor is not yet complete, as land prices are skyrocketing beyond what public agencies can afford. For now, some wildlife does migrate using the riverine corridor of the Blackwater Creek and naturally wooded private land. But it is a narrow, circuitous pathway, and ease of movement is dangerously limited.

We reach the entrance to the forest by midmorning after driving through a light drizzle, drop our money in an envelope at the self-pay kiosk, and stop in front of the cattle gate across the road. Lisa opens the gate's combo lock using the numbers on our permit, and we drive in atop the hard clay and stone road, past the pine flatwoods and ephemeral ponds and toward the place where the terrain begins to gradually drop, about 2 miles in. From here, hardwoods press up against the road, and clumps of wildflowers like the spiky aster known as deer-tongue thrive in the understory. At Blackwater Creek, we stop on the old concrete bridge that crosses it to look at what seems to be a mud shoal in the water just downstream. The shoal turns out to be a yard-wide pod of insects, all clamoring to stay together—the ones at the edge likely wishing they were inside, away from the bass and bream rising for protein from below. On the upstream side of the bridge, a 7-foot gator as black as a truck tire lies on the flat mud bank of the shore. His armored scutes and tail and head seem sculpted from the dark soil, and his perfect stillness accentuates the effect. A limpkin, the wading bird with a curved beak perfectly formed to pluck snails out of their shells, teeters on stilt legs on the other side of the bank, searching for the animals that fuel her life.

Once off the bridge, we round a sharp bend and pull up next to the river. As we pull our backpacks out of the jeep, Lisa hears animal noises from just inside the thick woods, and we cautiously walk over to the edge. There, barely hidden by the saw palmettos and bamboo, four large tom turkeys are strutting nervously in tight turkey circles, crying in muted gobblelike squawks. We have disturbed them and the precise geometry of their bird day. We set off down the road, hiking deeper into the forest with the intent of visiting Moccasin Springs and another more hidden spring that only recently has been mapped. Shep is with us, and, after some rudimentary training on a leash last month, he is now trotting obediently to Lisa's left side. It perplexes me that I have been with this dog for as long as I have, and outside of sitting and giving me his left paw when he feels like it, he will not perform any utilitarian behavior, such as walking in tandem with me in the woods. In fact, when we are by ourselves, he will trot far ahead, so far that I often lose sight of him. He is a smart dog, and maybe he too appreciates the sensibility and aesthetic of a handsome woman and is willing to give up the excitement of ranging far ahead in exchange for the solace of trotting nearby. Lisa seems as companionable as any woman I've ever met. But I also wonder if she might be accomplishing the same thing with me, just me not fully understanding the concept as it is being performed.

The sweetgum and cypress on each side of the one-lane dirt road rise up into a protective canopy so that we seem to be walking through a large foliage tunnel. Years ago, the former owners of this land ranged cattle here and cultivated the fast-growing slash pine for timber. To allow them access to their animals and trees, they created this trail from fill, and its elevation allows us a high and dry avenue through otherwise low mesic and hydric hammocks. Everything at the edge of our green tunnel seems to be simmering with the primal biology of a subtropic forest. Crimson lichens splatter the thin trunks of the water oak, as if they have bled from them. Both the bay magnolia trees and the Carolina aster bushes bloom with great vigor, white and lavender blossoms pushing out respectively from the monotone of dark green. And there, rising from the soggy earth like a fungus, are the stiff leaves of the swamp lily, each petal on its snow-white blossoms tapering down into a fancy baroque tip, not unlike the way the bottom wings of a tiger swallowtail butterfly are configured.

I marvel, as always, at the patterns of nature and how economic it all is. In the architectural community, there is a small but growing movement to use nature as a guideline for energy-efficient design. If we used biomimicry as a guide, we might learn to harness energy like a leaf, grow food like a prairie, build ceramics like an abalone, self-medicate like a chimp, compute like a cell. But there is a conflicting paradigm that may not allow that wisdom to take hold. In our westernized society, natural systems are regarded as separate from human-made ones. The cleverness of those natural systems—of this great cathedral of wonder around me today—is that it evolves, adapts, and sustains. In contrast, our ego-driven strategies seem intent on exploiting natural resources rather than learning from them.

We hike to Moccasin within forty-five minutes and, once there, revel in the color of its water as we always do. It is a wondrous contrast to the dark Blackwater, as it arises from the ground from under a submerged limestone ledge and spreads itself out into a bluish pool in the otherwise gloomy swamp. Depending on the time of day, sometimes it is clear, sometimes cloudy. But it always seems unworldly, as if unpolished sapphire has turned to liquid. We stand at its edge and watch the small fish just under the surface—gambusia and killifish and sailfin mollies—and then, in deeper water, we spot three cigar-shaped gar hanging in the transparency of the spring like Alexander Calder mobiles. We sit nearby at the edge of the creek, eat granola bars, and drink water we have brought. It is overcast and gray, and there is no real gray like the gray of a Florida swamp, which makes you feel as if you are on the threshold of time, in an early epoch of adaptation and invention. We sit quietly, without talking. Long ago, a cypress tree fell across where the spring run enters the Blackwater, and somehow a branch from it has turned into a fine straight young tree itself, maybe 8 inches in diameter and over 20 feet high. It is a graphic lesson in the tenacity of organisms to survive. I take a photograph of it. It is my favorite tree, I tell Lisa, and she understands why.

After a few more minutes, we shoulder our backpacks and head up the sloping terrain that cradles the creek, back up a steep incline to the sandhills. At the top, the forest opens up into a wild, grassy hillock, and it is studded with prickly pear cactus, all of them in yellow bloom now. Around the cactus are no fewer than ten gopher tortoise burrows, each of them marked by a clay-colored mound of dirt at its entrance. We poke around a bit, looking for wildflowers. The purple fuzz of the mistflower is perhaps the most striking for its blooms appear as tiny cheerleader pompoms. Then we head into another foliage tunnel that takes us back into the dark swamp. On both sides, shallow gullies of blackwater are covered almost completely by bright green dots of duckweed clustered so closely together that it seems like a carpet.

One ditch, a small pond really, seems deeper and larger than the rest, and I see that it is rimmed with saw grass, the same subtropic sedge that characterizes the Everglades far to the south of here.

We walk another hour or so through the woods, passing a marked trail that leads down to Sharks Tooth springs. Sharks Tooth surges out of the bottom of the high bluff we are walking atop, dissolving its Miocene limestone composition as it does. Tiny sharks' teeth and other fossils from that ancient epoch tumble out of the karst from inside the bluff, giving the little spring its name. Although not examined for flow or other chemical characteristics, Sharks Tooth is known enough to at least be mapped, and to be on a trail. We hike beyond it today, heading deeper into the forest to find a spring that is off the map. The path we walk turns to white sand and the trees into ancient live oaks bristling with bromeliads and hung with moss. We are walking atop the remnant of a prehistoric sea dune, and our shoes sink into the sand as if we were on a beach. Finally I see the old dead snag that I use as my marker for the spring just to the south of this trail. "It's down here somewhere," I tell Lisa, and we leave the soft white sand and scuttle down under the thick branches, ducking the thick bronze webs of the giant golden orb spiders, down, down the sharp falling terrain toward the swamp itself.

Steve, my hiking buddy, first led me here last year after the careful study of a topographical map. The map was full of isobars, the lines that indicate a rise in the terrain, and they were tightly cupped around a huge rise mapped as Sulphur Island. Although not a true water-bound island today, it geologically had functioned as one when the sea levels in Florida began to drop thousands of years ago. Today, long after the oceans have returned to the polar ice caps, Sulphur Island remains, covering a limestone bluff of compressed sand, coral, and bones. The first time I came here, I had to hang onto the limbs of small water oaks and bay magnolias, grabbing the occasional frond of a sabal palm to keep from falling on my butt. There was no path here, not even one made by animals, and my only trail marker was the sense that the mound would, sooner or later, flatten out at the swamp below.

Our visit today is more of the same—an ungraceful slow-motion free fall down the heavily forested sides of a seepage slope. Halfway down, the thicket of saw palmettos disappears because the gradient is too steep for them, and the flat swamp below is revealed. There are boulders of limestone at the bottom, geological formations more associated with northern Florida, where the aquifer comes closer to the surface. Lisa spots the largest boulder, which seems for all the world to be in the shape of a bear cub, and she lets out a muffled Wow! A perfectly round solution hole in the limestone of the bear serves as an eye, while irregular contours in the rock create the illusion of ears. The ether of the clear water flows up and around the base of the bear cub, leaking out of three or four separate seeps at the base of the bluff. "It looks like a little bear drinking from the water," she says, clearly astonished by it all. The outflow is only a few inches deep, but it is steady enough to polish the fine grains of silica and shell and lime rock in the spring run so they glowed luminously when shafts of sunlight hit them.

I have visited this boulder and its springs during different seasons—by winter, with no foliage shade canopy, it is stark and bright, the rock itself clean and gray. By summer, with the thick crown of sweetgum and tupelo and oak above, and ferns, lichens and mosses below, the scene changes. The bear cub grows a rich coat of jade-colored mosses. The springs, insulated by the surrounding jungle, seem to actually resonate, refolding themselves into a gentle gurgle, as if the lime-rock bear itself has taken life and really is sipping from them.

I wonder at the sheer timelessness of such places, of how swamps and seepage slopes that sometimes feed them are among the least changed of our Florida terrain. As they are usually too moist to burn, these relic landscapes have largely escaped the affliction that has reconfigured Florida, from the panhandle to the Keys. What I see today is similar to what other humans must have seen from the very moment this outlandish, wonderful peninsular geography took its present form. Wetlands like this that still remain intact become our time machines, places that that can transport us back to the geological beginnings, and if they afforded no other benefit, that alone would be worth the price of admission. But they allow a multitude of riches—storing and filtering water, keeping our climate and landscape moist, and housing a vast biological storehouse of animals and plants. It is no wonder that, over the last few centuries, naturalists like the Bartrams, André Michaux, A. W. Chapman, and John Kunkel Small traveled to Florida as scientists journey to the deepest reaches of the Amazon or Africa today—to discover new species and new wonders.

We sit on a large, flat boulder next to the cub and spread out our picnic, sandwiches of dark bread with turkey slices and fresh tomatoes and provolone cheese. It is green all around us, an astonishing, all-encompassing verdancy distilled from the wildness of this place. We sit here quietly for another hour, listening to the muted thumping of a pileated woodpecker deeper in the woods, watching the light change as golden rays of sun weave their way through the thick canopy of leaves above. It is wonderfully antediluvian, the idea of change five thousand years away yet, and the primal exhortations of nature still pure and absolute enough to have appreciable energy. Despite what I intellectually know about what is going on in the world outside these boundaries, it still gives me hope, down in my heart. Nature, as Edward Hoagland once wrote, pre-dates thought, and it is true. I allow myself to feel that the Timucua and Mayaca are still here, in a shadow world, just on the other side of the trees. I try to believe that the bear rock will come alive by night when we are gone, and that the Indians will worship it and allow it to imbue their spirits with supernatural magic. I try to believe that I am living in a world in which mythology still fires our dreams and passions, where time and neon and asphalt have no meaning at all. And just for a moment there, I succeed.

I awoke before dawn today, and then drifted back into an early morning dream sleep. When I finally opened my eyes again, it was nearly 7:30 a.m. These postdawn dreams are more vivid for me than others, and often seem full of longing. In one, I was eight years old again and walking home from school. It was my birthday. When I rounded the last block near my street, I saw a shiny, new blue bike propped up with its kickstand on the lawn. I was beside myself with joy and ran all the way to the bike. When I got there, my folks both came out and wished me a happy birthday. My mom had baked a chocolate cake with vanilla icing, my favorite, and after I took my bike on a test run, we went inside and celebrated. That had happened almost exactly as I dreamed it, so many years ago. My folks were loving, supportive parents, and home was a refuge for me, always something to look forward to, Mom busy with projects in the kitchen and Dad, fresh-faced after showering from work, always willing to play catch or shoot some hoops in the backyard. They allowed me the gift of remaining a little kid for a long, long time, and when I first went out into the world in this way, it was jarring to find others around who were not. There is an entire litany of adult behaviors I found disturbing then, but the most painful was that few seemed to hold fairness in high esteem. Giving someone your word and then following through with action to realize it was not as revered as I had once thought it to be. Before my dad passed away a couple years ago, I asked him how he was going to vote in an upcoming election. He thought about this and then said he didn't really know. "It would be a lot easier to make a decision if they all told the truth," he said.

It did not surprise me when I read yesterday in the New York Times that a recent study with primates showed that even the capuchin monkey—when shortchanged with pebbles instead of being given an anticipated food re-ward—would react strongly to it by slamming the pebbles down in anger. The point of the study was that we have an innate, almost genetic predisposi-tion for fairness. And when it is not forthcoming, it is not unusual to feel cheated in some way. We assume that wetlands are protected now because we are told they are. But the U.S. Army Corps of Engineers regional office in Jacksonville issues an average of two thousand permits a year to dredge or fill tracts of wetlands 3 acres or smaller in Florida. Because the work is pre-sumed to have little impact on the aquatic environment, the work receives scant monitoring from other agencies.

But scrutiny reveals otherwise: A lawsuit filed in June 2004 on behalf on the Wetlands Alert Inc. and Floridians for Environmental Accountability and Reform revealed that the scope of destruction is often far greater than the process allowed. The big-box retailer Wal-Mart had routinely acquired a Corps permit to destroy less than an acre of wetlands for a new store on 29 acres in New Smyrna Beach. Yet, closer study by the regional water manage-ment district later showed the construction destroyed 10 acres of wetlands. Instead of rescinding the permit, the Corps simply required Wal-Mart to ap-ply for another permit that would justify the loss of the entire tract.

The entire process demonstrated the reality that public officials and well-paid lawyers for corporate-sponsored development can't always be trusted to perform ethically—unless forced to do so. Like the monkeys who slammed down their bogus pebble "reward" in anger, this lack of trust must have a deep and underlying effect on the ability of the community to connect in a functional, healthy way. Barely 30 percent of voting-age adults bothered to even turn out for the last election here, and perhaps, in part, this explains why. And it would be easier to pick a candidate if they all told the truth.

When I bought my home in 1990, there were four Cracker homes out on the "hard road," one set farther back into these woods than the others. The offset home was owned by a man who kept wild deer in a high-fenced pen in his backyard. I was never sure why he did this, and while at first it struck me as cruel to fence in wild deer, I later realized that these were likely local deer that had been displaced by development like the gopher. They were at least safe from being roadkill and seemed to be well cared for. But they were still wild, and if you approached the fence, they would move in unison, like a school of tropical fish on the reef, reacting to some deep unconscious flight gene that still called out to them. There was an elegant grace in that movement, and whatever else the deer's owner had in mind, he had allowed a masterwork to be created in the synchronistic dynamic of these wild animals.

The deer keeper was the first to go. The Florida Power and Light company required room to expand its substation as they needed more energy to fuel all the infrastructure that would one day arrive. He and his deer got condemned, via eminent domain, and not long after I moved in, they left. One of the Cracker homes there was later vandalized and burned to the ground by the forlorn delinquent children of some nearby renters. Not so long ago, I was sitting in my jeep waiting for the light at the Reinhart intersection to change and saw that the entire woods on the corner were being cut to the ground. It was a cool day, and I had the driver's side window open, with my elbow resting on the rim. Giant Star Wars–like machines I had never seen before were yanking the trees from the earth and shredding them. The slash pine, some of them 70 and 80 feet high, made the loudest, most discordant sounds when they were snapped into pieces. The noise sounded like large bones being cracked and splintered, over and over again. It so disturbed me that I rolled up my window, turned up the radio, and looked straight ahead, staring down the red traffic light as if nothing else mattered.

We are all living at the edge of a broad alluvial floodplain here. The St. Johns once meandered at will through the moist landscape, scrubbing itself with the soil and roots and leaves. Most of the wetlands on this south side of its lake were replaced long ago by farmlands. Some of these fields were still being tilled and planted when I first moved here. But the farming community of Lake Monroe is a phantom now, its fields covered in the last decade by apartment buildings. "Our final crop is asphalt," one ex-resident lamented once. One apartment complex, which sits atop the former fields adjacent to old Monroe Road, has been built in a southwestern motif. It sports a mission-like bell tower, complete with a faux crumbling-brick-masonry façade and adobe-colored walls. It is trying desperately to look as if it has some connection with the landscape. I wonder what the architects were really thinking? Sure, we'll design a just-pretend piece of the arid American Southwest, and you can put it here on a soggy Florida field that once grew celery, and before that, was a rich blackwater river delta. After all, who would ever know? It was like the sixteenth-century French artist Jacques Le Moyne, who drew Florida alligators as 80 feet long, with external ears. Yep, it's stranger here than you can ever believe. Just look at what I have created.

It's finally clear this morning after several days of heavy rain. I let Shep out and walk with him through the backyard. He sniffs at the new moisture and the scents left by squirrels and rabbits. The soggy ground has not drained very well, and a couple dozen green oranges have fallen from trees and are starting to rot on the soggy ground. Ditches intended to drain during the rainy season are useless when pasture downstream is replaced with tire stores and sub shops and shopping plazas. The old trenches that once had meaning to some farmer are now filled or clogged because the new owners have scant understanding of their value. The maintenance of the ditches on a man's land was a tacit admission of the community of place, as was the acknowledgment that there were wet and dry seasons. I can imagine that it would be good to greet your downstream or upstream partner on a Saturday night when he went into town, and maybe buy him a cold soda or slap him on the back and be really glad to see him because he and his family were helping you sustain your lifestyle, and that meant as much as anything in the world to you.

Out in the front yard, I pull a few weeds in the "circle" near the driveway entrance. The circle is an arrangement of old chunks of concrete, maybe 10 feet in diameter, and was originally intended as a sort of a planter. The mineralization of age has given the concrete a certain veneration, as it has to the coquina pond nearby. Flowers were here once, but what grows now are plants and trees that have taken root on their own. There is a small magnolia, a very large sugar hackberry, a sabal palm, and a sort of domestic sisal, which is a deadly little demon with stiff stilettolike fronds. I've lopped off a small branch of the cereus cactus from the mother plant on the north side of the house and stuck it in the ground here. It's doing well, turning dormant by winter but blossoming in the warm summer months.

The highlight of the circle is a great old masonry birdbath that I regularly scour with bleach to keep white. In the dish of the bath is a little statuette of a naked boy holding a goose. When Mike and Carolyn Durak had first walked me around the yard years ago to help me understand its history, Carolyn asked Mike if he wanted to take the little statuette with them. It did seem to have great meaning to him, and I imagined him here as a little boy, when the property was a 5-acre farm, running around trying to catch a goose or a chicken, no I-4 at all, only one car passing every fifteen minutes or so up on the "hard road" of S.R. 46. It must have been idyllic then, out here in the countryside. Mike looked at the statuette, shook his head, and turned away. "No," he said. "It belongs here."

I check my mail and see Kelly in the yard across the street and call to her. She comes over and introduces me to Mark, a stocky, good-natured guy who seems to live there on and off. I ask him if he will help me fix a lock on my side door, and he says sure, just let me get my tools and a beer. I tell them the kumquats are ripe on the trees to the front, and the little tangerines on the tree to the back, and to help themselves. We talk a while, and Kelly tells me that Rucker, the developer who owns all the land to the north, drove out to Sewell recently and offered her $25,000 for her house. "That's what I paid for it, Bill," she says, heartbroken. She's owned her house almost as long as I've owned mine. I asked her how Rucker came across, since I have never seen him in person. She looked up, absently. "He had a really young wife."

I am just back from five days in Key Largo, which reminded me that sprawl is not limited to the Florida mainland. The lesson of the Keys is just more obvious because they are islands, with the very real boundaries unique to a spit of land surrounded by water. Like anywhere else, the most fascinating places in the Keys are the ones that are the most difficult to get to. We stayed at the Largo Lodge, a delightfully rustic series of cottages, all nestled inside a jungle of foliage—coconut palms and gumbo limbo and bougainvillea.

The day we arrived was Lisa's birthday, and I had arranged to have Steve Harris, a good friend, take us out on his sloop for a sunset sail. Steve's a Peter Pan of a guy, in his mid-thirties, with a master's in creative writing and a captain's license. He's working on a novel and tending bar at the Marriott. He takes pleasure in the little things, revealed in the moment. During an earlier visit a couple months ago, we paddled with him in a canoe out into the Blackwater Sound in the Gulf, winding our way through dense foliage tunnels cut into the red mangroves there. We started at twilight, and it was full night in no time. The tunnels were dark, and fireflies were everywhere, as if someone had hung a string of Twinkle Lites in the mangroves. By the time we turned to paddle back, bioluminescence—the same energy used by the fireflies—was glowing in the water, and each slice of our paddle strokes ignited it.

This time we brought our own kayaks and launched from the shore at the Lodge, headed across the sound named Tarpon Basin, aiming for a place where the mangroves were pinched into a narrow peninsula, just on the other side of the Intercoastal Waterway (ICW). The ICW, which skirts the Keys on the Gulf side, also marks the boundary of the Everglades National Park. It helps explain why the fireflies had been so abundant—unlike the islands connected by bridges, causeways, and roads, the Glades are not sprayed for mosquitoes. That means fish and other animals below them in the food chain don't get doused with poison; fireflies prosper for the same reason. We like our natural places tidy here in Florida, more like a pretty picture postcard than the real thing. Or as one of the characters observed in John Sayles's film Sunshine State: "Florida . . . It's nature on a leash."

When we poison mosquitoes, we poison lots of other stuff in the bargain. This doesn't much matter, of course, if you stick close to the Overseas Highway and visit only the neon-lit bars and sip your way into an umbrella-drink numbness. But if you take the road less traveled—or paddled—you can experience the real places that are still left, just as you can back in central Florida. And so we paddled back into a very real place, taking care when we crossed the Intercoastal Waterway to avoid the go-fast cigarette boats. We hid in a little cut as they roared by like giant airplanes, zooming down from Miami and Ft. Lauderdale, gold baubles swinging from the necks of their owners— moussed-out little men trying to make a big, loud impression. Once across the channel, we moved farther west into the edge of Tarpon Basin, skirting along next to the bowed roots of the thick red mangroves.

We stopped at one point to rest and drink Gatorade, and when we did, Lisa spotted what she thought was the fin of a dolphin barely 100 yards away. We slowly paddled toward it, and soon we saw it was several manatees— including a calf barely a yard long—and they were having a real time of it, frolicking back here in the shallows of the sound, atop the sea-grass beds, far away from the roaring boats. The fins—which were, in fact, flippers and tails—disappeared as we neared, and then, suddenly, I looked at the clear water under me and saw two manatees, one crossing atop the other, and the top one just inches from my kayak. Afraid it might surface under me, I put my paddle in the water to move slowly away. But the paddle startled the giant, and it flipped its tail to gain the momentum it needed to dive, smashing it against the hull of my boat and splashing me with a couple of gallons of water. My little kayak rocked precariously for a few seconds, and I back paddled as quickly as I could to get out of their way. Lisa and I had a good laugh about it after it was over, but I had to admit it scared me, and it took a while for the adrenaline surge to even out. The manatees went back to playing, still about 100 yards away, rippling the water with their snouts and tails. I looked closely and saw that the calf was the only one without prop scars.

We paddled some more, out through a cut, into Little Buttonwood Sound, a swatch of 5 square miles of water, all surrounded with a low mangrove forest, a vision of five centuries ago, and as far removed from the modern Keys as we could get. It was so quiet here that all I could feel was the beat of my heart. It was heaven. We floated for a while atop the clear water and the healthy sea grasses. We were farther from shore now, and the water, which was once green from the nutrients of the near-shore septic leakage, had cleared, diluted with the tides and the distance we had covered. And then the roar of the cigarette boats started off in the distance again, a low, chest-pounding vibration that shook the silence right out of the place. Manatees are said to cringe when they hear the sound of a boat motor, associating it with the props that have cut slices into their backs. I cringed, too, reacting to the raw insufferable explosion of sound in such a place. We started to paddle away, and I looked one more time for the manatees, but by now they had vanished.

I received a group email today from a "Jane" with the "Deltonans for Accountability" asking me to help save the vanishing Florida. The tone was urgent, desperate, full of passion and grief. It read: "Friends, I am forwarding this to you because it comes down to doing something that will make a difference for us and future generations in Florida. Fight the sprawl and big developments that are eradicating our beloved living and historic landscapes and our environmental health!!!! We really are down to pave it or save it. Most of the last of our real Florida is being disappeared. Florida is dying. Greed is killing her. What if we could be her hero? What if we could stop it?"

The email advised us to sign a petition that would put a new constitutional amendment to referendum. The revision—the Florida Hometown Amendment—actually would let locals vote on changes to their county's comprehensive plan instead of letting elected officials do it.

The next day, I receive an email to the group in response from an "Alan Foy." It reads: "Go to Hell. Go to hell. You are simply trying to put me and thousands of workers like me who have been keeping this economy going for the last three years while everything else went down the tubes out of work."

Today I see a spring I have never seen before. It is submerged on a backwater branch of the Wekiva. I sit there next to it in lawn chairs with Teri Sopp, a lawyer from Jacksonville, and her aunt Ruth. Teri grew up on the St. Johns and as a little girl played in Salt Springs up in the Ocala National Forest. She was thrilled with springs from the very first. Like me, she has never lost that primal childlike fascination with Florida's natural magic. It is a bond that connects us not only with nature but with each other. Sometimes Teri will call me out of the blue and tell me about things she has seen while kayaking outside of Jacksonville, the roseate spoonbills glowing like pink dots on the marsh, the pods of bottlenose dolphin chasing schools of baitfish. We watch this spring churn several feet under the surface, billowing up in great smoke plumes of fine clay sediment, turning in on itself and then disappearing into finely ground powder somewhere below.

Teri is worldly and educated, and in her professional life she routinely defends capital cases, like murder. But today, she is a kid again. Every so often she gives out a yelp of excitement, thrilled just with the way the spring is roiling. Ruth is a retired navy nurse who lives in Melbourne. She is sturdy and sharp-witted, skin finely etched from years of living unprotected in the sun of the subtropics. Ruth has driven a small RV—a sort of miniature Winnebago—here to camp in it on the lot she owns next to the spring on the river. Although more stoic, she is every bit as entranced as Teri and I with this miracle of water and light.

We stretch our legs out, facing the spring and its perpetual mystic churn. We drink cold Budweiser and shuck warm boiled peanuts Teri has brought with her. Ruth reminds us that we are actually sitting on a narrow island now, one mostly created from the fill of the river, back when anyone with a dredge or backhoe could just about do what they wanted without worrying about rules or laws against it. On other trips kayaking the Wekiva, I have noticed several engineer-straight, time-weathered canals dug from the main stem of the river back to higher ground, and they likely came from this same era—a half century and more ago when cheap earth-moving technology first became widely available.

When a former owner of this property was scouring out this branch of the river and adding fill to the island in 1969, he scraped the top of the hardpan and limestone below, Ruth says. In doing so, he breached the limestone in at least four different places in the river bottom. Each breach responded by spraying up water that had been held in the limestone under pressure. Of the newly created "springs," only this one survived, and over time, it became larger. When created, it was said to be only a foot or so in width; now it is 30 feet across at the surface. "It's been growing," says Ruth. "It gets bigger every time I see it. The edges seem to slough off and fall into the bottom." As a result, the bottom is also growing, deeper and wider. Ruth calls the spring "Turtle" because she always sees peninsula cooters hanging there in it as if suspended in air. Rick Roberts, the kayak outfitter who lives nearby, calls it "Powder" for the fine white silt that is suspended in it by the dynamic of its upwelling. A state geographer who has just completed mapping the springs of the Wekiva has officially charted it as "Nova"—not for the stars but for the name of the road that leads to it.

When the rays of the sun hit the water surface over the spring, it seems electrified, an island of turquoise incandescence in the midst of an otherwise shallow and tannic river branch as brown as tea. It looks not unlike a celestial nova, and I wonder if the road may have been named for the spring. Scuba divers were in here last week, Ruth said, and were able to descend to 30 feet, where they found an opening not much bigger than a breadbox. Above it, a great funnel-shaped bowl has eaten its way into the clay and rock substrate of the riverbed terrain. We wonder how much longer it will be before it works its way out of the branch itself and begins to consume the fill that is under our chairs. We decide it will be sometime away in the future, and for now, all that is of concern is how cold the beer is, and how savory the soft, succulent boiled peanuts. And how the spring itself draws us into it, pulling shards of our unconscious back to its very beginning. It is as if it is helping us remember something we thought we had long ago forgotten. "Something about the water," says Ruth, smiling now, her time-etched face radiant in the late afternoon light. "I just have to be near it. I don't know where I got it from."

Chapter Ten

The art of losing isn't hard to master;
so many things seem filled with the intent
to be lost that their loss is no disaster.

Elizabeth Bishop, "One Art"

Yesterday I saw a man fly through the air. Today, during a bad storm, a live tree toppled over, blocking Sewell Road. The gopher tortoise that once dug a burrow at the edge of my backyard has returned after an absence of more than a year. Termites have continued to make their own tiny burrows into the wood of my house, causing the floor to sag just as my yard now sags with the collapsed veins of the karst below. And someone has sprayed the tree trunks in the woods to the south of me with an aerosol can, leaving each with a stripe of bright fuchsia-colored paint on its bark. At first I thought the spraying was an act of vandalism. Then I realized it was a way to inventory trees in preparation for development of the land.

The flying man, of course, was the most inescapable vision. I was driving the dangerous and congested I-4 back from Longwood yesterday when, less than a quarter mile ahead, I saw a van abruptly careen across three lanes. It then tumbled off the road and down a slight embankment to the parking lot of a rest stop. As it rolled, great gusts of white smoke billowed from its undercarriage, and a middle-aged man wearing dark pants and a t-shirt flew out of a passenger door, cartwheeled high into the air, and then came down hard on the concrete. Blood and bone splattered about him when he landed for human bodies are very fragile creations. He shuddered like a deer might shudder when it is fatally shot, and then did not move. He was dead, and there was nothing anyone could do about it. I had to slow because motorists were pulling off the road around me, some good Samaritans to try to render aid, bringing blankets and pillows from their trunks, and some simply to gawk. I looked because I couldn't help myself and felt a combination of profound nausea and shame when I did. Reminded once more of the transient and ephemeral nature of all things here, I kept driving.

Today a bad summer storm moved across the landscape with lightning and thunder and rain blowing in horizontal sheets. Shep, who is terribly afraid of the riflelike bursts of thunder, cowered as he always does, pushing his little body against my legs as I sat in a chair, watching the storm through the imperfect old glass of the living room windows. The storm cocooned the house in a sort of white mist, drowning out all noise but that of the wind and the hard rain against the metal roof. I petted Shep's head to comfort him. Yet I was strangely comforted myself by the storm because it momentarily gave me the illusion of safety from everything that rages outside my ever-diminishing world.

When the storm was over, I tried to drive out to the grocery store and found that a large wild black cherry tree had fallen across Sewell Road, just south of S.R. 46. The downed tree was over 30 feet long from top to bottom, and it was still green with leaves and thick with sap. It was too thick to drive over or to budge by myself. I carefully backed up, turned around, and went back to get an ax from my garage. I sharpened the blade with a grinder and drove back up to the tree, chopping it in two with a series of strong overhead strokes from the ax. When I went to carry one half of the tree off the road, I found it was still too heavy for me to move. Then Kelly and her new husband, Steve, drove up behind me. Steve got out—he's a big brute of a guy with a friendly smile—and with little fanfare walked over to one-half of the tree, lifted it, and walked it off the road. He then did so with the other half. I was still sweating and covered with wood chips from the hacking and was glad they had come when they did. Steve and I shook hands, and Kelly said, yeah, if we had waited for the county to get around to it, it would have taken a while. I agreed, but also I felt good in that—in some vague way—we were imitating the acts of cooperative goodwill that others here in this place had once shown for each other. It was a fleeting thing, of course, and made even more so by the new knowledge that the thick swatch of woods from where the chuck-will's-widow sings—perhaps the most enduring natural portion of Sewell Road—may soon vanish.

The poet Richard Hugo once said that writers often gravitate to "the edge" because they gain the perspective needed to do their most incisive work—whether the geographic edge of a continent or the edge of mainstream culture and "normalcy." I am certainly living on the edge, the cusp, the margin of what is accepted. There is scant recognition by most that the remnants of communities at the perimeter of development are even communities at all. When the momentum barrels through, all traces of the authentic are covered with fill dirt, and all of the wisdom that it may have once embodied in its landscape vanishes. When people ask where I live, I now tell them I live near the community that used to be called Lake Monroe. Anyone who has been here for a decade or more understands the general location, but newly arrived Floridians see only the newly extruded structures that sit atop the old delta farmland, and they are perplexed. What does this mean for us, really? Architect-professor Ronald Haase, the champion of Cracker architecture, says those who would leave a footprint behind on the land bear a greater burden now than ever. "Since the time of Pericles, the architect/sculptor was a technician and artist who was relied upon to express in stone and timber the best of humanity's aspirations. Such a responsibility carries with it the need to identify with a long standing tradition and not just the self-centered inclination of the moment."

But it is the moment that consumes me now. The markings on the trees clearly do foretell a future: I have just learned that the 20-acre grove-woods behind me will finally be developed. Phillip Hollis, the engineer who also is part-owner of the property has called and asked for a meeting with the other landowners on Sewell and Elder who are adjacent to property so he can explain the logistics of the development. There is one owner left on Elder, and she has now moved to North Carolina and is renting out her metal-roofed Cracker house. Only Kelly and I remain contiguous to the land here on Sewell. The developer has made it clear that he will also be asking for certain concessions from us in regard to how close his buildings can be to our property. We set up a meeting in three days. He suggests that we convene at the Cracker Barrel, a faux-country restaurant and store back behind the McDonalds near I-4. Before the meeting, Kelly's father dies, and she asks me to negotiate on her behalf. The out-of-state owner has already discussed the project with the developer and, since she is no longer living here, seems to have no concerns with it. The meeting will consist of me and four men who will direct the development of the land.

I arrive first and run into Hollis in the gift shop of the Cracker Barrel, a place that sells little geegaws that, in some distant and mass-produced way, suggest a country lifestyle. I initially met him a few months ago when he was considering another development for this land. We had a civilized conversation then for he is a very likable and good-natured guy. I learned that he enjoyed Boy Scouting as a parent and leader, and boating and the outdoors in general. He had a trace of a southern accent, but I guessed it was more Georgia than north Florida. He is about my age, but clean-shaven, and today is wearing a blue button-down shirt and khaki pants. He told me that when he was studying for his master's degree, he was mentored by a very respected groundwater engineer at the University of Central Florida. We chatted briefly about the Wekiva Swamp and the pressures on the springs there, and I was surprised to find we agreed on the need to protect recharge areas for its springs. Unlike the developer to the north, who has tried to intimidate the remaining property owners, this man seemed candid and warm and compassionate. Despite our respective roles—as developer and as a contrary homeowner about to be impacted by it—I felt he was quite a nice fellow.

As a developer, Hollis is not required to meet with or gain approval of adjacent property owners for his plan. But he is also smart enough to realize that if he doesn't have our support, we could become loose cannons at public hearings when elected officials consider the plan. He has even done some background research on me by visiting a Web site where information about my environmental work has been posted. Before we met, Hollis had stressed that he wanted to be "a good neighbor," even though he would not be living here as a neighbor at all. Oddly enough, Rucker, the real estate speculator leasing the ramshackle homes to raw transient tenants to the north, had also expressed his desire to be a "good neighbor." He did so right before threatening to install a retention pond next to my property, thus boxing me in and forever restricting the appeal of my land. I guess good neighbors come in all sizes, depending on how you spin it. The real issues to be examined at our meeting in the Cracker Barrel are drainage and the "buffer" between his new development and our remaining residential land.

I have already talked with the director of planning at Sanford about these issues. He told me the burden is on developers of City land to "not impact the quality of life of those who were there before them." The planner seemed sincere and well-informed, if a bit guarded. Nonetheless, that philosophy must be a tremendous challenge in real life as any intense development transforms the adjacent landscape in immutable ways. It especially does when it takes place on the relatively flat karst terrain of Florida. As we grow, we drain, dry, and then, in certain special places, we sink. The wisdom of botanist Small, who noted this cause-and-effect phenomenon seventy-five years ago, is still irrefutable. But our collective memory in Florida is perilously short.

Ice tea and sodas are brought to the table, and we move them aside. Hollis stands and unrolls the detailed plans for "Flagship Park." Since he is part-owner of the project now, he has hired another firm to do the actual engineering work. Two of the men are with this company, while the third represents the home builder, D. R. Horton, Inc. The business cards of the engineering company lists the specialties of their firm as "Transportation. Land Development. Environmental Services." In contrast, I imagine my card, if I had one, might read "giant pain in the ass." Nonetheless, they all seem like affable folks, not trying to bully or intimidate, and I try to respond in kind. There is a momentum here at work in this region that goes far beyond this table, and there's little anyone can do to stop it. The dialogue will only be about the minutiae of the project. Not long ago, Jim Toner, a regional columnist for the Orlando Sentinel, wrote of the sprawl along nearby Reinhart Road under a headline that read: "Big Boxes Graze in Pastures off Rinehart Road." Toner led his column with an account of the opening of a new Wal-Mart Supercenter. Unlike in other regions of the country where rural locals have rallied to vehemently oppose impacts the giant-box retailer will have on small business economics, the culture, noise, traffic congestion, and nature, this store opened without a single quarrel. The reason, said Toner, is that most of the local residents now live in new apartments and welcome work at Wal-mart. Or else they are cows, grazing quietly in remnant pastures there. "The cows, though they don't know it, are just biding their time chewing on grass until some truck picks them up and moves them . . . perhaps to make room for another big box," Toner shrewdly observed.

There are eight large schematics and charts spread out on our table, each of which shows different aspects of the project, from landscaping to building elevation. Dutiful as a cow grazing in his final pasture, I look through them as if it will matter. Together, the drawings make up a "preliminary subdivision plan," which must still be approved by Sanford before the details are fleshed out. Soils have been tested for permeability and even for aquifer recharge. A survey targets prospective buyers, and I learn that single female professionals and young couples will make up the mainstay of that market. There is even an "estimated school impact" of 26.32 students, divided by elementary, middle, and high school. All the buildings, parking lots, and roads will cover over half of the terrain with impervious surfaces. The mainstay of the landscaping buffer will be adjacent to our property and will include a thin, 6-foot-high "opaque screen" surrounded by low scrubs and newly planted trees. The structures will be two-story condominiums, built to look like homes in configurations of three. There will be 117 units grouped around a dry storm-water retention pond, which will be landscaped to resemble a shallow, grassy depression in the ground. Since laws do not require it, there is no estimate of how much potable groundwater will be required to quench the thirst of the people and their community lawn.

The grove-woods has been divided into forty-three quadrants, and all the trees over 6 inches in diameter have been inventoried, which explains the spray paint I saw earlier on the trunks. A city ordinance requires trees of this size and larger to be replaced, or "mitigated," if they are cut. In a chart entitled "Tree Table," every tree species is listed—most are laurel oak, sabal palm, and cedar. Some of the oaks, the dominant species, are as large as 20 inches in diameter. There are well over 1,500 trees here. Elevation of most of the existing property above sea level is 30 feet, while the proposed elevation of the new development is 5 feet higher. This implies that all the trees that now exist will have to be clear-cut and removed. At first I think the land must be raised for the same reason it is raised elsewhere here in the delta—because it historically has been part of the floodplain linked to the St. Johns River. But Hollis tells me that years ago Smith Canal was very effective in draining the original pine flatwoods. The jerry-rigged series of neighborhood ditches around it must have helped as well, but no one is quite sure how much.

Yet even without the pines and the upland flow, this landscape is underlain by soils that don't drain well. Like a flatwood, portions of it still flood with heavy rain. It will remain a flatwood right up to the point where it is covered with fill. Then the only people who will remember it will be those who once lived here, or who saw the photos or heard of the stories that were told. I am a little numbed by it all, not unlike the way I have been numbed by the homeless, by the sinking house and yard, by the flying dead man. I ask why, if the land does not theoretically flood, it needs to be elevated and why all the trees need to be removed. I am told this is a simple economic decision on the part of the home-building corporation. The cost savings are explained in detail: A large retention pond must be dug to contain all the rainwater so that it doesn't flow off the property. The triplex units will encircle the pond. If a "wet retention pond" were used, it would have to be larger in area, whereas a "dry" pond could be smaller. A dry pond, by virtue of being grassy and not full of water, would also give the illusion of being a slight depression in the lawn—a "green space" where residents and their kids could play, say, soccer or baseball, if they wanted. While a wet pond could be dug into the existing terrain, a dry pond would have to be excavated atop a raised landscape. Although the clear-cutting of the entire wood and the transportation of 5 feet or so worth of soil onto the entire tract seem costly and a terrible waste of energy, it allows the builder to sell more condo units. In the long run, the builder actually makes more money. In the puppet theater of mitigation, destroyed trees would be replaced with other trees of the same size. Of course, there isn't room to replant all the trees on site, so those destroyed would be planted elsewhere or purchased for credits in a mitigation bank. The substitute trees would be set into the new ground not with the randomness that defines a wild forest but with great precision and linear planning. It would be the Joe's Crab Shack version of nature, an entire landscape morphed into rehearsed and safe geometry.

I am given an "Environmental Assessment and Site Plan Analysis," which has identified plants, animals, and birds, and has analyzed the potential for environmental harm. There is no reported "impact," except that a north-south ditch that now runs through the property will be piped and filled. Birds inventoried in the existing woods here include the mourning dove, the palm warbler, the red-bellied woodpecker, the Cooper's hawk, and the Carolina wren, while animals include opossum, gray squirrel, and armadillo. Although I have most recently seen four active gopher tortoise burrows, none were reported in the analysis, nor was the chuck-will's-widow or barred owl. As there were no "listed" or protected species identified, there was no need to devise a strategy for sustaining them. The existing forest was described as "mixed hardwoods." All the drawings and tables appear to be in order, except for the buffer and the tortoises. I tell the engineering team that I would like a solid, high, thick stucco wall, rather than a thin plastic fence, that I would like an 8-foot screen to shield our property from dust and debris during construction, and that I want the work to take place only during those hours approved by the city, and not too early or too late. I tell them that I also would like a plan to acknowledge the existence of any gopher tortoises. The men hem and haw in an affable way and finally agree. The catch is that Kelly and I must sign a letter to the city stipulating we will allow them to build closer to our property lines. In turn, they would allow the same when our land was eventually developed. Quid pro quo. We smile and shake hands.

I am now part and parcel of the Florida real estate development experience, no more or less culpable than anyone else. At this point, I feel almost nothing. Hollis orders a small dish of vanilla ice cream and eats it. I think he might be a nice guy to go fishing with. We chat some more about superficial things, our conversation as vague as the little pretend-country souvenirs back in the gift shop. And then we leave. I have come face to face with the impending end of Sewell Road. It is as if one of the cows grazing in a relic pasture over on Reinhart suddenly realizes that there is more in store for him than an unending field of bahia grass. His placid bovine consciousness is shattered by a moment of stark clarity, and that moment reveals a cattle truck rumbling over the horizon toward him, bearing down hard.

The ménage of wild plants that are my yard is high and needs cutting, and the exterior siding needs painting. The mowing is less of a problem as it affords exercise and brings in birds to hunt for newly upturned food. The painting is another thing entirely. It takes an act of faith to consider it, a suspension of belief, a delusion that this house will be around long enough to make painting it worthwhile. The few homeowners who still live here have virtually stopped maintaining their homes, except for the barest levels of necessity. Mark across the street replaced some termite-damaged siding, and after a few months got around to priming the new wood. Kelly does some yard work and has planted some caladiums near the front porch, and old Jones drives down from Deltona to periodically cut his own lawn. But we seem to be sleepwalking through it all.

In a way, I envy the people who rent the apartments that were built atop the fields of cabbage and melons, as they are blissfully unaware of the historic prerogative of the place. And, of course, they can continue to occupy their "units" as long as they want, to the end of their lives if they so chose. For me, continuing to live on Sewell Road has started to feel as if I am camping out in the forest—I know it is mine only for a few more nights, that I must soon break camp and leave. Then, too, Rawlings once pondered the validity of the "ownership" of any land. As she did, she realized that the answer cannot be found in any legal title or deed in a county courthouse. The land, she wrote, "belongs to the wind, the seed, the everlasting supremacy of the seasons and of time." It doesn't belong to realtors, except for a little while, and it certainly doesn't belong to the lessees who inhabit larger corporate-designed retail shops and stores and plazas here. And it doesn't belong to me.

I think of Mike Durak as a boy, and Zona Beckwith as a little girl, each in their own time on Sewell, before the road even had a name. They were the offspring of adults who planted and gathered crops, raised livestock, awoke to the winter dew on the fronds of the sabal palm and the new buds on the spring wildflowers. Although as adults they surely knew better, when they were here as children, the home and the land belonged to them and to them alone. And perhaps deep in their hearts, they will always think of it that way, even now. I make the decision to paint my house one last time, carrying my ladder and bucket and brush with me as I work my way around its exterior. I use a wire brush and scraper to knock away the peeling skin of the old paint, every so often stopping to run my fingers over the smoothly hewn cypress frames around the windows and on the eaves. This is a home that has been built and rebuilt and fixed and repaired and loved since 1928, and when I touch the fibers of its texture, it is as if I am feeling something visceral that still lives through its collective memory.

I took Shep in yesterday for his annual rabies shots and check-up. I changed vets about two years ago, shifting from a very efficient, hyperactive, white-coat–wearing man down in Lake Mary to a more country vet not far from where I live. His name is Mills, and I like him a lot. In weather like this, he wears a t-shirt, hiking shorts, and sandals. He weighed and did all the things vets do to dogs and seemed genuinely impressed at how healthy Shep was. Shep is older now, white around his muzzle and eyelids, but he is still solid and fit. I said, "He goes with us a lot on hikes in the woods and trots along almost the entire way." Mills asked where we hiked and I told him, and we talked more about hiking and how he now has come to appreciate the challenging relief in the terrain in North Carolina. I say, "Yeah, a mile there is worth three or four here in the flatlands." We talked a little about travel to wild places around the world. I don't like to bring up this stuff to people I do not know well because it sounds like I'm bragging about a been-there, done-that t-shirt travel experience. But I did mention that I had journeyed to some remote parts of the earth and that they had left a big impression on me—the Galapagos, the White Sea of Russia, the Amazon, the Everglades of Florida. And he said, "If I had it to do all over again, I'd go into the wildlife end of it all, where I could be in the field." I told him of some wildlife biologists I once met who spent most of their time tracking and collaring the Florida black bear up in the Ocala National Forest, and Mills says, "Yeah, I'd like something like that."

Mills said, "I'll be right back," and instead of going to get some overpriced medicine like the other vet would have done and trying to scare me into buying it, he came back with a copy of the Nature Conservancy's magazine and showed me a photograph of Indonesia—treed, hilly islands surrounded by turquoise water. We looked at it and agreed that, yes, that would be a fine place to be. And he slapped me on the shoulder like an old pal and shook hands, and Shep and I left. I drove away feeling good for a change, the way I feel, oddly enough, when I go to my dentist because he too is a genuine person who cares and is country enough to slow down and to enjoy his life. Sprawl will likely roll over both my vet and dentist some day. For now, they are still here and that is somehow comforting. But the professionals who come to take their place likely won't have the same relaxed, tranquil style, and the new residents who live in Flagship Park and Dunwoody Commons likely won't even know what they have missed.

At this time, we have a governor who has discovered a way to solve the crisis of water in our state. Historically, we had lots of water, and the philosophy was to drain it away. Flood control districts were set up to do just this. In the Everglades alone, more engineering gates and canals were built than in all of the Suez Canal to allow south Florida to continue to sprawl westward, eating up acre after acre of historic saw grass. The portion of the Everglades protected inside a national park—about 1.5 million acres—is only about one-seventh of the historic Glades itself, a sprawling ecological system that once stretched all the way to the lakes that drained southward, just below Orlando.

We have worked hard to channel off the single element that has most distinctly defined the peninsula of Florida for the last twelve thousand years: Water. Once a God to the Timucua and Mayaca and Seminoles, then an expletive to the settlers, water is now desirable again—but for most this is only practical economics. Author John Rothchild, who gave us our first realistic history of Florida in Up for Grabs, defined our wetlands—our magnificent glades and marshes and tropical swamps—as "pre-dredged real estate." That's how Henry Sanford's friend Hamilton Disston saw it when Disston planned to buy most of the soggy interior of Florida for 25 cents an acre and drain it dry in the late nineteenth century. Disston didn't have the technology we have today, and while he turned miles of pastoral, meandering rivers and streams into arrow-straight canals, he botched his larger mission. Taking his failure to drain Florida personally, he ended up back up north somewhere, blowing out his brains in a bathtub, a method that seems at least considerate of others who had to clean up the mess behind him. Less can be said for his drainage vision—a muddle we have not yet reconciled.

Just when we get to the edge of understanding—when we finally realize that without water, we would be a desert—the affluent supporters of the current governor declare we have no water problem. Indeed, the governor's "Council of 100" has decided we have a water-delivery problem. There's plenty of water, most of it in the ground in rural northern Florida. But our population has sprawled mainly in south Florida and along the coast, where groundwater isn't as sweet or pure and is also seasoned with salt. As a result, this advisory committee of wealthy developers, agriculture executives, and sugar growers has urged a straightforward solution: Run pipelines from water-rich north Florida to water-poor south Florida. North Florida, rural and less prosperous, has little political clout, while south Florida is awash in money and power. To fund this delivery, the state should rob conservation land-buying accounts like Forever Florida. Thus liberated, the funds could be used to construct conduits to pump potable water to the sprawl created atop barrier islands and sumps that old-time Crackers believed to be uninhabitable. Mark Twain once said that we live in a plutocracy, a government by the wealthy. I wish he could have visited Florida today. He would be more lost than he ever was in King Arthur's court.

A weather forecast earlier in the week told of a dry cold front moving through, so I call Steve and see if we can make it out to the state forest for a hike. The more distressing life becomes here, the more I find myself retreating to the woods for solace. We haven't been out since last spring—way too long, considering the amount of time we've spent hiking together over the last seven years or so. Steve jumps at the chance, and we make plans to meet by noon on Thursday at the forest entrance.

I arrive first, backpack full of water, granola bars, a peanut butter sandwich, a clear plastic bag to collect seeds from wildflowers, a small compass, and a folding knife. I always carry a knife with me for use not as a weapon but as a tool—much like I sometimes wear a knife when diving. This one was my dad's; it has a shiny, yellow enamel case and four blades, each sharp and smaller than the other. I have slipped it into an outer pocket of the knapsack, and it gives me great comfort just knowing it is there. Dad and I walked in the woods not far from our house when I was growing up, and I guess it's like having a part of him with me in some small way. It's a reminder, too, of his quiet encouragement to not be afraid of the woods where we walked or the waters where we fished. Dad's beliefs were revealed in his actions. Great sweeping aphorisms were unnecessary. He only hinted that squeezing people together in big cities held far more risk than the vast countryside ever did. He grew up in the country, too, with lots of space to roam. The idea of so many people living on top of each other seemed unnecessary and chaotic to him.

It's in the high seventies today, and the humidity is low. I'm in khaki shorts with generous pockets, a t-shirt with an old, blue-checked flannel shirt over it—thin and comfortable from years of wear—and a great pair of low-cut, water-resistant hiking boots. I always look forward to Steve's company not just because of the familiarity, but because he considers life deeply and thoroughly, from many different angles. Steve always looks for the details and seems to process them as honestly as he can, without pretense. When I hike or paddle with Lisa, she does the same. It creates a quest for wholeness, and guides our relationships to intimacy. The methods she and Steve use to process information are widely different—she sees detail like an artist recording the exacting and astonishing twists and coils of nature as it quietly reveals itself. Steve teases out the infinitesimal parts intellectually, stacking and reorganizing in his head to consider origins and methodology. Steve and I debate often about springs, about where they lie in the landscape, about how they got here. We differ, as always, about direction, Steve deferring to the map and compass, and me, as always, forging into a new soggy, vine-tangled place simply because it feels right.

I drive into the forest, following the jeep path as it descends gradually toward the swamp. We cross the old concrete bridge atop the Blackwater Creek, and then ride the ascending terrain back up on the other side. We park and get out, shoulder our packs, and head into the forest. Bear tracks appear with regularity in the sand as do great piles of scat. It is November now, and the bears are on the move again, as active as they will ever be out here in these dense woods, following the same trails we use because the paths are open and unencumbered, little primitive superhighways taking them easily from one end of the dense subtropical forest to the other. When Lisa and I last hiked, the scat had just begun to appear, and I had stopped to more closely examine one pile. Unlike the droppings of some animals, bear scat is loose, only slightly moist, and almost entirely odorless. I picked through the pile with a little twig, and saw it was mostly berries and large brown undigested seeds, not unlike those of a pumpkin—maybe a wild squash? I had cleaned one off with the sand, and held it up to get a better look. Lisa eyed me suspiciously and took half a step back. "Now," she said, as if addressing a small boy, "don't you eat that." It was not an unreasonable request, for after all, I do sometimes seem to lose myself so thoroughly that actually tasting such a seed wouldn't seem out of the question. Instead, I snapped it in two parts and sniffed it, trying to get a hint as to what bush or plant bore it. Knowing the fodder of wildlife is a key to figuring out where they roam, and what habitats they rely on to survive, all contributing to our larger understanding of the place itself. Yet, when I broke that piece of seed, I didn't think of any of that. I was simply curious. Perhaps it's like trying to examine the seed of a relationship—between good friends, lovers, between people and their place. Sometimes the seed itself has no scent, and exists only in the context in which it appears before you in the world. Sometimes it functions as fully and as perfectly and as spontaneously as a found object—a wildflower, an animal track, a nest, a shed skin, all clues to something that has happened before you were there, that has changed ever so slightly, and now has become something else yet again by your examination of it. Relationships, like place, change, adjust, transform, but in the best of worlds, they do so gradually, organically, with some grace and wisdom to inform them.

When the canopy over the trail opens, the glorious winter sky appears. The winds of the dry cold front have done their job well and every shard of cloud is gone, leaving a sky of solid cerulean from end to end. High above, there are two black-headed vultures circling, and in the distance, I see the distinct outline of a red-tailed hawk, frozen for now in his own elliptical orbit in the everlasting blue. As we walk, Steve tells me of an unpublished William Bartram manuscript he stumbled over when visiting the Pennsylvania Historical Society recently. It was scattered in several different folders in the archives there and had to be pieced together by guessing at the chronology. Written in the small but precise handwriting of "Billy," the manuscript was formatted as a letter or a public answer to a question, which Steve tells me was the preferred essay style of that era. It was less about the specifics of his Travels, and more about the meaning of God and how he is revealed to us in nature—of how Bartram's own Quaker understanding of the cosmos had led him to this belief. In Bartram's gentle world, nature was to be communed with, and not exploited. Humans had no more status or standing than a wildflower or a black bear. We walk a while without talking, and I think some on this, think how much I would love to see an original manuscript in Bartram's hand, think of the judiciousness of this philosophy, of the lessons imbedded in it. I worked once with a former priest who was a social worker with young schoolchildren in the ghetto of a large northern city. He had learned the nuances of handwriting analysis, and tried to coax his charges to change their behavior by gradually imitating a longhand style representative of a healthy, balanced life. In the midst of all the disarray of their painful broken lives, it made as much sense as anything else we tried to do. But I remember it now and wonder: If I traced and retraced the original writing of Billy Bartram, would the own untold secrets he once found here and never expressed be somehow articulated to me?

There is a single spring run called Sulphur that drains off into Blackwater Creek, and while we have visited several small springs along its run on other hikes, we have yet to find the headspring of Sulphur. Steve thinks there may be no single source, but that it might arise from higher swampy land west of here around the creek itself. That makes sense, of course, but I push for the single-source option; it gives us something tangible to search for that we have not yet found. I suggest we simply forge over the sloping terrain to the bottomland and follow the base of the bluff until we stumble over a spring or two. If we stay up on the high sandy island and simply rely on the map to guide us, we may well miss the random spring that doesn't conform to the contours of the map, I say. Steve laughs his deep, good-natured laugh, mostly in acknowledgment of what he expected me to say. It confirms my own prejudice by which the vernacular spirit trumps the logical map every time. But when I find a break in the trees that could indicate the presence of a descending animal trail and light off for it, he follows without protest. Down over the edge of the ancient sea bluff we go, following a narrow animal trail through the thicket of sabal palms. This trail abruptly ends about halfway down the incline in a gridlock of saw palmetto, and I remember that other animal trails have dissolved in much the same way. I wonder where these animals go, and if they do this just to confuse us—if so, they have done their job well, because I am always confounded by it.

We are deep in the forest now, far beyond its boundary back on busy S.R. 46. The traffic noise associated with the edges of such preserves has long faded. While the most obvious sign of our distance inward is the complete silence of the place, there are other dynamics are work here. I tell Steve of an ecological phenomenon that is predictable enough to even be assigned a name—the Edge Effect. That's because the margins between the natural and human-built world have a distinction: Compared to the deeper woods, they suffer increased sunlight, higher temperatures and evaporation, and less moisture in their soils. Travel along the roads at these edges produces air pollution, noise, soil erosion, and even changes the population dynamics of plants and animals. Aggressive bird species like brown-headed cowbirds and blue jays thrive at the edges, as do raccoons, certain snakes, and other predators. More sensitive bird species move deeper into the woods, to where we are now, to avoid predation. On other hikes to the middle of the forest, we have seen ovenbirds, hooded warblers, and even scarlet tanagers, birds seldom spotted at the edges. Indeed, while only 1 percent of our entire country is covered with roadways, the impact of those roads affects 20 percent of the landscape with related noise and pollution. When I finish my riff on edges, Steve looks at me. "Makes sense," he says. I think, briefly, of the irony between the ecological impacts at the forest edge and the anthropological ones that I experience back on Sewell.

We split up, me going around one side of the thicket of palmettos, Steve to the other. I duck under low limbs, pull back the serrated stems of the menacing little palms, am bitten once by a crab spider, and after raising blood twice from deep scratches on my legs, finally arrive at the bottom. A hundred yards away, I see Steve making his final descent and call to him. We join up down here and walk away from the bluff and out into the margins of the swamp. We've had little rain for the last few weeks, and the ground under us is soggy rather than wet, a swamp in its seasonal dry phase. But traveling through it is still much the same as walking in a swamp—we must step from logs to slightly higher clumps of vegetation, or we will we sink down a half foot and more into the spongy boot-sucking bottomland. Thick vines of muscadine and summer grape hang from the trees, and the moist trunks are splotched with patchy lichens the color of old scars. A variety of tillandsia mosses, some with spiky red flowers, bristle from crooks in the branches, thriving on nutrients in the air. The longer, trailing Spanish moss was once so predominant in Florida that an entire industry that used it as stuffing for mattresses thrived here in the nineteenth century. But now our air conveys pollution from auto exhaust. Mosses have been dying off just about everywhere except in the more remote places, on isolated country roads and deep in the swamps.

We are in a hydric hammock—a great layer of fertile humus nurturing large hardwood trees, ferns, and palms—and it's cool down here in the early winter shade. I run into another stand of thick foliage and see it is the threatened needle palm, fronds like a palmetto but thicker and undivided. I think of the rare butterfly orchid and look for it on the trunks around me, but to no avail. Green mosses cover the exposed roots of the hardwoods, and I see these trees have mimicked the successful anchoring technique of the cypress by turning the bottoms of their trunks into elegant buttresses. We step around and through this Devonian gloom, sunlight nearly gone now in the triple canopy except for a haphazard shaft of it now and then.

Steve is a few steps ahead of me now, and after he passes through one of the light shafts, I look down and see a giant water moccasin curled in the buttress of a swamp tupelo. His head is as triangular as an arrow point, and he seems almost in a stupor from the warmth of the sun. I stop in my tracks and call to Steve. I tell him to look over his shoulder. He does, but the snake is so well camouflaged that it is not easily seen. Then Steve focuses. The snake seems to have formed itself from the molecules of light and dark, subtle natural colorations and inscrutable, timeless reptile consciousness merging perfectly. I think it could be a phantom, that if we glanced away, it might be gone. "Geeeez," says Steve, finally. "He's a big one" and I agree. We look at each other.

"It's not that I'm afraid of snakes," I say, "but I take this as a sign." And I really do. The great Florida naturalist Archie Carr listened to Bartram, and Bartram listened to the Native Americans, who in turn listened to the sweet mystery in the wind and the eternal wisdom in their spirits. All in all, it was not a bad place to seek advice. The wind isn't speaking right now, but my spirits tell me to change course. "Ah, let's go in the other direction, a little more on higher ground," I say. The snake doesn't seem to have moved this entire time but remains curled, fully watchful as a rock or a tree is watchful, not unkindly or maliciously, but because not a particle of its being would allow it to do any less. We are far less inscrutable, and painfully obvious in our human conceits. But we are at least trying to listen, to be mindful to the crunching we now make as fallen cypress sprigs and bay leaves and the discarded skins of anoles crack and splinter under each step we take toward higher ground. Before we saw the moccasin, we seemed to be making hardly any sound at all. Now its presence has keyed our senses, making us more fully aware of the timbre of our movements. Once back on the high trail, Steve finally puts away the map, and we look for other signs.

We are between hunting seasons, and sportsmen from the last hunt have left the bright pink fluorescent strips of soft plastic called "flagging" tied to trunks and branches. The flagging is there to help mark their way in and out of the woods, a more reliable form of a breadcrumb trail. But there is so much flagging around me in the woods today that it looks like some sort of parade has been through before us. "Why don't these guys just learn to use a compass?" I ask out loud, to no one. As we go, I pull all the flagging from the trees and stuff it into my backpack. But when we come to a curious arrangement of it, I stop. The new plastic, hung in great strips on a small sabal palm island in the middle of the swamp, is matched by older, faded strips that seem to mark a trail that leads back down the slope. I know that a geographic information specialist with the state has been trying to map the springs of the larger Wekiva system—indeed, he had contacted me earlier, asking for photos of Island Spring, the submerged spring in the middle of the river itself. "Maybe this old flagging leads to one of the springs he found," I say. Immediately, I head back down the steep slide of the slope, stuffing my moccasin premonitions. Steve, noncommittal, follows. I pass a young tree trunk raked by a bear staking his territory. I put my hand on the raw underbark, feel the sap there, and forming my hand like a paw, scrape it across the surface. I make my version of a bear sound, raaaauuuullllllwwww, as if it were I and not the bruin who left this mark. Steve looks at me curiously and says nothing.

As we go deeper, I smell the distinct scent of sulfur, a sign that a spring is nearby. And sure enough, tucked away at the very bottom of the bluff, is a clear pool of water maybe 30 feet across. I smile widely—it doesn't get any better than this!—and shake Steve's hand. "It's a beauty," he says, picking his way around its low shore. We scrutinize it closely, see that small gambusia have found their way all the way upstream from Sulphur Run to this boil. There are two slight depressions in the pool, either of which could hide the vent for the spring. We debate the merits of both. Finally, we agree that a slight churning of the water's surface over the deeper of the two is the source. It is close to the edge, and so I crouch there, hanging onto an arching algae-covered trunk of a sweetgum tree, and look down into it. The upwelling seems to be coming from under the roots of the tree itself, perhaps from a small limestone crevice there. Around me in the clear water, the tiny spiky balls of the sweetgum are scattered. A leopard frog leaps a heroic distance into the pool creating a loud splash, and somewhere nearby in the understory, an unseen animal rustles. A barred owl, awakened by all this commotion in the middle of his sleep, calls out repeatedly with his deep, hollow-reeded exhalations. Down here the thick swamp air has appreciable weight. "We'll name this Sweetgum Spring," says Steve, smiling now. We are both covered with sweat and twigs and dirt, insect bites and scratches with tendrils of red blood. And we are fully exultant at the wonder of it all.

Chapter Eleven

What remains of the self unwinds and unwinds, for none
Of the boundaries holds.
Mark Strand, "In Memory of Joseph Brodsky"

A hurricane with 130-mph winds just made landfall on the southwest coast of Florida and is headed this way. It has been named Charley, and if it stays its course, it will come directly through central Florida, becoming the worst storm to hit here since Hurricane Donna in 1960. The anticipation of natural catastrophes like this seems to unite a disparate community like almost nothing else, creating a bond that we otherwise would not have. That bond, of course, is fear, and it is the one element that we have tried so diligently to remove from our relationship with nature. With this storm, fear reenters the equation, and although it won't be a sustainable fear that affects our ethic and imagination, it is enough to galvanize everyone for now.

I do what I can to make ready, moving the kayaks inside the utility shed next to the garage, storing lawn furniture, and loading up on ice and batteries. I back my vehicle to the mouth of my driveway where it is the least likely to be hit if the old water oak next to the house falls. I turn on television and watch as the weather radar shows "bands" of storms preceding Charley moving northeasterly across the peninsula as splotches of green. Already, people in Punta Gorda, where the storm came ashore from the Gulf of Mexico, are dying because they were trapped in their trailers. Charley peeled away the thin metal sides and roofs as if opening giant sardine cans. Other poorly built houses are being turned into piles of giant pick-up sticks. I take a great deal of solace in knowing my home was hand-built of heart cypress, by people who cared for themselves and for their families.

Although the hurricane isn't predicted to arrive until 11 p.m. or so, the first band of thunderstorms associated with it hits us at 6 p.m., lashing the yard with torrents of rain and bursts of wind. Dead branches and clusters of leaves fall, slapping against the wet ground. In a half hour, the wave passes over, and all is calm until the next one arrives. I think of the homeless who live back in the woods, and I pack up three plastic parkas with some water and granola bars, and sticking it all in my knapsack, head out for their camp. The forest is already patched with pools of water from the heavy rains, and I slosh through to the other side until I reach the Smith Canal. The water in the canal is dangerously high, nearly to its top. It is full of gray storm water, which is being transported with great haste down to the St. Johns River. Sediments, toxic metal particles, pesticides, fertilizers, oil and grease pathogens, nutrients, and trash all stream together. Normally low, sluggish, and full of blackwater, the canal now conveys rain that falls on parking lots and rooftops and roads of new developments uphill, a brew far more noxious and of a much higher volume than it was ever intended to carry when built decades ago.

I walk the open path next to the canal, back to where I know the last camp of the homeless ought to be. Elected commissioners for the City of Sanford recently passed a law outlawing panhandling. As a result, many of the homeless have moved on, becoming somebody else's problem. One camp is farther back in the woods, making it harder for the police to find. I can't see it today from the path, but I know its general location from having spotted the glow of campfire there not too long ago. I head into the woods to where I think it should be, and the sky darkens once again, promising that the edge of the new storm band will not be far behind. I poke through low-hanging limbs, all saturated with rain, and finally reach the camp. It is a series of blue plastic tarps, suspended on ropes secured to some trees. There are several cheap white plastic chairs, charred wood from a fire, and empty boxes and beer and food cans lying around. A bouquet of plastic flowers has been stuck into the dirt next to a large soiled pillow. A toy tiger has been hung on a tree nearby, perhaps as a sort of mascot. Half of its lower body has been pulled apart, and its cotton stuffing puffs out. I sit in one of the chairs and wait, thinking perhaps I may have scared the transient campers away by my sudden arrival, and maybe they will return. But no one appears, and the wind begins to pick up again.

I leave the provisions I have brought on one of the chairs and thread my way back through the woods. It is nearly dark now, and I run into branches and blunder through spider webs and trip over small logs. When I am within 100 yards of the edge of my property, the sky opens up again and rain falls in torrents. I go inside, change into dry clothes, and wait for Charley. Shep is quaking from the rumbles of the thunder and is relieved to see me. Just before midnight, the hurricane suddenly arrives with a vengeance, distinguishing itself from the early storms by its sheer brute force. I look outside and see lightning bolts spider-web their way between the clouds. They are colored an unworldly sea green. Larger limbs fall atop utility lines and across the driveway. Some hit the solid steel roof of my house and tumble to the ground. The sound of the wind is harrowing, almost like a thing alive. No wonder the Timucua designated a separate god just for hurricanes. Despite the pounding, the house does not tremble, save for the rattling of the old windows.

I finally sleep, and by morning the sun is out, and the air is new and fresh. Branches and leaves are everywhere, and water has filled the ditches and even puddled up around the yard. Utility lines are down in the road, and a large tree limb leans against the roof of the Metts home. I turn on a battery-powered radio and learn that a few people in the region have lost their lives, including a man who drove into a 35-foot-deep sinkhole that opened in the road down near Lake Wales. The power and telephone service may be gone for days. While many homes were destroyed, my house is not damaged, not even a broken window pane. I turn on the Ultramatic Caloric gas stove and heat up a flour tortilla with cheddar and boil some water for a cup of yerba maté, a highly caffeinated herbal brew popular in South America. Ethnobotanists, the people who study the link of plants to culture, say a form of maté was used by the Timucua as the "black drink" during religious ceremonies to provide clarity. It is a strange breakfast for a strange day, but I figure I can use all the clarity I can get. With Shep at my side, I walk back through the woods to check on the damage there. Large oaks have been snapped in half. The homeless camp is still deserted. Smith Canal is surging like a narrow, deep river.

Today I read in the newspaper that a homeless woman was arrested by police from the City of Sanford just before the storm. The woman was the rough-hewn blonde I had met in the woods when I brought Christmas food and gifts, the one who had hugged me and asked me to pray for her. She had been charged with violating a city law against having an "open container." An official arrest report written in cop-speak reveals that a police officer observed the suspect sitting cross-legged on the grass under the shade of a tree next to a hedge. The hedge was in front of Don Pablo's, a franchised Mexican restaurant at the entrance to the mall. She was reportedly eating a hot dog and drinking a can of Natural Ice. When she was asked to stand up, the officer "could smell a strong odor of alcoholic beverage coming from her facial area." Her hands were then cuffed behind her back, and she was taken to the county jail, where her bond was set at $163.

The day after she was arrested, she died. A sheriff's spokesman said her death was likely related to a "pre-existing condition." No other information was made available. Her name was Cheryl Ann Vantine. She had just turned forty-seven. I now understand that the plastic flowers placed in the ground back in the woods had been a memorial for her, an act of mourning by one of her homeless friends. The merchants who pay large square-footage rents on the old cow pasture that is now a mall have assumed a territoriality in which perfectly coifed landscapes cannot be marred by the blight of the homeless. Sitting under a tree and drinking a beer here may have been acceptable two decades ago, but not now. Sprawl is exclusionary, no room for anomalies that may interfere with the relentless urge to consume. It strikes me that unbridled porcine consumption is really what sprawl is all about. Swilling an overpriced beer and eating an overpriced burrito in Don Pablo's is perfectly okay, nothing odd in that the restaurant, the road leading to it, and the rest of its grid was subsidized by taxpayers in the name of economic prosperity. In his classic 1958 novel Surrounded on Three Sides, John Keasler sounded one of the first modern laments about the deceptive illusion of progress in Florida's runaway growth: "What the hell is Florida for if you can't sleep in it?" one character asks. "To Hell with progress."

I return again and again to Rawlings's account of her time at Cross Creek. Despite the years that divide us, I am struck by the equilibrium our historic landscapes shared. During my time here, we have had the chuck-will's-widow, the redbird, the red hibiscus, the Turks-cap, the blackberry vines, the magnolia tree with its leaves "shining as dark polished jade," the migrating robins in winter, the mourning doves, the egrets, and the mockingbirds, even the pileated woodpecker, the "Lord God bird" of the Creek. At some point, the families who have lived here kept cows and pigs and a garden with hogwire fencing, and if no one ran catfish trotlines as they did at the Creek, certainly all had fished. I know I certainly have. The population had a sustainable relationship with the land, one that did not overwhelm its resources. "At one time or another, most of us at the Creek have been suspected of a degree of madness," Rawlings also wrote. Madness then may have been Cracker knowledge uncluttered by the pretense of civilization, a pure sensibility not yet contorted by the pressure to conform. Madness now, at least for me, is growing outrage over being surrounded on three sides by manipulative and unsustainable growth.

Since Charley, three other hurricanes have moved through, all in the same season. I lost power for ten days during one. But the only damage my old house suffered was when a tree limb bashed into the heavy concrete cap over the fireplace chimney and sent the 80-pound slab tumbling down the steel roof to the ground.

Change now is more pressing than ever, gathering like a tropical storm churning its way toward me. Pretending it won't happen is no longer an option. Once more I find myself saturated by the present, and it sends me hurtling back into the past. I talk with Zona again, and she tells me a few more stories and visits once more. She admits candidly that she was a little girl when she lived here, and it was a long time ago. The memories are fading, the way a newspaper page loses its color when left in the sunlight. She asks me how I fared in the hurricanes, and I told her I did well. She said "that old house has been through many a storm."

I do a book-signing for my new anthology at a little independent bookstore in the historic downtown of Sanford, where, if you squint just a bit, you can still imagine that time has not changed too much at all. Most of the buildings are from the late nineteenth and early twentieth centuries, two-story brick structures with ornate molding rimming the roof lines. At the book-signing, there is wine and cheese and a warm air of unforced camaraderie among the patrons, owner, and employees that I seldom encounter at the bloodless chain bookstores. Zona and Art come, as do Lisa and some of my friends. Fred, a judge, is here, along with Linda, an artist who is his wife. There seems to be a balance between the geniality of the evening and the historic nature of the building we are in. It is a fragile, endearing quality, this genuine friendliness, and like other retro values that still endure here, transformation of the community will test its limits.

I meet Michelle Thatcher, who is the director of the nonprofit Seminole Soil and Water Conservation District. Michelle, originally from Seattle, moved here with her family four years ago. She tells me that her office gets by on a shoestring, squeezing a handful of modest grants into projects like managing conservation land, setting up educational butterfly gardens at local schools, and encouraging homeowners to redesign their yards to save water. The intent of it all is to sustain the earth in various ways. If the downtown is time-locked—at least for now—so too are efforts such as these, for they illustrate an ethic that once connected natives to their place. Michelle, a striking woman with an untamed mane of blonde hair and an infectious cheerfulness, brings out a rare first-edition copy of botanist Small's prophetic book From Eden to Sahara. The book has been out of print since 1929, and I handle it as I would a fragile orchid, of the sort Small himself used to collect from this once-wild state. She thinks it would be a grand idea to bring the book back to publication now, given the growing pressures of sprawling growth on natural places and our unique lime-rock aquifer just below. "Isn't water what Florida's all about?" Michelle asks.

There are cities, counties, a state—even an entire "water management district"—that should have strategies to account for our most precious resource in this bioregion. Yet, every year—as botanist Small predicted over six decades ago—we have less potable water. And every year, as we continue to grow, we drill wells deeper into the ground, searching for those diminishing veins of life. Springs continue to dry, sinks continue to form, and the native veneer of the landscape continues to peel away, like the tops of mobile homes unfurled by hurricane winds. "What will be left when my kids are my age?" she asks.

I contact Mike and Carolyn Durak one last time and encourage them to tell me stories they have not yet told about what they call the "old homeplace." I don't hear from the Duraks for a couple weeks, and then I begin to receive a series of written reports from Mike about its history. It is clear he has put some time into thinking about this and relishes the chance to remember out loud, one last time. As I read his accounts, it occurs to me that beyond self-sufficiency and a connection to place, of all the characteristics this historic neighborhood shared with the Creek, its eccentricities may have been among its most endearing. They were the sort of behaviors that set Old Florida residents apart from those living in the gated and sterile communities that are coming to define the New. Mike writes: "My father and mother bought what is now two-thirds of your property on June 4, 1938, from John J. and Sarah Maude Mathews [Zona's parents]. This parcel included the 50-foot house lot and the 50-foot lot immediately to the north. They paid $1,200 for this property. Then on February 18, 1939, my folks purchased the 50-foot lot immediately to the south of the house from A. D. 'Dewey' Mathews and his wife. This is the lot where the garage now sits. A. D. and John J. Mathews were brothers. They worked for the Atlantic Coast Line Railroad in Sanford. They thought they could build their houses next to each other and enjoy each other's company. Well, it did not work out that way. For whatever reason, Dewey put his house on wheels and rolled it to State Road 46. It is the house on the northeast corner of S.R. 46 and Sewell Road. John sold his house to Dad and Dewey sold his now vacant lot to Dad. The north side lot, included in my Dad's original purchase, had been purchased by John after the house on it was rolled across the street and became the Fredricks' home. It is now owned by the Metts. This was the time of house roulette."

Mike remembered the families who lived here when he was a child—the Fredricks; the Dunns; an "Uncle Jack," who lived alone in another Cracker house up on the hard road; Mr. Hunter, who lived near Uncle Jack; and Miss Logan. Miss Logan lived by herself in a wood and metal-roofed home on the southwest corner of Sewell and the hard road. In Mike's reminiscences of the "old homeplace," everyone knew everyone else, and all was still right with the world. One man was an avid fisherman; one man worked so hard his wife had to mow the lawn; one man had bad shocks on his car that could be heard when he turned off the hard road onto Sewell. Houses migrated about for various reasons. It sounded like a slightly out of kilter Mayberry RFD.

"Miss Logan lived alone with her cat Blueboy. Blueboy was a very large Maltese cat with a bluish tint to his gray coat. He ruled the neighborhood. Miss Logan made sweet tomato relish that was the best in the world. It was no secret when she was making the relish, you could smell the aroma up and down the street." Her house was the one bought by the developer Rucker— the one he rented to the married cousins, one of whom led a band with electrical guitars in the flooded yard, in the rain.

"All of the oranges and grapefruit in your yard came from seed. Dad always said that the seeds of the sweet orange trees had come from Hamlin oranges. They made the sweetest full-bodied orange juice! You will note the citrus are all planted on ditch-banks. If you planted them anywhere else, they would die of root rot. The big yellow grapefruit is the Duncan. My, were they good! The sour orange came from root stock. Mom planted them all along the ditch south of the garage. We used them as a substitute for lemons or limes. In the summer we prized them for 'sour orange-ade,' sweetened up with sugar. They were used to make a sour orange meringue pie (like a key lime pie). That bamboo was always in the chicken yard, which controlled its spread. The chickens picked at new shoots unmercifully. New shoots just did not succeed. After Dad quit having chickens, the bamboo became a threat. It wanted to take over, and was formidable to chop back. Sewell itself was a sand road with two ruts. The entry to the road had board and post structures on both sides to mark where the road crossed the ditch that ran along SR 46. They were painted white. The big horizontal boards that tied the posts together were great fun to sit upon and swing on while waiting for the school bus."

The nearby country store that Zona had remembered was also there in Mike Durak's time. "It sat on piers and had wood floors, but the siding ran almost to the ground. You could drive up to the front of the store from either SR 46 or Monroe Road. It formed a large covered area where cars could drive under in bad weather. At the end of this covered area sat two gas pumps of the Pure Oil Company. The pumps had the standard glass globes of the day on top. The globes had light bulbs inside that were turned on at night to highlight the blue and white star of the oil company. We simply called it the Corner Store."

Like most of the neighbors, the Duraks kept a cow or two and milked them early—around four—each morning. In one fond recollection, Mike tells a story of him and his dad pushing and pulling Beauty, one of their cows, nearly a mile toward Lake Monroe to breed her with the neighborhood bull. It was summer and cool and quiet in the early dawn. As they walked along the lonely country roads, Mike recognized every celery field, and every neighbor who lived along the way by name. For a while, they walked next to a creek that flowed with "a beautiful ribbon of clear water" and it cut down into the sand, under a wide canopy of oaks. It was named Elder, and upstream it had once flowed through my backyard. "There was mist in the air and a heavy dew on the weeds and grass that hugged the side of the road. The only sounds were the shuffle of our feet in the sand." They passed a grand house owned by a botanist, and then another owned by Mike's music teacher from school. "I felt very important to have my music teacher living in my area of the world." Beauty was finally led into the bull's barn, and she was mounted by the bull. "Mama marked the date on the calendar and counted the days to the next possible heat, but that date was uneventful. Beauty was bred."

And there was that lush countryside, which in Mike's world seemed to spread out forever, full of the verdant enchantment that distinguished the rare native Florida landscape. "Due west of the celery field behind the house were 10 acres of slash pine. The pines were big, straight and beautiful. As a kid, I thought the deep dark pine woods were the home of ghosts and goblins. As I got older I loved to walk through the big trees. Some of the larger ones had to be over 100 feet tall. It took three of my arm lengths on some to go around their circumference. The trees were being bled for turpentine."

In addition to Mike's having lived here as a boy, his education as a land planner also gave him a historic perspective on the politics of growth that few others had. Planning and zoning in the 1960s may have seemed an intrusive business for the iconoclasts of the Old Florida, but it was the first organized attempt to acknowledge the natural sustainability of a sparsely populated state and to prepare for the anticipated growth pressures that would one day arrive. Water was at the essence of the landscape, and Mike fully understood this. "When I was a kid, potable water was abundant. Everyone in our area had an artesian 'flow well.' During dry periods in the 1940s, when not a drop of rain had fallen at our place, Daddy could always tell if it had rained in the uplands; the level of pressure in our wells would increase in the same day. Many houses in the area did not need a pump. And I still could wash the top of my van with well water in the 1970s and 1980s! The water in the hose would flow to a height of seven or eight feet above the ground surface.

"When I was working for Seminole County as a transportation planner in the 1980s, studies were circulating that the piezometric surface (the pressure on the groundwater) was decreasing. This was first attributed to the lack of rainfall. The idea that the reduction of recharge could be the result of development was only considered only when municipal well fields were threatened."

Although Mike used great restraint in retelling the story of his landscape, I could tell he was aggrieved by it all. He was a conservative man in many ways, a farmer's son. He had an undying work ethic and believed, almost religiously, in the free-enterprise system's capacity to reward hard-earned achievement. But he also saw the backroom dispensations that had been made. He saw how the rules had been bent, the playing field rendered uneven.

For instance, equations that specified the size of "retention" ponds to capture the toxic storm water and to allow some percolation back into the ground erred greatly on the side of the developer. "As a result of such compromise, runoff that should be retained is being discharged downstream in rapid and larger volumes." Natural waterways, like the St. Johns and Wekiva, which receive the brunt of this discharge, have become loaded with sediment and toxins as a result.

In his remembrances, Mike considered once more how the lifeways had been inextricably shaped by the singular environment of place. "Celery really was king. First Street was lined with celery fields. The farmers lived for the most part on the land they farmed. The houses were well built, usually two-story and spacious. They were equipped with the latest in modern conveniences, but their yards were tiny. The fields came right up to their doorsteps. They were not in the business of yards—they were in the business of celery. Many of these farmers farmed only 10 to 20 acres and got rich doing it. Sanford was the celery capital of the world. Seminole High School students were the Celery Feds. School dances were held above the City Hall which was known as the Celery Crate.

"All the fields had a sub-irrigation system in place made out of underground terra-cotta pipes. All it took was an artesian well and you could water a ten-acre field on demand. Once drilled, the artesian wells were basically free to flow, so little thought was given to conservation. There was always plenty of water just waiting to bubble out of the ground."

But the relationship the farmers first had with the land seemed to lose its balance as the demands of modernization increased. It was an era when hydrology and conservation were foreign words. And the working conditions for the field hands were not something the Chamber of Commerce would ever brag about. For Mike, the sustainability of the historic landscape began to diminish, and the culture it had shaped began to transform, tilting like a gyroscope that has lost its spin and grace. "Most of the farmers did not handle the water wisely. They would over-water the fields, letting the excess water run down the ditches, sometimes for days. Many times they would forget to turn the wells off after the crop had been gathered. The resource seemed endless and was used and abused. The leaching action of these waters, running unimpeded through the soils, finally took its toll. The waters slowly removed the basic nutrients from the fields, making it more and more expensive to maintain the soils' fertility.

"Mr. Lundenburg was the only farmer I knew who took the time to plug the 'pockets' at the end of the field. He would first plug the pockets, then turn the wells on for the time it took the water to reach the end of the field. He would then turn the wells off, and pull the plugs to lower the water level in the field, step by step.

"Of course the farmers didn't do the hard work on the land themselves; that was done by the black farm hands. It was only a step up from slavery now that I look back on the situation. Poor pay, poor working conditions, and inadequate school opportunities kept most of these people in the field. Many a business that wanted to settle in Sanford was turned away so that there would be no competition for the area's labor pool. Many a black man would be denied the opportunity to 'move up' because of these economic attitudes.

"The days of celery were numbered. The land became poorer due to excesses and abuse. The use of blue stone (copper sulfate) to control fungi on the celery was widely used. The buildup of copper in the soil became so pervasive over time that many fields were useless for farming. After World War II, trace elements came into widespread use in the muck lands south of Lake Okeechobee after they were drained, making farming of celery on thousand-acre farms in that area possible. The economy of scale of these muck lands put growing celery on 10- and 20-acre fields in the Sanford area on the ropes.

"Some farmers turned to beef cattle. Some turned to farming cabbage, squash, peppers, and cucumbers, trying to tailor their operations to a niche market. The McCalls, who owned the land east of Lundenberg's 10 acres, between Elder Road and Upsala Road, planted their 20 acres in citrus. Mr. Lundenberg turned to citrus as well. That was when we discovered who owned the pine woods. It was Mr. Lundenberg. He clear-cut the pine forest, and made railroad ties of the trees. Mr. Lundenberg had always been a friend of the land in my young eyes. His farming practices seemed to be a model for the conservation of land and water. The waste and destruction he wrought on those pine woods dispelled that image forever. He burned the debris, bulldozed the stumps and reshaped the once pine land and celery field into alternating rows of hills and valleys. He planted the citrus, and irrigated the trees with the old sub-irrigation system that was still in place. While the first 10 acres had made good celery fields, even that did not make good citrus land. It was not a well-drained soil type like the sandhills. Now it became apparent why Mr. Lundenberg had never cleared his pine forest for farming celery. It was even more poorly drained. This was flatwoods soil. The citrus trees died of root rot and other diseases associated with high groundwater conditions. With trees in place it was impossible to maintain the sub-irrigation system. So over time the ground water situation grew worse. An orange tree would grow for maybe five or perhaps ten years after planting, start to really produce, and then die. Replanting became the norm.

"The Interstate 4 corridor in those days was the outback of Seminole County. It was citrus groves, woods and rural home sites. Dirt roads predominated. Then growth started out rather slowly—a new subdivision here, a new shopping mall there. Urban growth began to spread from Orlando into Orange County and the surrounding counties including Seminole. The County and its communities had wished for growth so hard and for so long that nothing was allowed to detract from this newfound prosperity. The developers took full advantage of their naiveté and did basically what they pleased. Local government woke up to the fact that new growth was not free. The County and almost every town got themselves a land use planner or two. But the politician, influenced by the power of landowner greed and by the developer's desire to minimize his costs, modified the recommendations of planners to suit their political needs.

"The sandhills to the south had always been considered by the celery farmer of little value. These same sandhills had suddenly become the land of choice for the developer. The land was well drained, and easily cleared. They had new value. The woods became the urban landscape of today.

"Sanford, the center of political power when celery was king, lost its political grip. As the center of population and power continued to shift to the southern parts of the county, Sanford and north Seminole County became just another area fighting for its share of the development pie."

Even the legal protections that made the Wekiva so special were defaults—successful only because there "was a supply of comparable properties elsewhere at the time with no restrictions on them." Now with the supply of other lands built out, "the developer is challenging the police powers of the Wekiva area. And what they are finding are holes in the regulations they can use to their advantage." Mike finished with a final note about our road. It is profound in what it foretells, for it clearly marked the turning point in the Duraks' decision to leave "our Florida behind" years later. "Sewell Road did not have a name. It never crossed anybody's mind that it needed a name. The name 'Sewell' came into being for 911 purposes. No one in our area was named Sewell. No one from the county or the 911 consultant asked us what it should be named. The road naming coincided with the change to a more urban, less personal mentality that began to sweep the county at that time."

I picked a handful of kumquats from the two trees in the front yard this morning, popping a couple into my mouth. They were bittersweet, still cool from the night air. It was early, the glow of the new sun just beginning to spread itself over the horizon through the limbs of the longleaf to the east. There was just enough of a glow to backlight the webs of the golden orb spiders, magnificent mazes of slender bronze thread, woven carefully in the night. Today the air is newly crisp and refreshing. The white, daisylike blooms of the Spanish needle and the lavender of the four o'clocks—nearly as sweet as honeysuckle—are bushing up at the edge of the yard, beyond where I mow. The perfect little violet trumpets of the wood sorrel poke up anywhere they can. All of this is covered with the fresh dew, and when the sun rises up just a little more and shines through the canopies of the pines to the east, it casts a glow on the wet, warmer foliage, making it seem as if the entire yard is releasing a fine amber mist.

Shep always seems invigorated by seasonal change, and as I lose myself in my fruit quest, he is busy romping through the cool grasses and wildflowers, an animal that defines his life by the smells that surely were left here just for him. The oranges are still yellow, but when I pull a branch down and squeeze my fingers around one, I see it is full and nearly ripe. Out under the tin-roofed pavilion over the brick barbecue, I use my pocketknife to cut the orange in half, and then in half twice again—creating eight wedges of the single fruit, just like my grandmother used to make for me when I was a little boy. She called the triangular little pieces of orange a "tea party," and that is how I still like to eat it, holding the skin of each piece by the edge and peeling away each triangle of sweet fruit from the rind with my teeth. I sometimes wonder if she learned how to cut oranges that way when she first lived in Florida with my grandfather as a young woman, when the wild land seemed to stretch out forever, into the prairies and scrub and swamp.

I guess now it doesn't matter. The earth-moving machinery is growling its way into the old grove now, preparing to remove my last large buffer against the world. It just started last week with a lone bulldozer blazing a path around the entire perimeter of the woods to the south. I was inside my kitchen when it approached the edge of my land. The force of the excavation actually made my home quiver from the floor up, in ways the hurricanes never did. I walked outside and watched the trees fall—the live oaks, the sabal palms, the hackberry, the cedar. I had heard the bone-fracturing sound of the cracking of tree trunks several years ago when the machinery was clear-cutting the woods back at the corner of Rinehart and S.R. 46. It churned my stomach then, but the effect now is far more pronounced. The trembling of my home seems to foretell some deeper shuddering at the core of my soul. A pileated woodpecker, Rawlings's Lord God bird, soars out of the woods, and scads of tiny migrants—warblers of some kind—zigzag out from limb to limb. I wonder what the wrens and others that are now nesting will do.

When the dozers stop for the day, I walk back onto the land. I know there is one remaining camp of homeless still left, four large tents grouped together with large blue tarps strung over them. In contrast to earlier camps, it seemed orderly, almost tidy. I am curious as to what has become of it. When I reach it, I see bare ground where at least one tent had been pitched. On the ground is an empty carton that once held Tropicana Twister lemonade drinks. A neat block-script message has been written on the bottom of the white carton with a felt-tipped pen, a note from one of the campers to the others: Kenny and Linny: You can see the bulldozers and loaders. So as you can tell, we have to move now. I got us a couple of days, but it is time to go. Any or some help would be appreciated. Somebody needs to talk to me or I will just look after me.—Macon.

Within two weeks, the excavators have moved so proficiently over the terrain that all the trees have been uprooted and piled into great lumps of trunks and dirt and leaves. There is nothing whatsoever left of the woods that were here. The excavated trees were gathered into one large heap and then mulched into tiny shards, which together grew into small mountains near the Smith Canal. The sunlight, once muted by the little forest, now baked full force on my land. For days, the air was full of the curious scent of the mulch. I imagined that it smelled of sap, black earth, box turtle shell, squirrel nest, bromeliad, the final song of the chuck-will's-widow.

When I was a boy, I came home from school one spring afternoon to find my mother sitting at the kitchen table, crying. It was unlike her to do this, and I was perplexed and upset by it. I asked her what was wrong, and she told me that the ancient sassafras tree that grew next to our house had been cut down. My neighborhood was still being created, and the new owner of the lot was preparing to build a house on the property. The sassafras was clearly in the way. It was a majestic tree with an impressive crown and roots that, when you dug them up and bent them until they snapped, released the sweet scent of root beer. "You boys grew up playing under that tree. We had our cook-outs out there. Dusty [our dog] is buried there. You built your little fort there." I thought some about that, but I was a teenager, shallow and insensitive to the context of a past and a future. "Awww, Mom," I said, wanting to comfort her, but oblivious to the depth of her sorrow. I couldn't understand my mother's pain, of how one can become attached to those iconic relationships in a landscape, and of how the taking of them can seem so brutal. I do now.

I am packing most of my life into boxes for the move from my house. But there is so much I will be leaving behind. I look up absently and hear the hawk cry and see it once more soaring high overhead, the crimson in his feathers glowing in the morning sun. I want to tell Mark I have seen it again, but he is planning to leave for South Carolina soon, and is seldom here anymore. I go to the garage and pull out the old bamboo cane fishing poles the Duraks once used. I bring them outside in the sunlight, as if making an offering to the supremacy of all that once was. They are brittle, covered in dust, their energy gone. I got us a couple of days, Macon wrote. But it is time to go. The noise of the construction work rises, and the earth shakes some more, for obliterating the landscape is hard work. The one-eyed bunny, spooked, runs swiftly across the yard, slips into a tall stand of dog fennel to the north, and vanishes, as completely gone as he will ever be. He is only a phantom now, running swiftly like all of us, into the quiet and unyielding depths of the past. Zona, Mike, Mark, Kelly, Lisa, me. Soon only the clouds will remember him, as they shift and transform and then dissolve into the everlasting blue. They will remember him for the briefest moment, just as they remember us all.

Bibliography

Archaeological Site Form. "Katie's Landing." Site Number 1177, Florida Site File. Florida Department of State, Bureau of Archives and Records Management. Tallahassee. April 11, 1991.

Arrest Report number 200450004900. Sanford Florida Police Department. Defendant: Cheryl Ann Vantine. August 9, 2004.

Barnes, Steve. 2003. "Sanford Sets Its Future in Past Glories." *Orlando Sentinel*, October 5.

Bartram, William. 1996. *Travels and Other Writings: Travels through North and South Carolina, Georgia, East and West Florida. Travels in Georgia and Florida. 1773–1774. A Report to Dr. John Fothergill. Miscellaneous Writings.* Philadelphia: Library of America.

Beach, Jimmy. Program manager, Roads. Seminole County Public Works Department. Sanford, Fla. Personal communication with the author. December 5, 2003.

Beckwith, Zona. Correspondence with the author. November 3, December 30, 2003.

Beebe, William, ed. [1944] 1971. *The Book of Naturalists: An Anthology of the Best Natural History.* Princeton, N.J.: Princeton University Press.

Belleville, Bill. 2000. *River of Lakes: A Journey on Florida's St. Johns River.* Athens: University of Georgia Press.

Berry, Mike. 1990. "Developers Seek Rezoning for Mall." *Orlando Sentinel*, August 31.

Berry, Thomas. 1990. *Dream of the Earth.* San Francisco: Sierra Club Books.

Blackman, William F. [ca. 1930]. "The Wekiwa Ranch: The Astor Grant." Brochure. Winter Park, Fla.

A Blueprint for Action. 2002. Report. Orlando: Wekiva Coalition. November.

Brown, Robin C. 1994. *Florida's First People: Twelve Thousand Years of Human History.* Sarasota, Fla.: Pineapple Press.

Burchell, Robert, and David Listokin. 1995. *Land, Infrastructure, Housing Costs, and Fiscal Impacts Associated with Growth: The Literature on the Impacts of Traditional Versus Managed Growth.* Washington, D.C.: Brookings Institute.

Cabell, Branch, and A. J. Hanna. 1943. *The St. Johns: A Parade of Diversities.* New York: Farrar and Rinehart.

Cabeza de Vaca, Alvar Nuñez. 1983. *Cabeza de Vaca's Adventures in the Unknown Interior of America.* Edited by Cyclone Covey. Albuquerque: University of New Mexico Press.

Campbell, Joseph, with Bill Moyers. 1988. *The Power of Myth.* New York: Doubleday.

Carr, Archie. *A Naturalist in Florida.* Edited by Marjorie Harris Carr. New Haven: Yale University Press.

Cooper, Helen A. 1986. *Winslow Homer Watercolors.* New Haven: Yale University Press.

Cox, James, Randy Kautz, Maureen MacLaughlin, and Terry Gilbert. 1994. *Closing the Gaps in Florida's Wildlife Habitat Conservation System.* Tallahassee: Office of Environmental Services, Florida Game and Fresh Water Fish Commission.

Cruickshank, Helen G., ed. 1986. *William Bartram in Florida.* N.p: Florida Federation of Garden Clubs.

The Dark Side of the American Dream: The Costs and Consequences of Suburban Sprawl. A Sierra Club Report. 1998. College Park, Md.: Sierra Club.

Denton, Cheryl. 1992. *The Wekiva River Basin: A Resource Revisited: A Technical Report of the Friends of the Wekiva River, Inc.* FOWR, P.O. Box 6090, Longwood, Fla., 32791.

Dellert, Christine. 2004. "Wal-Mart Pays Big For Loss of Trees." *Orlando Sentinel,* February 1.

Dennis, Jerry. 1996. *The Bird in the Waterfall: A Natural History of Oceans, Rivers, and Lakes.* New York: HarperCollins.

Dennis, John V. 1988. *The Great Cypress Swamps.* Baton Rouge: Louisiana State University Press.

Durak, Michael, and Carolyn Durak. Correspondence with the author. October 30, 2003; January 9, 10, 12, 15, 2004; February 26, 27, 2004.

Economic and Mobility Impacts of the Orlando-Orange County Expressway Authority. 1977. St. Petersburg: Center for Urban Transportation Research. University of South Florida.

Environmental Assessment and Site Plan Analysis: Flagship Project Site. 2004. Bio-Tech Consulting, Inc. Orlando. March 16.

Fernald, Edward A., and Donald J. Patton, eds. 1985. *Water Resources Atlas of Florida.* Tallahassee: Florida State University, Institute of Science and Public Affairs.

Flagship Park: Buffer Sections, Buffer Concept Plan. 2004. Miller, Einhouse, Rymer, and Boyd. Maitland, Fla. June 24.

Flagship Park: Preliminary Subdivision Plan. 2004. Vanasse, Hangen, Brustlin, Inc. Orlando. June 25.

Fishman, Gail. 2000. *Journeys through Paradise: Pioneering Naturalists in the Southeast.* Gainesville: University Press of Florida.

Florida Rivers Assessment: The St. Johns River. 1989. Tallahassee: State of Florida, Department of Natural Resources.

Florida Springs Conference: Natural Gems, Troubled Waters. Abstract of Papers and Posters. 2003. Gainesville: Florida Department of Environmental Protection. February 5–7.

Galloway, Devin, David R. Jones, and S. E. Ingebritsen, eds. 1999. *Land Subsidence in the United States.* Reston, Va.: U.S. Department of the Interior. U.S. Geological Survey.

Gannon, Michael, ed. 1996. *The New History of Florida.* Gainesville: University Press of Florida.

Gibson, Russ. Director of Planning and Development Services. City of Sanford, Fla. Personal communication with the author. September 9, 2003; June 8, 2004.

Gilbert, Terry, and John Wooding. 1994. *Roadkill Problem Areas for Black Bear in Florida.* Tallahassee: Florida Game and Fresh Water Fish Commission. February 24.

Gimenez, Rebecca (Durak). Personal communication with the author. January 8, 2004.

Gopher Tortoise Incidental Take Permits. N.d. Tallahassee: Florida Wildlife Commission, Office of Environmental Services.

Gopher Tortoise Protection (Florida Only). 1998. U.S. Army Corps of Engineers. Jacksonville, Fla.: Jacksonville District.

Green, Deborah. 1994. *Wekiwa Springs State Park Habitat Tour.* Longwood, Fla.: Self-published.

Grosso, Richard J. 2003. *Statement on the Florida Hometown Democracy Initiative.* Ft. Lauderdale, Fla.: Nova Southeastern University, Environmental and Land Use Law Center, Inc. April 15.

Haase, Ronald W. 1992. *Classic Cracker: Florida's Wood-Frame Vernacular Architecture.* Sarasota: Pineapple Press.

Harper, Francis, ed. 1958. *Bartram's Travels: Naturalist Edition.* New Haven: Yale University Press.

Harris, Larry D., and Bill Suchy, writers. *Landscape Linkages.* 1988. Winter Park, Fla.: Ironwood Video.

Hawken, Paul. 1993. *The Ecology of Commerce: A Declaration of Sustainability.* New York: HarperBusiness.

Historic Byways of Florida Series: A Facsimile Reproduction of the 1887 Edition with an Introduction by V. O. Coshow. 1981. DeLand, Fla.: Saint Johns-Oklawaha Rivers Trading Company.

Hudson, Charles M., ed. 2004. *Black Drink: A Native American Tea.* Athens: University of Georgia Press.

Imperiale, Nancy. 1990. "Effort Fails to Stop Sanford from Paying for Mall Roads." *Orlando Sentinel,* April 10.

———. 1990. "Sanford Is 'Blighted.'" *Orlando Sentinel,* November 27.

"Inmate Who Died Is Identified." 2004. *Orlando Sentinel,* August 13.

Into Tropical Florida, or a Round Trip upon the St. Johns River [ca. 1880]. Jacksonville, Fla.: Passenger Department of the Debary-Baya Merchants Line.

Jenks, J.W.P. 1884. "Hunting in Florida in 1874." Textual Collections. A State University System of Florida PALMM Project. 2003. Gainesville. [Internet]

Keasler, John. [1958] 1999. *Surrounded on All Sides.* Gainesville: University Press of Florida.

Kilsheimer, Joe. 1993. "North Seminole Residents Are Bracing for a Boom in the Area around Seminole Towne Center's Site." *Orlando Sentinel,* December 19.

Kraus, Mark L. 1996. "Wetland Mitigation Banking in Florida: Issues and Concerns." Winter Park: Audubon Society of Florida. Oct. 18.

Lanier, Sidney. 1875. *Florida: Its Scenery, Climate, and History.* Philadelphia: J. B. Lippincott and Company.

Legacy 2002: Greater Orlando Indicators Report. 2002. The Healthy Community Initiative of Greater Orlando. Orlando, Fla.

Matthiessen, Peter. 1994. Lecture at the University of Central Florida. January 13.

———. 2001. *The Birds of Heaven: Travels with Cranes.* New York: North Point Press.

McGurk, B. E. 1998. *Estimating the Potential Impacts to Spring Flow in the Wekiva River Basin from Projected Future Ground Water Withdrawals.* Palatka, Fla.: St. Johns River Water Management District.

McKinney, Dennis. 2003. "Wetlands Pollute, Says Study Okayed by EPA; EPA Biologist Resigns in Protest." *Public Employees for Environmental Responsibility.* PEER.org. October 23.

McMurtray, Jennifer. Personal communication with the author. December 15, 2003.

———. 2003. *The Conservation-Minded Citizens Guide to Transportation Planning.* Report. Washington, D.C.: Defenders of Wildlife.

"Merge Lanes Ahead: Street Design." 1996. Fact Sheet Number 4. Tallahassee: 1000 Friends of Florida.

Milanich, Jerald T. 1994. *Archaeology of Precolumbian Florida.* Gainesville: University Press of Florida.

———. 1995. *Florida Indians and the Invasion from Europe.* Gainesville: University Press of Florida.

Milanich, J. T., ed. 1972. *Francisco Paraja's Confessionario: A Document for Timucu-*

an Ethnography. Tallahassee: Department of State, Director of Archives, History and Records Management.

Moore, Thomas. *The Re-Enchantment of Everyday Life*. 1996. New York: Harper-Collins.

Mueller, Edward A. 1986. *St. Johns River Steamboats*. Jacksonville: Self-published.

Myers, R. L., and John J. Jewel. 1990. *Ecosystems of Florida*. Gainesville: University Press of Florida.

Newman, Joe. 2003. "Panel Will Tackle How to Protect Wekiva's Riches." *Orlando Sentinel*, August 24.

———. 2003. "Wekiva River Basin's Residents Face an Uncertain Future." *Orlando Sentinel*, December 14.

———. 2003. "Wekiva Land Buy 'Critical.'" *Orlando Sentinel*, December 19.

———. 2003. "Special Report: Paradise Sold. State Law to Fight Sprawl Often Flouted." *Orlando Sentinel*, December 29.

———. 2004. "As Leaders Mull Options, River's Health Suffers." *Orlando Sentinel*, January 25.

———. 2004. "Wekiva's Future Looks Clearer." *Orlando Sentinel*, January 30.

Nozzi, Dom. 2003. *Road to Ruin: An Introduction to Sprawl and How to Cure It*. Westport, Conn.: Greenwood Publishing Group.

Oppel, Frank, and Tony Meisel, eds. 1870–1910. Reprint, 1987. *Tales of Old Florida*. Secaucus, N.J.: Castle.

Pittman, Craig, and Julie Hauserman. 2003. "North Has It, South Wants It: Special Report, Florida Water." *St. Petersburg Times*, August 10.

Planning for Tomorrow: A Citizen's Guide to Smarter Growth in Florida. [N.d.]. Tallahassee: 1000 Friends of Florida.

Pritchard, Peter, and Herbert W. Kale. 1994. *Saving What's Left*. Winter Park: Florida Audubon Society.

"Promoting Smarter Growth at the Local Level." 2000. *Foresight: Newsletter of 1000 Friends of Florida*. Tallahassee: 1000 Friends of Florida. Winter.

Purdum, Elizabeth D. 2002. *Florida Waters: A Water Resources Manual from Florida's Water Management Districts*. Brooksville: Southwest Florida Water Management District. April.

Rawlings, Marjorie Kinnan. [1939] 2002. *The Yearling*. New York: Scribners.

———. *Cross Creek*. [1942] 1996. New York: Touchstone (Simon and Schuster).

Recreation Guide to District Lands. 2000. Palatka: St. Johns River Water Management District's Office of Public Information and the Division of Land Management.

"Red Alert: The Wekiva Basin Needs Immediate Action from the Governor." Editorial. 2004. *Orlando Sentinel*, August 8.

Robison, Jim. 1990. "Fisherman's Paradise of Wekiva Keeps Soldiers' Mess Well Stocked." *Orlando Sentinel*, March 22.

————. 2001. *Images of America: Altamonte Springs*. Charleston, S.C.: Arcadia.

————. 2003. "Sanlando Springs Still Is Fountain of Stories." *Orlando Sentinel*, September 28.

Robison, Jim, and Mark Andrews. 1995. *Flashbacks: The Story of Central Florida's Past*. Orlando: Orange County Historical Society and the *Orlando Sentinel*.

Rosenau, Jack C., and Glen L. Faulkner. 1977. *Geological Bulletin No. 31, Revised: An Index to the Springs of Florida*. Tallahassee: Florida Department of Natural Resources, Florida Geological Survey.

Salamone, Debbie. 2002. "Florida's Water Crisis: A Drying Oasis" (chapters 1–12, special section reprint). *Orlando Sentinel*.

Sargent, Robert. 2003. "Florida's Water Crisis: Rain Can't Meet Demand." *Orlando Sentinel*, July 28.

"Seminole County: Presenters Copy." August 9, 2001. Bond solicitation. Sanford: Seminole County.

Seminole County Vision 2020. 2001. Seminole County Comprehensive Management Plan. Sanford: Seminole County.

Small, John Kunkel. 1929. *From Eden to Sahara: Florida's Tragedy*. Lancaster, Penn.: Science Press Printing Company.

Soil Survey of Seminole County Florida. 1990. Washington, D.C.: U.S. Dept. of Agriculture Soil Conservation District.

Stephenson, R. Bruce. 1997. *Visions of Eden: Environmentalism, Urban Planning, and City Building in St. Petersburg, Florida, 1900–1995*. Columbus: Ohio State University Press.

Straton, Jim. 1999. "Beltway Fight Revives: Foes Vow Again to Protect Wekiva River Basin." *Orlando Sentinel*, June 6.

Tibbals, C. H. 1990. "Hydrology of the Floridan Aquifer in East Central Florida." Paper No. 1403-E. Washington, D.C.: U.S. Geological Survey, U.S. Government Printing Office.

Toner, Jim. 2004. "Big Boxes Graze in Pastures off Rinehart Road." *Orlando Sentinel*, February 26.

Trombalak, S. C., and C. A. Friswell. 2000. "Review of Ecological Effects of Roads on Terrestrial and Aquatic Communities." *Conservation Biology* 14: 18–30.

Turner, Richard L. 1994. *The Effects of Hydrology on the Population Dynamics of the Florida Applesnail (Pomacea paludosa)*. Special Publication SJ94-SPC. Palatka, Fla.: St. Johns River Water Management District.

Van Sickler, Michael, and Janet Zink. 2003. "The Hidden Cost of Living." *St. Petersburg Times*, December 12.

Walker, Gregg. 2003. *Wildlife Use and Interaction with Structures Constructed to*

Minimize Collisions and Animal Mortality Along State Road 46 Lake County Florida. Summary of Final Report, BD162. Tallahassee: Florida Department of Environmental Protection. October.

Warner, Bethany. 2001. "Suburban Sprawl Spreads Incivility, Book Author Says." *Washington (D.C.) Times,* April 25.

"Water Sense: Availability of Water Should Be Tied to New-Growth Approvals." 2004. Editorial. *Orlando Sentinel,* January 4.

Wekiva River Conservation Area Land Management Plan. 2004. Palatka, Fla.: St. Johns River Water Management District. June 27.

Wekiva River Writers. 1988. "The Wekiva River: Scenic and Wild." Apopka, Fla.: Wekiva River Writers.

White, O. E. 1957. "Magmatic, Connate, and Metamorphic Waters." *Bulletin of the Geological Society of America.* 68: 1659–82.

White, William A. 1970. *The Geomorphology of the Florida Peninsula.* Geological Bulletin No. 51. Tallahassee: Bureau of Geology, Florida Department of Natural Resources.

Williams, Angela T. 2001. "Affidavit for Blanket Authorization to Test Tortoises for Upper Respiratory Tract Disease." Memorandum. Tallahassee: Florida Fish and Wildlife Conservation Commission. February 16.

Wilson, Edward O. 1992. *The Diversity of Life.* Cambridge: Harvard University Press, Belknap Press.

Wilson, Edward O., and Stephen R. Kellert, eds. 1993. *The Biophilia Hypothesis.* Washington, D.C.: Island Press.

Wooding, John B. 1990. *Recommendations to Reduce the Impact of the Orlando Beltway and S.R. 46 to Black Bears in the Wekiva River Area.* Tallahassee: Florida Game and Fresh Water Fish Commission.

The WPA Guide to Florida: The Federal Writers' Project Guide to 1930's Florida. [1939] 1984. New York: Pantheon Books.

Bill Belleville is the award-winning author of *River of Lakes: A Journey on Florida's St. Johns River*, *Deep Cuba: The Inside Story of an American Oceanographic Expedition*, and his anthology *Sunken Cities, Sacred Cenotes, and Golden Sharks*. His byline has appeared in *Sierra*, *Oxford American*, *Reader's Digest*, and *Islands*, and elsewhere. He lives in Sanford, Florida.

Related-interest titles from University Press of Florida

Al Burt's Florida: Snowbirds, Sand Castles, and Self-Rising Crackers
Al Burt

Florida Frenzy
Harry Crews

Death in the Everglades: The Murder of Guy Bradley, America's First Martyr to Environmentalism
Stuart B. McIver

Green Empire: The St. Joe Company and the Remaking of Florida's Panhandle
Kathryn Ziewitz and June Wiaz

Highway A1A: Florida at the Edge
Herbert L. Hiller

Journal of Light: The Visual Diary of a Florida Nature Photographer
John Moran

Land of Sunshine, State of Dreams: A Social History of Modern Florida
Gary R. Mormino

"A River in Flood" and Other Florida Stories by Marjorie Stoneman Douglas
Edited by Kevin McCarthy

Saving South Beach
M. Barron Stofik

Seasons of Real Florida
Jeff Klinkenberg

Some Kind of Paradise: A Chronicle of Man and the Land in Florida
Mark Derr

Surrounded on Three Sides
John Keasler

The Tropic of Cracker
Al Burt

The Wide Brim: Early Poems and Ponderings of Marjory Stoneman Douglas
Edited by Jack E. Davis

For more information on these and other books, visit our Web site at www.upf.com.